The Basketball Handbook

Lee H. Rose

HUMAN
KINETICS

Library of Congress Cataloging-in-Publication Data

Rose, Lee H.
   The basketball handbook / Lee H. Rose.
       p. cm.
   Includes index.
   ISBN 0-7360-4906-1 (softcover)
   1. Basketball--Coaching--Handbooks, manuals, etc. I. Title.
   GV885.3.R67 2004
   796.323'2--dc22   2004009346

ISBN: 0-7360-4906-1

Developmental Editor: Jennifer L. Walker; **Assistant Editor:** Mandy Maiden; **Copyeditor:** Bob Replinger; **Proofreader:** Annette Pierce; **Indexer:** Bobbi Swanson; **Graphic Designer:** Nancy Rasmus; **Graphic Artist:** Kim McFarland; **Photo Manager:** Dan Wendt; **Cover Designer:** Keith Blomberg; **Photographer (cover):** Doug Pensigner/Getty Images; **Photographer (interior):** All photos by Kent Smith unless otherwise noted.; **Art Manager:** Kareema McLendon; **Illustrator:** Tim Offenstein; **Printer:** Versa Press

Human Kinetics books are available at special discounts for bulk purchase. Special editions or book excerpts can also be created to specification. For details, contact the Special Sales Manager at Human Kinetics.

Printed in the United States of America   10   9   8   7   6   5   4   3   2   1

Human Kinetics
Web site: www.HumanKinetics.com

United States: Human Kinetics
P.O. Box 5076
Champaign, IL 61825-5076
800-747-4457
e-mail: humank@hkusa.com

Canada: Human Kinetics
475 Devonshire Road Unit 100
Windsor, ON N8Y 2L5
800-465-7301 (in Canada only)
e-mail: orders@hkcanada.com

Europe: Human Kinetics
107 Bradford Road
Stanningley
Leeds LS28 6AT, United Kingdom
+44 (0) 113 255 5665
e-mail: hk@hkeurope.com

Australia: Human Kinetics
57A Price Avenue
Lower Mitcham, South Australia 5062
08 8277 1555
e-mail: liaw@hkaustralia.com

New Zealand: Human Kinetics
Division of Sports Distributors NZ Ltd.
P.O. Box 300 226 Albany
North Shore City
Auckland
0064 9 448 1207
e-mail: blairc@hknewz.com

To Eleanor, Mike, and Mark.
They lived it every day.

CONTENTS

PREFACE

The purpose of this book is to give coaches and players the understanding and tools they need to be successful in basketball. This book is for coaches at all levels who are seeking ways to improve and for players who are interested in developing an all-around game. In all my years of coaching I've never met a player who didn't need to improve in some area. I've been around good players, excellent players, and great players, but never a perfect player. Whether it's free-throw shooting, dribbling, passing, rebounding, setting screens, using proper shooting technique, or some intuitive trait such as selflessness or good decision making, even a great player can improve parts of his game. This book addresses those areas and more.

Middle school and high school players who want to know what's expected of them when trying out for a team can quickly go to the offensive skills section or learn about defense by checking the defensive tactics segment. If they want to know how to improve their vertical jump or increase their speed, it's here. Players who will soon attend college will find helpful drills covering the fundamentals, as well as vital information on what to look for and what they can expect when selecting a four-year institution.

The further one advances in organized ball, the more one is expected to contribute. Those who have good habits understand that the more effort they give, the greater the benefits. This axiom is true in sports, but more important, it's true in life. Players and coaches need to understand that the disappointment in losing relates directly to the amount of energy expended in trying to win. Ask yourself why young players excel in high school but fall behind as they progress to college. Too often it's because they focus only on the skills that come easy for them and disregard the importance of being well rounded. Coaches and players need to bring to the game a firm understanding of what it takes to be successful and then devise a plan that accomplishes the desired goals.

The first four chapters of *The Basketball Handbook* discuss the importance of establishing principles that help both coach and player stay focused; identify roles for players, coaches, and teams; present a fair and consistent evaluation process; and conclude with a sport-specific conditioning program that assures practice-ready results. The book moves from the philosophical to the technical by defining the necessary offensive and defensive fundamentals with drills and diagrams that promote development. Regardless of the level, these drills can be helpful. For coaches, the drills and diagrams provide excellent teaching aids for practice. Nineteen years of success have proved the effectiveness of the no-middle team defense and LA offense.

When applicable, I have included personal coaching stories to illustrate a point, but this book is not about my coaching career or the college institutions or pro teams where I have worked. This book is about helping coaches and players understand the fundamentals of the game and how to apply that knowledge to their particular needs. For the past three years, I've been a coaching supervisor to the NBA's minor league, the National Basketball Development League (NBDL). In that role, I critique professional coaches, offering concrete suggestions that will help them develop expertise in their trade. This handbook addresses many of the issues that I cover with the coaches. I hope that by reading this book, players and coaches will come across new ideas that will enhance and improve their game.

Talent alone does not guarantee winning, but talent sharpened by fundamentals certainly offers a better chance. Players and coaches who excel in basketball understand that energy unleashed randomly is rarely constructive, so they come to the game seeking ways to improve—ways to get that edge that provides success. Successful coaches have a plan for the team and for each team member. Players need the same kind of road map for their game as they seek improvement. Each drill worked on in practice and every offensive and defensive strategy employed should have a specific purpose. *The Basketball Handbook* provides proven drills that enhance development for both player and coach.

Today's head coach is involved with a veritable Rubik's Cube of issues, problems, and personalities, all of which he has to manage. To be successful, a coach must maintain the confidence and support of the players, work effectively within the school or institutional system, delegate responsibilities to and provide leadership for his assistants, and establish a civil relationship with the media. He must do all of that while performing the traditional coaching responsibilities of selecting the team, determining player rotation, setting offensive strategy and making play calls, managing the clock, setting defensive matchups, developing zones and zone attacks, and handling countless daily problems. At times, coaching is like running on a fast-moving treadmill with no stop button.

Young coaches must develop their own coaching philosophy. Coaches want to win, so they are naturally attracted to whoever is hot at the moment. Whether they are copying hairstyles or trying to emulate coaches with reputations for being hard-nosed disciplinarians, patterning themselves after others has its pitfalls. All coaches borrow various plays, drills, styles, and strategies from other coaches, but each coach should be himself and know his own strengths and weaknesses. *The Basketball Handbook* will help coaches analyze their philosophy, challenge their rationale, encourage thinking outside the conventional box, and provide useful tools as they expand their understanding.

Coaches open to new experiences and new challenges will find unlimited opportunities to grow and expand. When Willis Reed asked me to be a member of his coaching staff, little did I know what would transpire. I had a truly unique experience as a Nets assistant coach. Peter Vecsey, who was a sportswriter for the *New York Post* at that time, referred to me as the Nets' token, in reference to the fact that I was the only white among the team's 12 players and 3 coaches. This situation also occurred in my last year with the Charlotte Hornets. This rare opportunity gave me insight into the particulars of being in the minority. Clarence Page, a Pulitzer Prize–winning columnist who is black, once wrote that most people like to be listened to, but nobody likes to be listened to more than the members of groups that historically have had a rough time being heard. "If you want to win the members of such groups over," he explained, "remember that it's not how you define equality that counts, it's how *they* define it." Willis Reed was a first-class man—a man of integrity, character, civility—and wonderful to work for. Coaches who continue to grow need to be open, receptive, and flexible.

Many coaches in the game have been called purists. John Wooden, Hank Iba, Adolph Rupp, and Dean Smith are possibly the most noted perfectionists when it comes to the fundamentals of the game. These men emphasized teamwork, not individual showmanship. They remained traditionalists in their attitude toward passing, pivoting, screening, shooting, ball and player movement, and defensive play. Oscar Robertson, who may have been the most fundamentally sound superstar ever, said in a February 15, 2004, *New York Times* article, "Basketball is not a vertical game. The game is won between the foul line and the basket, an area where so few players today choose to, or are unable to, operate. Dunking is such a tiny part of the game. My answers to these youngsters are always the same: Concentrate on mastering all the fundamentals and becoming a complete player."

Just as pillars are important to bridge construction, so are fundamentals important to players and coaches. Most coaches love to scrimmage, but that doesn't mean that you start practice with a full-court game. Before you can go up and down the court, you must teach and practice fundamentals of offense and defense. A major purpose of this handbook is to elaborate on the most important offensive and defensive fundamentals and explain how each works to support the team.

At age 29 I became the head coach of my alma mater. When considering the principles that I wanted to instill in my players, the first thing I did was reflect on my experiences as a player and assistant coach. What was important to players? Having started as a player in elementary school, junior high school, senior high school, and college, I'd been in many locker rooms and heard all the stories. The main thrust of negative comments always involved one topic: Players want to be treated fairly.

The more I contemplated that idea, the more I realized that nothing means more to players than fair and consistent treatment. Players must feel comfortable with the evaluation process. The less subjectivity involved, the better they like it. The best tool I found for gaining their confidence was a weighted, graded system that evaluated everyone on the same objective scale. I developed a weighted performance rating system and will explain how it works and the benefits derived from its use.

Another pillar in the foundation of a good basketball team is being in good physical condition to begin the season. The idea that teams can play themselves into good condition is flawed. Smart thinking says that teams get in shape and then play. In today's sport-specific culture, coaches should have a firm understanding of oxygen debt, plyometrics, and current physical training techniques. Players want to know how to increase their vertical jump and improve their speed, and successful coaches make it a point to be ready with the correct answer. I designed the eighths running program strictly for basketball players. The program is challenging, competitive, motivating, fair, and effective. Coaches and players will like the unique features and the outstanding results it produces.

I'll conclude by emphasizing that *The Basketball Handbook* can serve as a reference book for both coach and player. The information presented here is the culmination of almost a half-century of active involvement in basketball. The drills, taken from college and the NBA, are the ones that have endured the test of time and proved most effective. Coaching is many things. The following story illustrates what it is to me and captures what I enjoy most about the game.

One day a power plant that supplied electricity to a large Southern city came to a screeching halt. A few portable generators were available, but no one in the city had planned for such an emergency, so hospitals, schools, restaurants, and health care centers were all in dire circumstances. The CEO of the power plant immediately called an emergency meeting with his entire management team of foremen and supervisors. The CEO exclaimed, "We must get help; someone must know how to fix this problem." His most dependable foreman stepped forward and said, "I know a guy, Joe Smith from New York City, who says he can fix our problem." The CEO replied, "Well, call him and get him here as quickly as possible." So, the foreman called Smith, explained the situation, and told Smith that they were sending the company jet to pick him up early the next morning. After a three-hour flight, the foreman picked up Joe in the company limousine, and they headed toward the plant. As they pulled off the tarmac, Joe said that he needed to stop by the closest hardware store to pick up a ball-peen hammer. This done, Joe put the hammer in his small, black tool bag, and they drove to the plant, arriving at 11:00.

Joe Smith got out of the limo and went straight to the boiler room of the power plant. He walked beside the walls and studied the big pipes, where he would occasionally stop and listen. After about 30 minutes he stopped, pulled out his ball-peen hammer, listened intently, and struck the pipe once with his hammer. Immediately the plant came alive, and power surged throughout the city. Joe Smith collected his bag and his hammer, returned to the limo, and received a ride back to the airport.

The next day, an invoice for the work was delivered to the CEO. It read: "Balance Due: $100,005." The CEO asked his secretary to get Mr. Smith on the phone. Asked to explain the bill, Mr. Smith replied that $5 was for the purchase of the hammer, and $100,000 was for knowing which pipe to hit with the hammer. That's what coaching is—knowing which pipe to hit.

Enjoy the book.

ACKNOWLEDGMENTS

First, I would like thank the players I have coached. For a coach to win, he must have talented players, and I was indeed blessed with talented players. But more than that, I coached men of strong character. To each of you I say thank you for being part of my journey and this book.

My deepest appreciation goes to the unheralded assistant coaches who contributed so much to our success. Following, in chronological order, are the four institutions where I coached and the assistants, in alphabetical order.

Transylvania	Don Lane, Bob Pace, Ron Whitson, Roland Wierwille
UNC Charlotte	Everett Bass, Mike Pratt
Purdue	Everett Bass, Roger Blalock, George Faerber, Billy Keller, Jeff Meyer
South Florida	Everett Bass, Jan Bennett, Lewis Card, Gordon Gibbons, Mike Lederman, Mike Lewis, Jeff Meyer, Mike Shirley, Mark Wise

I owe a great deal of gratitude and appreciation to two special people who kept me on track with their continuous encouragement and support throughout the writing process. The manuscript took just over two years to write, but the experience, knowledge, and theories were collected over a lifetime of coaching. The concepts and stories are mine, but without many people giving freely of their time and energy, this book would never have made it to print. I want to recognize and thank the following:

Jordan Cohn: For the past 10 years, Jordan has been encouraging me to write about the technical aspects of basketball. In 2001, he came to me with a publishing house, Human Kinetics; a name, Ted Miller; and a phone number. Throughout the arduous process, Jordan's experience as an author kept me on course with organizational ideas, proposals, and revision recommendations. I am eternally grateful for his contribution.

John Kilgo: John and I forged a lasting friendship when he was the announcer for the UNC Charlotte 49ers during our run to the Final Four in 1976-77. I am indebted to him for the invaluable suggestions, perceptive insights, and basketball knowledge that he shared as an author and radio and TV commentator. His involvement came when the task seemed almost overwhelming; he has my thanks and deep respect.

I am profoundly grateful to Human Kinetics, principally **Ted Miller** for his patience, direction, enthusiasm, and belief in this book. Thanks to **Jennifer Walker** for her editorial expertise and astute perceptions in guiding a struggling novice through a maze of daunting projects and revisions. To **Mandy Maiden**, assistant editor, thanks for a great job, especially with all those tedious diagrams. Thanks to **Bob Replinger**, copyeditor, for finding more mistakes than the law allows.

I have many people to thank for giving their time and energy in supplying research facts: Chris Ekstrand, Jason Roose, Ryan Blake, Drew Perry, and Mike Lewis. Thanks to Natalie Knorr Best for her reading, research, and constructive comments. To photographer Kent Smith, Athletic Director Doug Maynard, Coach Shonn Brown, and the student-athletes at Charlotte Christian School, my sincere appreciation for providing facilities and players for the photo shoot.

During my formative years I received wonderful training and encouragement from my coaches: Briscoe Evans at Morton Junior High; Elmer "Baldy" Gilb, John Heber, Walter Hill, and Dr. C.T. Sharpton, the principal, at Henry Clay High School; and Harry Stephenson, C.M. Newton, and Jack Wise at Transylvania College.

Shared values and mutual respect were the basis for the relationships I had with those for whom I worked. It is my pleasure to recognize Dr. Irvin Lunger, Dr. James Broadus, Dr. Dean Colvard, Dr. Frank Dickey, Dr. Doug Orr, Wayne Duke, Bill Wall, Vic Bubas, Tay Baker, Fred Schaus, and Dr. Dick Bowers. NBA colleagues Bob Weiss, Willis Reed, Lenny Wilkins, Marty Blake, Matt Winick, Larry Riley, and Herb Kohl, owner of the Milwaukee Bucks, were always encouraging and supportive.

Eleanor Rose: I want to thank Elo for her steadfast confidence and her unselfish commitment of time, energy, and wise counsel. She read and reread every word, every drill, and is one tough critic. As partners for these past 45 years, we found that few things in our lives equaled the emotional roller coaster we rode while writing this book.

KEY TO DIAGRAMS

Offensive player	○
Offensive player relocates	◌
Offensive player with ball	●
Coach start drill with ball	●
Defensive player	X
Pass	– – ▶
Dribble	/\/\/\/\^
Screen	──────┤
Player movement	───▶
Pivot	♂

CHAPTER 1

Five Guiding Principles

I grew up in West Irvine, Kentucky, a coal-mining town seated at the edge of the Appalachian Mountains. At the time (1936) the game of basketball, especially University of Kentucky basketball, was a religion unto itself. Coach Adolph Rupp's "Big Blue" won an unbelievable string of NCAA championships in 1948, 1949, 1951, and 1958. His almost clockwork success fascinated me. I can still hear radio play-by-play announcer Claude Sullivan calling out plays and scores, linking me to the magic and action that was Kentucky basketball. I listened intently to each game, kept score, and lived and died with the Wildcats.

When I was nine, my family moved to Lexington. Our house was located just two blocks from where Kentucky played its home games. I couldn't wait to get a closer look at the Wildcats and was thrilled with my first basketball job—selling soft drinks at UK games.

Watching UK's glorious championship teams of Ralph Beard and Alex Groza to "Rupp's Runts" of the mid-1960s taught me that each player and coach had to commit to playing within a set of fundamental beliefs to gain team and individual success and that commitment was just one layer to the success of a team. The legacy of UK and of all basketball shows us that no single tried-and-true formula results in consistent winning, because so many variables are tied to the individual skills and experiences of the players and the knowledge and teaching ability of the coach. Although no one plan is effective in producing consistent winners, I have learned in my half century as a player, coach, and administrator that five guiding principles applied correctly and with determination produce consistent, winning teams:

1. Play hard
2. Play smart
3. Execute the plan
4. Be unselfish
5. Maximize strengths and minimize weaknesses

As a lifelong student and a teacher of basketball, I spent 19 years as a college head coach and 8 years as an assistant, paying my dues, and served five NBA head coaches as the top assistant while formulating these five fundamental principles. I found that regardless of level—high school, college, or professional—the coaches who employed these five principles gave themselves and their teams the best opportunity to win. These five guiding principles are the foundation for this book and should influence all coaching and practice sessions.

Principle 1: **Play Hard**

In 1958 I graduated from Transylvania University—a small, academically sound school in Lexington that had its own rich basketball history and tradition. We learned quickly to be comfortable and secure in our own shoes, because being located in the same city with UK, we knew that we would always be in its long shadow. After serving as captain of the basketball team and earning my degree in physical education, I sought a job in coaching.

For me, money wasn't the issue; an opportunity was what I was searching for. I jumped at the offer to coach high school in the small town of Versailles, Kentucky, located about 12 miles from Lexington. For teaching five classes, coaching three sports—basketball, football, and baseball—and driving the school bus to athletic events, my salary was $3,200 annually. Fine with me. This was my chance to coach basketball, and it was a golden opportunity. Besides, I was too busy to complain.

Many people have a story like mine that involves working hard. But if basketball is a person's dream, to play it or coach it or both, hard work and dedication

Lee (pictured in the first row at left) with his Transylvania team.

© Transylvania University

have to be part of the equation. I'm not much impressed with young men who say they want to coach but then turn down an opportunity because they don't want to live in a small town off the beaten path. To get your break in coaching or in playing basketball, you have to be willing to start small and work hard. Period. Anything less than total effort on the part of high school and college players and coaches will not produce consistent winning. Players and coaches at those levels must do several things to ensure maximum effort on a consistent basis because, when everything else is equal, effort usually determines the winner. David Hunziker, our student clock supervisor at Transylvania College, showed us by example that slacking off was unacceptable. Though stricken with cerebral palsy, he took great pride in handling his duties without a slip, was a key member of our staff, and set a great example for our team. He was such an inspiration to everyone in the program that none of us could imagine complaining or letting up.

The following points summarize ways in which to work hard:

• **Maintain focus.** Like most things in life, winning in basketball requires a keen, sustained effort. Forget the short cuts and distractions. Unless you are incredibly lucky, there aren't any. Winners realize that they must stay focused, work their way to the top, and understand, going in, that discouraging setbacks will occur along the way. Whether working on individual skills alone on an outdoor court or taking part in a team practice in the middle of the season, total concentration is essential to learning, retention, and execution. Injuries such as turned ankles and pulled muscles are commonplace in practice when players lose concentration and don't maintain intensity.

- **Be efficient.** One way a coach can avoid player distractions is by keeping practices interesting, productive, and upbeat. Individual sessions should move briskly, preferably with a clock regulating the amount of time spent on each drill. Drills should not exceed 5 minutes, except for scrimmages. Blocks of time ranging as high as 20 minutes can be devoted to a specific aspect of the game (shooting, defensive footwork, boxing out) as long as drills vary throughout the period. Variety keeps players from becoming bored and helps them maintain concentration. More is accomplished in less time, and practice is more productive for everyone involved.

- **Compete every day.** Whether you're a high school freshman trying out for the junior varsity team or a top NBA player battling for a roster spot or a place in the starting lineup, a practice environment that promotes healthy competition can help you flourish. High school players can find opportunities to compete as close as the local church league, YMCA, or even the neighborhood hoops. College players and beyond can take even the simplest offensive drill to the next level of competition. For example, individual shooting drills should end with a winner. Keep tabs on who is first to make a certain number of shots and declare a winner. Once a winner emerges, change the drill. For team shooting drills based on curls, fades, and pop-outs off pin-downs, say that the first team to make five baskets wins. Having worked with great NBA shooters such as Dell Curry, Glen Rice, Dale Ellis, and Ricky Pierce, I can tell you that such competition drives them.

- **Seek extra work.** The time before and after practice is player improvement time, or PIT. Whether working on ballhandling, rebounding, defense, or shooting, players who put in an extra 15 to 30 minutes a day will improve faster than those who show up right at the start of practice and leave as soon as it ends. PIT also provides an excellent opportunity to improve coach-player relationships. Players who master skills and feel better about their coaches will be more motivated from one practice to the next. Many coaches are making PIT an integral part of practices rather than optional. PIT is essential for young NBA players as well as veterans who aren't getting significant playing time.

Principle 2: Play Smart

Energy unleashed randomly is rarely constructive. Dr. Jim Broadus, the dean of education at Transylvania College, was a frequent visitor to our basketball practices. An analytical man, he was always questioning why we did certain things. For instance, he wanted to know why, in our press offense, we worked against seven defenders. The players' intense concentration fascinated Dr. Broadus, and he wondered if they could duplicate it in the classroom. We discussed the difficulties in teaching competition and cooperation. He was always interested in the teaching process and enjoyed the give and take between player and coach. His questions underscored the importance of why a particular drill and plan was better than another. Further, his questions emphasized that you should do everything with a purpose—that you should plan your work and work your plan. Staff meetings and the practice court are where you develop the plan and where players learn to succeed by playing smart.

The following points summarize ways in which to play smart:

- **Focus on intelligence.** In deciding how to run his program, a coach can drive his team, push it, or lead it. Although a coach usually favors one style over another, all three methods will probably surface during the long season. The most effective coaches understand that the cornerstone of a winning program includes not only basketball success, but also academic success for each player. To maintain a flourishing, well-rounded program, the coach should become involved in the total educational process.

- **Practice with a purpose.** Players cannot play smart without understanding the fundamentals, and they learn the basics in practice. Teams that are not fundamentally sound and dedicated to the same purpose and goals will have a hard time playing, especially when they face adversity. Some players who make the game look easy, such as former New York Knicks star Walt Frazier, might leave the impression that they are playing by instinct and guts, but statistics reveal another story. Frazier, a 13-year NBA veteran, averaged 18.9 points and 6.1 assists per game. Like many outstanding players, he improved his production to 20.7 points and 6.4 assists while playing in 93 playoff games. Practice sessions offer players the opportunity to experiment and come to know their strengths as well as develop a shared purpose with other team members.

- **Develop a solid foundation.** The coach must seek to develop the foundational offensive and defensive skills of players, from the high school to the professional level. As young players rise through the ranks, much attention—usually too much attention—is given to points scored. The leading scorer is not necessarily the team's best player, although that wouldn't always be apparent to those who read newspaper accounts of games.

  A player who scores a lot of points is not necessarily a good shooter. Shooters might be scorers, but it doesn't always work the other way around. In many instances, a big, young player scores many points simply because he is bigger than his defenders. With stars twinkling in his eyes because of the media coverage he receives for scoring points, he might not understand that he needs to improve his passing and dribbling or increase the range on his jumper. The coach must remind him of what he needs to work on, because as the player moves up the basketball ladder his lack of overall skills will catch up with him. The game requires much more than just scoring points. Good defensive habits are essential. Players need to learn early to stay in front of their man, stay down on jump shooters, avoid reaching and grabbing on dribble penetration, and use good rebounding techniques. The players who go on to good college and professional careers have developed both offensive and defensive skills to become complete players.

- **Keep fouls under control.** Once players have learned the foundational skills, they should begin to realize that fouling and putting the opponent on the line is costly. Intelligent play is impossible if players foul because they lack fundamentals or play out of position because of lackadaisical effort. Coaches need to drive home the point that excessive fouling is often a path to defeat. After all, a 15-foot shot directly in front of the basket with no one guarding shouldn't be too hard for a top player. I had a system at UNC Charlotte, Purdue, and South Florida whereby I substituted a player as soon as he picked up his first foul. That rule serves a couple of purposes. First, the substitute feels that he is an important part of the team because he knows that he's going in as soon as the starter at his position fouls for the first time. Knowing that he's going to get into the game, the substitute concentrates more in practice. He doesn't have the mind-set that he's just a substitute and doesn't need to work hard in practice. Second, as the starter leaves the game after one foul, he receives a strong message that random fouling hurts the team. By sitting awhile, the player has time to focus on not picking up a careless second foul. This policy also includes sitting the starter after his second and third fouls to avoid early foul problems.

• **Get the ball to the right player.** Coaches and players should work hard in practice to ensure that the right person receives the inbounds pass in late-game situations. A team protecting a lead late in the game should make every effort to get the ball to the best foul shooter because they know that the opponent is going to foul as soon as the inbounds pass is completed. The old NBA Charlotte Hornets used a play called "The Line" to inbound the ball against pressure. Players would line up single file and then break randomly to open areas on the floor. Opponents would foul the player receiving the inbounds pass. We realized that Glen Rice, our best free-throw shooter, should be our first option in those situations. If we succeeded in getting the ball to Rice, opponents were reluctant to foul him because he shot 85 percent from the foul line. Not fouling immediately took time off the clock, which played into our hands. Know your best options and use them.

Principle 3: **Execute the Plan**

A game often boils down to two or three possessions in the endgame. Close games usually go to the team that executes with poise late in the contest. Knowing this, coaches spend hours working on late-game situations. They emphasize getting the proper passing angles, setting good screens, balancing the floor in a manner that makes it difficult for the opponent to guard the offensive players or get a double team, and having every man on the court work hard in his role so that he or a teammate can get an open shot. Coaches and players learn that mental mistakes breed physical errors; thus, good teams focus on the task, play with intensity, and keep a positive mind-set.

Just getting a shot in late-game situations isn't enough; the goal is to get a high-percentage shot. Doing so takes discipline and poise, which come in part from proper preparation. All the men on the court—passer, screener, decoy, and shooter—must perform their roles correctly for the team to reach its goal. One of the truths of basketball is that the failure of one man to do his job can negate the work of four teammates who did theirs perfectly. Basketball is the true team game, with five players working as one to accomplish a single purpose. And if we're paying attention, all of us—coaches and players—will learn something new in every game that will help us down the road.

The following points summarize ways in which to execute the plan:

- **Don't experiment in games.** After trailing Jacksonville for most of the game, South Florida (my team) used a full-court, 1-3-1 press to pull within two points with five seconds to go. Jacksonville fouled our center, who went to the free-throw line for two shots and a chance to tie the game. The press had worked well, so we decided to stay in it. But we needed to adjust our alignment because our center was shooting the free throws. If he made the free throws, his new role would be to take the up position in the press to guard the inbounds passer, while the small forward needed to rotate back and guard the basket against any long pass or layup attempt.

Our center made the two free throws to tie the score and then took his proper defensive position guarding the Jacksonville player who was throwing the ball inbounds. The entry pass went to Jacksonville's guard, who immediately attacked the sideline off the dribble. Instead of attacking the wing defenders, he threw a long pass to Jacksonville's center, who hit an uncontested layup at the buzzer. Our small forward had lined up correctly before the foul shots were taken, but when Jacksonville threw the ball in, he left his assignment under the basket and ran to midcourt, his usual position, forgetting that he had exchanged spots with the center.

As South Florida's head coach, I learned two important lessons from this experience: First, don't try things in a game that the players have never practiced. Second, remember that although some players are capable of making adjustments on the fly during the heat of a close game, others are not as adaptable and need to stay within their comfort zones. Failure to execute in the endgame cost us a possible victory.

- **Play your trump card at the right time.** Most good teams know the value of proper execution. Baseball teams practice the suicide squeeze, even though they seldom use the play. Football teams practice the quarterback sneak, although they use it sparingly. Basketball teams work on full-court, short-clock situations almost daily. Teams should spend time practicing minute details because such situations might arise in any game. When I was head coach at Transylvania, we were in the finals of the Kentucky Intercollegiate Athletic Conference tournament against Union College of Barbourville, Kentucky. Union had home-court advantage by virtue of being the higher seed. Much was at stake, because the winner would advance to the National Association of Intercollegiate Athletics (NAIA) playoffs and the loser's season would end.

Transylvania had the ball out of bounds in a tie game 94 feet from the basket with four seconds left in regulation. We had practiced a play all season for precisely that situation, and when the players came to the time-out huddle they already knew what our strategy would be. Still, for the play to work, each player had to carry out his assignment. Our guards were positioned opposite each other on the sidelines at midcourt. Our tallest player, Bob Ecroyd, lined up at our free-throw line, and our center was at midcourt. On the call of "Hike," Ecroyd set a back screen for our center as our two guards took three hard steps into the backcourt then pivoted and ran toward the frontcourt as the ball was thrown to Ecroyd at midcourt. Ecroyd's first option was to pass to one of the guards, but that option wasn't available. His second option, which he executed, was to drive to the basket and shoot. The ball banked in at the buzzer, and we were on our way to Kansas City and the NAIA national tournament. The back screen, the sprinting by the guards, their reverse pivots, the long pass to Ecroyd at midcourt and his catch, dribble, and shot all culminated in perfect execution. The true essence of coaching is execution.

Principle 4: **Be Unselfish**

I've never met a coach who enjoyed coaching a selfish player, and I've never met a player who enjoys playing with a selfish player. Basketball players learn early that shooting and ballhandling are the skills that coaches look for when selecting teams. Unfortunately, as coaches select the better players for Amateur Athletic Union (AAU), middle school, and high school teams, selfish play is already built into the system.

The following points summarize ways in which to be unselfish:

• **Share the ball.** High scorers make the teams, are voted to all-star teams, and receive media attention from those who don't understand the game on any level other than point scoring. Given this situation, it's not surprising that many young players become selfish. They look at taking shots and scoring as *the* way to succeed.

Coaches spend hours teaching players about shot selection. Bad shots can destroy a team in many ways. Effective coaches teach players that poor shot selection can cause several problems:

- The team is in poor offensive rebounding position; no one knows when to go to the boards.
- Bad shots make the team vulnerable to fast breaks and easy baskets for opponents. Who rotates back?
- Poor shot selection destroys team morale; the shooter puts selfish interest above team success.
- When players take bad shots, teammates have no incentive to make screens and cuts.
- The fire-at-will, one-and-done offensive approach leads to chaos, confusion, and team problems.

Basketball should be fun for all. The coach should clarify at the beginning what a good shot is and what a bad shot is. Players need to know their parameters.

Ball handlers are taught to move the ball, hit the open man, and pass ahead on fast breaks. Selfish players might choose to hold the ball rather than pass ahead to a teammate in transition, thus destroying the advantage of having numbers on their side in a fast break. Think of some of the great players who you've seen. Michael Jordan, Jerry West, and Larry Bird come quickly to mind. You'll recall that they didn't have to dominate the ball to be effective. In fact, they went out of their way to involve their teammates and spread the scoring load, making it harder for opponents to guard them. That approach is not only unselfish basketball but also the smart way to play. Good coaches design half-court sets that highlight player and ball movement. When this movement stops, the offense breaks down. For their own individual good as well as for the success of the team, players should share the basketball. They'll find that making a good pass that leads to a teammate's basket is just as much fun as scoring themselves.

• **Help teammates on defense.** Defense is the cornerstone of good basketball. Good defensive teams can often hang in there with teams that have better talent. And even teams with exceptional talent know that there are going to be nights, especially on the road, when their shots aren't falling. The way to win on such nights is through good defense. Keep the other team from shooting a high percentage and your chances of victory skyrocket. Good athletes who are willing can learn to play effective defense, and good defensive teams are almost always in the game.

What does a player need to play good defense? Defenders bring high energy, toughness, unselfishness, enthusiasm, and the ability to move their feet. The best defensive players always stand ready to lend a helping hand to a teammate who gets beat. Great camaraderie can be built on defense. The beauty here is that the unselfishness seeps over to the offense and helps foster unselfish behavior there. Defense can be fun, and the best defensive teams take pride in their defensive effort. Coaches can learn many things about a player from watching him play defense.

Here are nine hustle indicators that players should use when trying out for a team:

1. Get down in an athletic position and assume a defensive stance.
2. Slide the feet without crossing them.
3. Sprint to catch up and get level to the ball when you fall behind.
4. Contain by staying in front of the dribbler.
5. Contest every shot your man takes.
6. Deny ball-side cuts.
7. Box out on rebounds.
8. Dive on the floor for loose balls. Such conduct is contagious.
9. Take no plays off. If you need rest, ask the coach to remove you from the game. Don't try to catch your breath on defense.

• **Eliminate the virus.** Sooner or later, selfish players will poison the team. Coaches must move quickly and decisively to eradicate the selfish virus. If a coach lets one team member get by with selfish play, then other players eventually are going to say, "He lets Joe do it. Why shouldn't I?" Then your team is doomed.

Bill Russell, the great center of the Boston Celtics, dominated with unselfishness. One evening I was seated next to Tom "Satch" Sanders, a Boston teammate of Russell's. I asked him what made Boston so effective. He said it was because of Russell. "He controlled the ball 90 percent of the time for us but scored only 10 percent of our points," Sanders said. Russell understood that players succeed by winning, not by individual scoring statistics. Although the NBA has produced many star players, only the truly unselfish ones such as Russell, Michael Jordan, Larry Bird, Magic Johnson, Isiah Thomas, and more recently, Shaquille O'Neal, David Robinson, and Tim Duncan have provided the necessary leadership to win the NBA title.

Principle 5:
Maximize Strengths, Minimize Weaknesses

Players bring different skills to the game. Some are scorers and shooters, others are good ball handlers, some are best at rebounding, others excel on defense, and still others provide overall leadership and enhance team chemistry. Good coaches know what each player on their team does well and not so well, and serious players want to know the truth about their skills, whether they're playing on an AAU team, at summer camp, or on a school team.

As players progress from middle school to high school to college and into the NBA, coaches and scouts cull out those who are selfish. One NBA team charts 67 different parameters of defense and grades players daily on those measures.

The following points summarize ways in which to maximize strengths and minimize weaknesses:

• **Record workout results.** Figure 1.1, a first-look evaluation form used for tryouts and practices, provides the coach with specific information for accurate comments when discussing a player's strengths and weaknesses.

A coach analyzes and determines his team's assets and liabilities through record keeping and workouts, eventually refining the players' roles (see chapter 2) to build a cohesive unit. Roles define the shooters, the rebounders, and the defenders. Most of the time these roles are self-evident. When players understand and accept their roles, the potential for conflict diminishes. Perceptive coaches still understand that players can disagree about style of play. Guards, naturally, prefer an offense that features the perimeter shot as the first option, whereas the big men want their touches in an offense that emphasizes going inside first. Highly talented teams enjoy the luxury of being able to attack inside and outside, but the coach of less talented teams must make clear what style

Observation Chart

Name _____   Scale 1- 5 (5 is best)

Offensive skills		**Defensive skills**	
Shooting	(4)	Proper stance	(1)
Perimeter shots	(2)	Contains	(4)
Dribbling	(4)	Contests	(2)
Passing	(1)	Gives help / support	(2)
Moves ball ahead	(1)	Stops dribble drive	(2)
Offense rebounding	(1)	Defense rebounding	(4)

Discussion points

Strengths		**Weakness**	
Shooting	(4)	Proper stance	(1)
Dribbling	(4)	Contest	(2)
Contain	(4)	Help / support	(2)
Defense rebounding	(4)	Stops dribble drive	(2)
Hustle	(4)	Perimeter shots	(2)
Attitude	(3)	Passing	(1)
		Moves ball ahead	(1)
		Offense rebounding	(1)

Figure 1.1   Observation chart.

will dominate. The head coach seeks input from assistants on style of play, but the final decision is his.

Just to make sure that there is no confusion, the coach, not the player, has the final word on what role the player will play to help the team succeed. In the team's first meeting of the season, the coach must cover several issues, such as policies, regulations, and discipline. At this time, all players should fill out a form about their strengths, weaknesses, and their individual goals for the year (see figure 2.2 on page 27). Compiling and reviewing their responses should help reduce the potential for conflicts and get everyone pulling in the same direction.

• **Use statistics.** Used properly, statistics can help define strengths and weaknesses. Statistics and charts (see chapter 3) compiled during practice are valuable resources in establishing roles for players. Tracking a player's progress is an important way of showing him where he needs to improve and where he stacks up against other players at his position. Statistical systems can measure individual players and teams over a season or a specific number of games. Getting this information is part of the process, but more important is knowing how to apply it. Valid statistics is one tool that helps coaches identify their team's strengths and weaknesses. They are not an end-all, but used properly, they provide valuable guidance. Statistics track a player's progress in certain areas and, along with other things that happen in practice, can determine playing time.

• **Finish the game with your best players.** One of the biggest challenges for coaches and players is to make sure that the best players are on the floor at the end of close ball games. Players should be quick to recognize when a teammate is in foul trouble and make adjustments to help on defense, crash the boards, or sprint back to cover the basket to give help. Joe Barry Carroll, a seven-footer and a number-one NBA Draft pick in 1980 from Purdue, was so valuable to our team that when he picked up his fourth foul, we had to find ways to keep him in the game. We might change the defense or adjust matchups. The coach must be aware of personal fouls, fatigue, injuries, and who his best pressure free-throw shooters are so that he finishes with the strongest possible team on the floor. This is exactly what UConn did in its 2004 NCAA semifinal win over Duke, when Emeka Okafor was held out for almost 16 minutes in the first half of the game in order to be available for the second-half finish.

Plan the work and work the plan is good advice for anyone attempting to be successful in any enterprise. During the early planning stage, it's important to establish trustworthy principles that serve as the foundation on which to build a successful basketball program. These five guiding principles—play hard, play smart, execute properly, be unselfish, and maximize player strengths and minimize player weaknesses—enable the coach to begin on a solid foundation with a clean, unambiguous road map. With our principles firmly in place, we move to the important roles that players and coaches undertake as leadership qualities unfold.

CHAPTER 2

Roles

A winning basketball team has many roles for players to fill. Obvious position-specific roles are defensive stopper, rebounding leader, and ball handler. Other roles relate to status in practice and games, such as whether a player is a starter, rotation player, or support player. Perhaps just as important are roles that go beyond the court and player, roles that truly define the energy of a team, such as leader, motivator, encourager, and team player. And highly skilled and gifted players in high school must take on the added role, or responsibility, of being a decision maker when choosing a college.

Just as players take on these multiple roles, coaches too must wear several hats both on and off the court—they must be leaders, tacticians, drill sergeants, negotiators, and disciplinarians. The coach may also fill the role of being a mentor, advisor, and player advocate. In this chapter, we will discuss these varying player, coach, and team roles and talk about ways to bring out the best that each role and player can offer your team.

Players' Roles

Regardless of the level of competition, players function best when the coach defines their specific on-court responsibilities. There can be no ambiguity. Each player should know exactly what is expected of him, and the coach should make sure that his players know, understand, and accept these expectations. Right from the first day of practice, the coach needs to evaluate each player on his individual merits (see chapter 3). After evaluating and placing the player into his role, the coach creates a written plan and consults with the player to define a specific course of action aimed at capitalizing on individual strengths and improving deficiencies.

The following discussion describes and defines the five specific playing positions and their roles.

Point Guard   *Coaches who really appreciate point guards are the ones who've had to try coaching without one.*

Characteristics:

John Stockton
© Icon Sports Media

- A coach on the floor like the great John Stockton.
- Has peripheral awareness and makes good decisions with the ball.
- Unselfish—thinks pass first, shot second.
- Primarily a ball handler and distributor who knows who is hot.
- The more speed and quickness he has, the better.
- Should be able to separate and create space when dribbling.
- Directs the offensive and defensive formations.
- Pushes the ball for fast breaks and calls half-court plays.
- Maintains constant communication with the coaches.
- Vocal leader on the floor.
- Discusses rule interpretations with the officials.
- During dead-ball situations such as free throws and out-of-bounds situations, he passes on information to teammates concerning strategy and matchups.
- Knows the time on both clocks, the score, the number of time-outs, and whom to foul.
- Size is a plus, but it is secondary to knowledge and skill.

Two Guard   *A scoring touch.*

Characteristics:

- Position requires great skills and perimeter shooting.

- Primary role is to score points; can sacrifice defense for offense at this position.

- Typically they are big, from 6-3 to 6-7, and athletic, like Kobe Bryant, Allen Houston, Tracy McGrady, and Michael Finley.

- Size is not an absolute restriction; smaller guards like Allen Iverson and David Wesley are exceptions who thrive as shooters.

Tracy McGrady

- Should be able to handle the ball, beat opponents off the dribble, penetrate, and finish at the basket.

- Should have good catch-and-shoot skills coming off pin-downs and baseline screens.

- The better the ball handler, the more difficult he is to defend.

- Good open-court player because of ability to pull up for open shots.

- Should be a good free-throw shooter because in late-game situations he is involved in handling the ball and taking last-second shots.

- Needs to be a good one-on-one player to be highly effective.

Small Forward   *Diversity, size, and scoring.*

Characteristics:

- Highly skilled player who has many of the two-guard skills.

- Bigger, stronger version of the two guard, with ability to play inside on the low post and outside on the perimeter.

- Has the ability to rebound and take it and fill the lane in the fast break.

- Good open-court player with ball-handling, passing, and decision-making capability.

- No standard size; can range from 6-5 to 7-0. The term "small forward" is

Kevin Garnett

somewhat inappropriate, especially with players like 7-0 Kevin Garnett and 6-11 Dirk Nowitzki.

- The more skills the small forward brings to the team, the more difficult it is for opponents to match up.
- Successful teams need at least three players who score in the upper teens to 20s; the small forward should be one of them.

Power Forward   *Power and strength.*

Characteristics:

- Big and powerful, with emphasis more on strength than finesse.
- Requires a player to be physically strong, rebound aggressively, protect the basket, block shots, and be a competitive defender.
- Needs to have a midrange jump shot out to 17 feet and a low-post game.
- Not required to score big numbers but should consistently score in the 8 to 10 points range with a good field-goal percentage.
- NBA crossover players like Karl Malone and Tim Duncan, both dominant scorers, are exceptions, not the rule, for the power forward position.

© Icon Sports Media

Karl Malone

- Should be a team player willing to sacrifice scoring for defense and rebounding. P.J. Brown, who played for the Charlotte and New Orleans Hornets, is an excellent example of what it takes to play this position.
- Players at this position often convert from the center position as they progress from high school to college and from college to professional ball.

Center   *Offense separates the great ones.*

Characteristics:

- Ideally, big, strong, mobile, good ball handler, with scoring touch around the basket.
- Better ones are excellent passers with peripheral awareness, good rebounders, and shot blockers with quick jumping ability.
- As low-post player, needs soft hands, good footwork, and body balance.

Shaquille O'Neal

© Icon Sports Media

- Best ones are good free-throw shooters, permitting their teams to go to them late in games. Glaring exceptions are Shaquille O'Neal and Wilt Chamberlain, with lifetime free-throw averages of 53 percent and 51 percent respectively.

- Should have a trademark go-to move that is practically unstoppable; could be a skyhook, stepback jumper, explosive power move, or face-up jump shot with drive options.

- An old Kentucky saying goes "Great centers don't come down the pike very often." Table 2.1 shows how the big-time centers have statistically dominated the game. All won NBA championships, and their lifetime averages reflect their statistical dominance.

To reach maximum efficiency, every team needs its players to accept their assigned roles on the court. Once players are assigned a position, they are usually placed in one of three distinct roles: Players 1 through 5 are classified as starters; players 6 through 8 are top reserves, or rotation players; and players 9 through 12, or 15, are role, or support, players. Each group has its own important jobs and objectives. Roles for the starters and top reserves are well defined and reflect the characteristics noted in the preceding discussion.

Table 2.1 Statistics of Big-Time Centers

Name	ppg	rpg	Seasons
Chamberlain	30.1	22.8	14
O'Neal*	27.5	12.4	10
Abdul-Jabbar	24.6	11.2	20
Olajuwon	23.6	11.6	15
Reed	18.7	12.9	10
Russell	15.1	22.5	13

*still active

Players generally accept these roles because they know they will play in the games. It's a different story for the support players, as will be pointed out later in this chapter. Support players will quickly learn that they won't play much in games, but their actions and attitudes on and off the court can still have a huge effect on the team's well-being and chances for success.

Players' Personal Qualities

Player roles are never static. In many situations, a player's role can change suddenly. The change often occurs when a player's skills improve, but at other times injuries can force a player out of the lineup, or the coach may give a fresh face an opportunity to make good, causing some sticky realignments. Semester grading periods can affect team composition as some athletes fail to follow through on their academic responsibilities. Discipline can also take its toll on a team, whether it comes from the school, home, or coach. Regardless of one's position or the role he plays on the team, following the rules, staying ready, and being available are the most important things a player can do. Let's look at some other role issues that affect every team.

Resilience

Had you told anyone in Kinston, North Carolina in 1970 that hometown high school player Cedric Maxwell would become the MVP of the 1981 NBA playoffs, your sanity would have been questioned. After his outstanding college career at UNC Charlotte, Maxwell led the Boston Celtics to the NBA title, four wins to two in the championship series against the Houston Rockets. He averaged 16.1 points and 7.4 rebounds in the playoffs while hitting 56.8 percent of his field goals. Maxwell's story is a good example of a key player trait—resilience.

Maxwell tried out for the varsity basketball team as a skinny high school sophomore and was told he should play in his homeroom's after-school basketball program. That would have been enough to insult and embarrass many young people into giving up. It only strengthened Maxwell's resolve. He had certain gifts such as good speed and quickness and unusually good ballhandling skills for a person his size. However, he had some physical limitations that couldn't be glossed over. He simply was not strong enough to compete with the older players. He took his coach's advice his sophomore year and played homeroom basketball. He tried out for the varsity again as a junior and was told to return to homeroom basketball. Maxwell loved basketball and wasn't about to give up.

Maxwell had one last chance to make his varsity basketball team as a senior. Fortunately, he had experienced a tremendous growth spurt and stood 6-7, with a corresponding addition of strength. A quick 6-7 player with strength and determination wasn't going to settle for a third year of homeroom basketball. Maxwell's ballhandling skills continued to improve and his overall game complemented his growth spurt. He was not only bigger, but his skills were better.

Maxwell had a good senior year for Kinston High School and earned a full basketball scholarship to UNC Charlotte, where he became MVP of the 1976 NIT as a junior and led his team to the 1977 NCAA Final Four as a senior. Boston took Maxwell with the eleventh pick of the first round of the NBA draft, a good choice indeed as he still holds several of Boston's field goal shooting percentage records.

All players have to learn to deal with disappointment and be able to bounce back. For support players in particular, criticism and discouragement can take their toll.

Their usual job is to scrimmage against the first team, which routinely results in a solid pounding. These daily thrashings are part of the role that players 9 through 15 must learn to deal with. All of us have egos, and it takes a tough-minded, resilient person to deal with daily defeats while keeping a positive attitude.

Inexperienced players who are still learning and making fundamental mistakes are likely to be corrected more than experienced players who have a better understanding of how to play and what is expected of them. Most experienced players have learned how to handle constructive criticism, and they don't let it beat them down or distract them. They hear it, learn from it, and begin to develop the tough skin necessary to move on.

Young support players must learn not to let criticism debilitate them. They should strive to view a coach's criticism this way: "Coach gets on me because he's interested and wants to see me improve. I should start worrying when he doesn't criticize me when I make mistakes."

An excellent example of a contributing player who made his team better is Ken Angel, a 6-8 power player who was on my 1977 UNC Charlotte Final Four team. Angel's role dictated that he seldom played in games, but he came to practice every day with a positive attitude and a commitment to work as hard as he could to make our starting center, Maxwell, compete and become the best player he could be. Angel's work in practice each day never showed up in a game box score, and although the casual fan didn't know of his contribution, his coaches and teammates did. He helped us improve, and he had every right to feel he was a part of the process that helped Maxwell become an All-American and later a first-round draft pick of the Boston Celtics. To reach its goals, every team needs three or four Ken Angels.

Players in support positions are usually the younger players who need to grow and develop. Consequently, getting to practice early when balls, space, and instructors are all available is a smart move. Players who arrive early establish good work habits and demonstrate willingness to spend extra time improving their game. Everyone profits from extra practice, but support players stand to benefit the most. Seldom do these players get headlines, have interviews, or even receive notice by the media. Every successful program at any level has dedicated support players who take pride in doing a job the best they can—a job that elicits respect from their coaches and peers.

Motivation

Competitive athletes bring their motivation to the team, both on and off the court. Motivation varies greatly among players. Some strive for the ultimate, to become all-stars, whereas others seek only to start or to improve enough to get into the rotation and obtain more playing time.

One motivated player who stands out in my mind was Joe Barry Carroll. After signing a contract to coach at Purdue University, I caught a plane to Lexington, Kentucky, to meet Carroll, Purdue's 7-1 junior center. Carroll was playing in an all-star game, and this was my first opportunity to visit him. I asked him one question, "What do you want out of basketball?" because I needed to know if

Carroll and I had the same expectations for the team and for him. He pondered the question and announced thoughtfully that he wanted to play in the NBA. "That's great," I said, "because we'll work hard together and get you ready." The Purdue team went on to the NCAA Final Four. With his excellent work ethic, desire for improvement, and personal motivation, he went on to become the number-one pick in the 1980 NBA Draft.

As shown by the preceding example, personal motivation is a key to everything that athletes do because it provides the incentive for their participation. Social acceptance is a major reason that some youngsters become involved in athletics. Recognition and career opportunities drive many players who want to improve their standard of living beyond high school. Imagine an entry level job that guarantees millions of dollars. How many generations might such wealth affect? The average salary in some pro sports goes as high as $3.6 million per player for those gifted enough to make it.

You can spot good motivational candidates by their commitment to excellence in character and by the way they care for their bodies. Generally, coaches do not have to discipline highly motivated players because such players lead by example and challenge others to follow.

You can encourage motivation by publicly recognizing those who excel by working hard and working extra. Motivated players come early to practice and stay late. You need not use a starter or star as your example of a motivated player with competitive character; anyone can assume that role.

Leadership

I am not aware of any teams or businesses that become successful without good leadership. To succeed, players and coaches must work together with the five playing guidelines—play hard, play smart, execute, be unselfish, and maximize your talents. Great teams usually have a player or players who emerge to fit the role of leader. First, such players lead by example, thereby gaining the respect of their teammates and coaches. Later, their teammates heed their words.

Leadership is a key role because leaders provide the dedication, desire, and commitment to establish and follow worthy goals. Leaders share the characteristic of motivation and with it bring character, a work ethic, a vision, and a value system underscored by integrity. You can spot good leadership candidates by understanding that leaders give and losers take. Maturity is also important because the players who learn to take "no" in the same manner that they take "yes" have a much greater chance of succeeding. You can encourage leadership in your team by establishing high standards and living up to them. From junior high school to the NBA, coaches and players must share leadership roles if the team is to achieve its full potential.

Responsibility

Coaches must give players the tools with which to succeed. Players appreciate and benefit greatly when coaches seek their input. One way that coaches can do this is by asking players to help set team rules for the current season. Coaches should make players aware of issues that affect the team and allow time for players to meet without the coaches so that they can discuss team matters and policies on their own. This approach puts them in a position of making sure that the penalty fits the crime, in case disciplinary action is needed. Although this approach provides an excellent learning experience in democracy, players have expressed anguish over the difficulty of working through the process.

Here's a blueprint: Assign every player to a committee, with the most senior player serving as chairman of his committee. The committees represent the various issues that the players encounter while representing their team. After establishing policies, the committees should present them to the entire team and coaches for debate. This committee experience encourages less outspoken players to become more involved. The objective is to have the players assume responsibility for leadership and self-governance. Providing leadership is the ultimate experience, and players can emerge from these sessions with a new perspective. Here are four suggested committees that relate directly to high school and college teams:

Committee	Policy responsibility
Practice	Conditioning, practice (late and missed) concerns, vacations
Grooming	Attire for home and away games, facial hair, hair length
Rules	Smoking, drugs, alcohol, curfew, dormitories, guns, insubordination
Academics	GPA requirements, exam schedules, study hall, cheating, missing class

A player's role depends on his individual strengths and weaknesses and a good understanding of how to go about improving.

Coaches' Attributes

Coaching requires a deft touch. If a coach has 15 players on his roster, chances are that they will have strikingly different physical, social, and behavioral attributes. What might be highly important to one player might not even register with another. The best coaches find ways to blend these different personalities and convince them to put the interests of the team first. That task might sound easy, but it isn't.

Most successful coaches have several traits in common, such as a keen eye that lets them observe what's going on around them, sharp intelligence, and the knack of spotting a problem in its early stages so that they can deal with it before it becomes a major distraction to the team. Although these attributes are key for strong coaches, the intangible emotional qualities of humility, respect, trust, optimism, and strength of character are equally important.

Humility

Head coaches need to have humility and the good sense to understand that they can't accomplish the goal to succeed without the full support and loyalty of the assistant coaches and all the players. In other words, the best coaches are careful to distribute the credit. You can do this by always praising the effort that support players bring to practice and games. When support players win a shooting drill, hit free throws, or make a good hustle play, coaches need to shower them with praise and positive encouragement. Tracking support players' academic progress and being quick to sing their praises when they excel in the classroom are excellent ways to recognize contributions. In general, anytime a player, especially a support player, can be singled out for doing a good job, from drill work to hitting a game winner, coaches should acknowledge his contribution. Show your appreciation by having them select which basket they want to defend, or let them go first at the water break or be the first to leave practice.

Mutual Respect

Teams gain strength when the coach is somehow able to put himself in the shoes of the players and understand their needs and wants, and when players grow to appreciate and respect the problem-solving issues inherent in the coach's position. Mutual respect goes a long way in helping a team achieve a goal. The ultimate goal of every coach is to gain the respect of his players. In no other profession is leadership so obvious and open to speculation. The coach lives by the slogan "Walk the talk" because everything he says is printed and aired for public consumption. The coach must be intelligent about the game, have good people skills, earn respect by his actions and his words, cultivate the media, and be loyal and honest to his players, family, and employer. Specifically, to earn his players' respect, the coach must pass the "standard test." After the team rules and penalties have been determined and implemented, the coach is on notice. Players want to know if the coach will apply the rules equally across the board. They find this out the minute the star player breaks a rule. If the coach administers the penalty according to the team penalty requirement, he immediately establishes team respect. If he fails to administer the penalty properly or waters down the penalty, he stands a good chance of losing their respect, never to regain it. The important issue for the players is finding out if the coach shows any partiality.

Trust

Trust comes into play every day in a team sport. For example, the following occurred on an NBA team, although it could happen at any level. The head coach had an open-door policy for any player who had a problem and wanted to talk. The guarantee was that the talk would remain private and confidential. Our captain and team leader was a fierce competitor and a classy man in every way. During an especially tough part of the schedule, the captain decided that he needed to discuss some problems with the head coach. A couple of games after that private meeting occurred, we played poorly and trailed at halftime. The head coach went into a tirade at halftime, and in the process identified the player and divulged the gist of their conversation—the one that the coach had promised would remain confidential. The coach had betrayed the player, who was embarrassed and humiliated by the breach of ethics. Every player in the locker room sided with the player, and respect for him soared. But the head coach lost the one thing a coach can't afford to lose—the trust of his players. His so-called open-door policy became the butt of players' jokes. When a leader breaks his word, he loses trust, and once lost, trust is virtually impossible to retrieve. When this coach lost the trust of his players, he lost his team.

Enthusiasm

Genuine enthusiasm has a favorable effect on players, so coaches should come to practice with a positive attitude. Coaches give confidence to players, and players should encourage their teammates, applaud good plays and effort, compete vigorously and physically, and always be good sports. Following a loss, a coach must get his players to learn from it but not dwell on the outcome to the point that it adversely affects the next game. The coach must not become negative when the season hits a tough spot. Enthusiastic team leaders inspire others. Showing enthusiasm is simple. The gesture can be as small as giving a high five as a player comes off the court or as large as stopping a practice, waiting until there is dead silence, and then praising an outstanding, unselfish play. The player might have made a good pass, taken a charge, executed an excellent box out, or helped a teammate up off the floor. By stopping and obtaining silence, the coach ensures that the players get the message.

Sometimes there are quantitative reasons, not excuses, why teams lose. Here are three valid reasons that affect losing coaches and teams in the NBA. All three deal with talent, or lack thereof, and are not necessarily reflective of the coach's ability. Coaches who take on expansion teams such as Vancouver or Toronto, or coaches who get caught in rebuilding situations such as Chicago or Atlanta, or unlucky coaches who lose star players to major injuries as did Miami with Alonzo Mourning and Orlando with Grant Hill, are simply not going to win.

Table 2.2, *a* and *b*, provides examples of the phenomenon of losing by showing the coaching records of former NBA players and highly successful college coaches. Many got caught up in expansion, rebuilding, and injury situations. Take a look at the following charts and you'll see many were caught up in circumstance beyond their capacity to control. Failure was predictable.

Mental Toughness

Teams have rules and policies that govern their programs. (See the "Responsibility" section earlier in this chapter.) The head coach should seek input in making team rules, but after the rules are established, it's his job to enforce discipline when violations occur: He can't delegate this task to someone else. Informed coaches

Table 2.2a Coaching Records of Former NBA Players

Coach	Team	Record		
		Won	**Lost**	**Winning percentage (%)**
Quinn Buckner	Dallas	13	69	.158
Brian Winters	Vancouver	23	102	.184
Sidney Lowe	Minn / VC / Mem	56	161	.217
Jim Cleamons	Dallas	20	70	.285
Magic Johnson	Lakers	5	11	.313
George Irvine	In / Detroit	100	190	.344
Wes Unseld	Washington	202	345	.369
Elgin Baylor	New Orleans	86	135	.389

Table 2.2b NBA Coaching Records of Former and Current College Coaches

Coach	Team	Record		
		Won	**Lost**	**Winning percentage (%)**
Tim Floyd	Chicago***	49	190	.205
Leonard Hamilton	Washington	19	63	.231
Lon Kruger	Atlanta	69	122	.361
John Calipari	New Jersey	72	112	.391
Jerry Tarkanian	San Antonio	9	11	.450
P.J. Carlesimo	Portland / Golden S	188	222	.458
Rick Pitino	NY / Boston	192	220	.466

*Statistics from team press guides.
**Statistics go through the 2003 season.
***Currently winning at New Orleans.

know that they will face criticism for handing out punishment, but they must be mentally tough enough to handle the chore fairly and quickly. If that discipline doesn't come when it should, clarity of purpose and fairness are out the window. Winning teams can't function without those two components.

Coach-Player Connection

Players benefit significantly when the head coach takes a genuine interest in their total college experience. By doing this, the coach makes his job much more rewarding. The student-athlete is in college primarily to learn things that will help him in his career after basketball, and his coach can serve as the catalyst in that quest. The coach should not settle for surprises from his players. He should make it a point of emphasis that players must keep up with their class attendance and maintain overall academic progress. If things slide, the coach should deal with the situation immediately.

To foster connection with players, coaches should meet with their players individually on a regular schedule, weekly if necessary, to talk about both basketball and nonbasketball topics. The coach may want to divide the team alphabetically into three groups of five each. The two assistant coaches and the head coach should meet individually with their particular group at a scheduled time, and the three groups can rotate to a different coach weekly.

These scheduled appointments remain constant throughout the year, and attendance is mandatory. Each player has an individual folder that rotates with the group; the folder includes an interview sheet with various issues to be discussed. Coaches write notes during the conversations. After completing the individual conferences, the coaches meet and discuss any problems that may have come up. The individual conference follows the outline shown in figure 2.1.

One question that should come up on a scheduled basis at these conferences is "What are your goals?" The answer to this question should reveal a great deal. What is the player's ambition? What motivates him? What is his value system? When team members help set the rules, they're more likely to obey them. The coach should realize that what players want and understand largely determines

---

Individual Conference

Name _____ Date _____

1. How are things at home?
2. Any problems? If there's a problem, how can we help / listen?
3. When was the last time you talked to your parents or guardian from home?
4. Review all classes and course work for previous week. (see class load below)
5. Record all test results.
6. Any outstanding work due / up to date on assignments?
7. Need any help with tutors / study table attendance up to date?
8. Any missed classes / if so why? (sickness) (injury) (travel)
9. Discuss dorm life / roommate / any problems?
10. Social life / dating / girlfriend problems / campus organizations / church life.
11. Any teammate conflicts / issues?
12. Any other problems you wish to discuss?
    - Class schedule (1. English) (2. History) (3. Spanish) (4. Psychology)
    - Players were scheduled 20 minutes apart over a two-hour block of time.
    - All unexcused missed classes were penalized.

Figure 2.1 Individual conference worksheet.

team success. The head coach should sit down with each player individually before preseason practice begins to discuss the player's goals.

Setting realistic, measurable goals helps players improve their performance with heightened motivation, more intense practices, and less boredom. Studies show that athletes who work toward performance goals outperform those without goals. Goals such as to play hard, have fun, and get in shape are difficult to measure. Others, such as field-goal percentage, rebound average, or number of steals, are more effective in improving performance because they are quantifiable. Coaches should help determine what goes on the form. Figure 2.2 is a sample to consider.

Protection of Player Interests

The final role a coach must play is that of player advocate. In a December 2002 article in *The New York Times*, George Vecsey wrote, "In the United States, people know all about the corruption, the phony admissions standards, the payoffs, the boosters who permeate college sports. University administrators know. Fans know. We all go along." Everett Bass, a loyal assistant coach with me at UNC Charlotte, Purdue, and South Florida would often return from a recruiting trip shaking his head and saying, "Coach, they're not dealing with a full deck out there."

Who are the guardians of our great game of basketball? Who are the gatekeepers that can stand as symbols to restore integrity to the game? Greed is like the camel poking his nose into the tent. If the camel gets his nose in and no one objects, he feels free to put his head in and have a look around. If this isn't met by objections, he feels free to put in one leg, then another, until he is completely inside the tent. At this point, someone may want to object as things get crowded and begin to smell. However, once the camel is in, it's hard to remove him. When he stands up, the tent collapses. The camel in the tent of college basketball involves institutions selling out to the big money offered by televisioin, a willingness to exploit players for the sole purpose of winning, and all involved turning their backs on what is right.

How do we reduce recruiting abuses, ensure civility, monitor morality, and see to it that the interests of players come first? How do we start to put reason back into college programs? All players and the game itself would benefit from the following reforms:

• **Eliminate freshman eligibility.** Few doubt that players who make the transition from high school to college benefit academically, physically, mentally, and socially by playing freshman or JV basketball rather than jumping into varsity competition. A few talented players will feel slighted by such a rule, but most freshmen need a year to adjust to the demands of college life and basketball.

• **Tie scholarships to graduation rates.** A meaningful reform would be to link athletic scholarships to graduation rates. Coaches would then be more selective in their recruiting and more involved in the academic progress of their players. Players who stood no chance of graduating would no longer be pushed through

Player's Goals

Name_____

I. Team goals:	(Please explain answer)
Winning season	_____
Win the conference	_____
Win the conference tournament	_____
NCAA / NAIA / NJUCO playoffs	_____
National rankings	
Team record	_____

II. Individual goals:	(Please explain answer)	
Be a starter	_____	
Be a rotation player	_____	
Make all-conference	_____	
Be an All-American candidate	_____	
Be a positive contributor	_____	
Statistical improvement	Projected	Last yr statistics
Field goals	_____	43 %
Free throws	_____	71 %
Rebound avg	_____	4.3
Assists avg	_____	.6
Turnover avg	_____	1.5
Personal fouls	_____	3.5
Points per game	_____	9.3
Shots per game	_____	12.2
Attitude (1-5 scale / 5 best)	_____	4

III. Academics	Projected	Last year
Grade classification	_____	Junior
Grade point average	_____	2.6
Major	_____	Math
First semester courses		
Accounting III	_____	
English Lit	_____	
Statistics	_____	
Physics	_____	
Academic counselor	_____	Dr. Smith
On time to graduate	_____	

IV. Playing strengths and weaknesses: Please list and elaborate:

Strengths	*Weaknesses*
1.	1.
2.	2.
3.	3.
4.	4.
5.	5.

Figure 2.2 Player's goals worksheet.

the admissions office if coaches knew that each scholarship would be renewable only at the end of the player's four or five years of eligibility. The player, coach, and institution would then share the responsibility of the student-athlete's graduation.

Team Roles

To achieve greatness, players and coaches must set high goals and then seek to accomplish them together, sharing the credit. An inspired person, player, or coach sees a guiding vision, a sense of purpose, and advances confidently with an upbeat disposition. Remember, before you can convince others, you must first believe in yourself. This belief happens through setting united goals, communicating clearly, and seeing the same vision.

Shared Goals

A few years ago, an NBA team had, on paper, an extremely talented lineup of starters returning. Sportswriters for a national publication picked them to win the Eastern Conference. The head coach was a man who did not have an understanding of the delicate balance that being the favorite and being saddled with unrealistic expectations called for. He fed the unrealistic predictions and basked in the undeserved attention. Early in the season, losses mounted. Chaos soon set in, and observers labeled the team as underachievers. Instead of finishing the season in first place, they ended in fifth place and lost in the first round of the playoffs, 1-3. After the mediocre season, everyone left for the summer feeling disappointed. The media's preseason predictions for teams—whether high school, college, or NBA—can present a delicate issue for coach and players. Nothing is harder for athletes than to be saddled with unobtainable expectations.

Team and individual goals must be well thought out, realistic, and created together. Players need direction on achieving individual goals, as well as instruction on how to improve. For example, if a player shoots free throws poorly, the coach should analyze his technique and offer specific instruction. Whether the problem is the base, release, flexibility, aim, or follow-through, the coach should let the player know exactly what he needs to work on. Team goals can vary—from holding teams under a certain number of points, to winning the rebound battle, to forcing the opponent into more turnovers. A good way to pull a number of team goals together is to institute a "hustle" board. A team creates a hustle board by listing three to five statistical categories (all nonshooting) that they intend to win each game. For example, the following five categories all depend on hustle and could be designated as goals: defensive field-goal percentage, offensive rebounds, steals, blocked shots, and getting the charge. Following each game, the team, along with the coaches, can analyze the game and chart their strengths and weaknesses. Only after evaluating his team's talent and comparing it with local and national teams can a coach make an educated guess about what might happen during the season.

The setting of team goals and preseason expectations is at best an inexact science. Some teams are good enough to set a goal of winning the national championship or a high school state championship. What happens if your team goal is the conference championship and you find yourself mathematically out of the race with four or five games to play? Do you say it's all over, or do you set a new goal to be the best team you can be for the remaining games?

A pragmatic perspective suggests that teams can have long-term and short-term goals, and coaches had better be able to adjust on the fly. For some teams, an appropriate goal might be, "Let's get better each day." For others it might be, "No opponent will play harder than we do." Set goals that players and teams have a chance to accomplish. Even then, it's a good idea to stay away from specific win-loss numbers. Media expectations are a coach killer, and intelligent coaches avoid making preseason predictions or going along with those made by someone else.

Communication

Players and coaches need to work to be good observers. The coach with a keen eye can identify a player who may have lost interest or an assistant coach who has grown frustrated with the team's effort and execution. During such times, he may be able to solve the problem by asking this simple question: "How can I help?" This offer indicates that he cares and is willing to help, and it opens the door for communication that can transcend basketball. Loyalties can develop that prevent minor episodes from becoming major. A definitive solution to the problem might not be immediately forthcoming, but showing care and concern can go a long way toward building a successful team.

When I was head men's basketball coach and athletic director at UNC Charlotte from 1975 to 1978, Dr. Frank Dickey, the school's provost, was my immediate boss. Dr. Dickey, whom I admired greatly, gave me the best advice I'd ever received from an administrator: "When you encounter problems, and there will be problems, bring them to me and let's solve them together." He offered wise advice with absolutely no arrogance. Imagine how many problems could be avoided in athletics if administrators gave the same advice to their staffs, coaches, and teams that Dr. Dickey gave to me. "How can I help?"—a simple question that carries a powerful message.

Clarity

For coaches, players, and, ultimately, the team, clear instructions—about such things as which play to run, the defensive call, or when practice begins—can prevent misunderstanding. A clinician once said, "Whatever you do, don't let one play at the end of the half or game cause you to go off on a player or your team. Things will be said in the heat of the moment that you'd wish you'd never said." Preventing this is not easy, but it's far better to say nothing than to compound a difficult situation. Analyzing the game goes one of two ways. After a win, analysis is easy. A loss makes it difficult. The best policy is to address a loss the next day after viewing the film and discussing the problems with assistant coaches. Be clear in your thoughts and comments and be consistent in your relationship with your players. For both players and coaches, being clear means eliminating anything that might cause confusion. For the coach, clarity means that he has defined the players' roles so that the players stay within their defined strengths. Confusion occurs when players with defensive roles suddenly try to be scorers and offensive players decide to gamble on defense, thereby giving the opponent easy baskets. Coaches should always try to eliminate any gray areas where misunderstanding could lead to poor execution.

A wonderful example to demonstrate this issue occurred when UNC Charlotte played in the NIT in 1976, the first time that the school's basketball team had ever made the postseason. The NIT field consisted of 16 teams in those days, and all games were played in New York's Madison Square Garden. Postseason play in college basketball is cut and dry: Win or go home. Every team that went to the NIT got off the airplane hoping that they'd be in New York for the duration of the tournament. Nobody wanted to play one game and then pack up the next morning to go home. UNC Charlotte was the 16th and last team selected for that year's NIT.

We didn't have much time to celebrate when we learned that our first-round foe would be the University of San Francisco, which had been ranked as high as sixth nationally earlier in the year. San Francisco led by two points with 16 seconds left in regulation, and we had the ball at side court. During our time-out, I asked our players who wanted to take the last shot. Three players put their hands up; two didn't. The situation could not have been any clearer than that. One of the two who indicated that he didn't want to take the last shot took the ball out of bounds, and we used the other as a screener.

The play we called was designed not for one shooter, but for three. We had three guys who had the confidence to say they wanted the shot, and it didn't matter to me which of them took it. Kevin King, a 6-7 freshman, got the ball on the low post, executed a show-the-ball fake and step-under move, and hit an open 15-footer that sent the game into overtime. We won 79-74 and advanced to the second round. Clarity, mutual trust, and good player execution got us all the way to the NIT finals.

When players and coaches are able to fit into definite roles, the team profits and the coach-player relationship flourishes on mutual respect. This process develops because of intelligent leadership and efficient management skills. Successful basketball coaches define guiding principles, set meaningful goals, outline conditioning requirements, implement an objective evaluation procedure, oversee a planned development program while teaching the fundamentals, and cover all the strategy involved in basketball. Effective coaches work diligently to help players expand their game and refine their roles as they grow and improve their skills. In the next chapter, we examine how coaches evaluate players and assign them particular roles using a process called "the performance rating system."

CHAPTER 3

Player Performance Rating System

Five people who watch the same game will likely give five different responses when you ask them detailed questions about the performance of any player on the court. Most people can identify the high scorers during the game, but when you ask, "What did you think of his defense, his ability to play the passing lanes, his rebounding technique, his use of screens, his rotation out of double teams," you'd get varied opinions. Everyone has a unique personal perspective that includes subjective preferences and selective attention. So, your analysis might lead you to favor player A, whereas I might be more impressed by player B.

Clearly, a legitimate method of analyzing basketball players' performance benefits everyone. Whether used to determine who makes the cut, who starts, or who is contributing the most to winning games, the assessment system should be nonjudgmental, accurate, reliable, and data based.

To overcome the partiality, I created a performance rating system, or PR. Simply put, the PR is an objective evaluation system that removes guesswork when a coach evaluates and selects players. I created it after realizing that basketball players compete for playing time every practice, so accurate and fair statistics should be kept during practices as well as in games to determine a player's production.

Advantages of the Performance Rating System

The benefits of the PR system for coaches and players are numerous. Overall, coaches and players appreciate it for the fact that it creates an environment for individualized success that is fair, competitive, and motivating. For me, the process served as an invaluable evaluation tool when coaching three USA teams in international competition, especially in the 1984 World University Games in Kobe, Japan.

Competitive Success

My staff and I had eight days of practice in which to get 12 players to play as a team. USA select teams are put together by a USA Basketball committee, with two players at each position and two skilled specialists chosen from a shooter, defender, big man, or point guard. All players in this instance were starters on major college teams, representing Kansas, Kentucky, Auburn, St. Joseph's, Louisville, Nebraska, Missouri, Virginia Tech, Alabama at Birmingham, South Florida, and Miami of Ohio. All reported to practice expecting to start.

We explained the objective evaluation system to the players at the first practice. The players liked the concept and quickly grasped the weighted values assessed for each statistical category. They appreciated the fact that all five starting positions were open and that no one had been given a starting role. Twelve highly competitive athletes left the locker room satisfied that the evaluation process was fair, equal, consistent. Each felt that he could win a starting position based on his skill and production. Competitors like to start on an even playing field. All that the good ones ask for is a fair chance with no favored treatment; if that is granted, no one feels victimized by the selection process.

Eliminating subjectivity from the evaluation showed these players the importance that the coach placed on integrity. That was a top priority. The real beauty of using this system, for both the coach and the players, is the clear message that there will be no free passes, handouts, individual agreements, or entitlements. The only way a player gets playing time is to earn it by his production. A daily PR demonstrates the player's consistency and reflects his position ranking on the team. Players cannot slough off in practice and maintain their position in the lineup.

Motivating Success

The PR system proves to be an effective motivational tool for players and coaches. I felt the real effect of the system in the amazing improvements we made at the

University of South Florida. Ranked 248th out of 252 NCAA Division I teams, South Florida was coming off its fourth straight losing season with a 6-21 record when the coaching change occurred in 1980. One of our first moves was to initiate the PR system.

The players loved it, and some would not leave practice until the PR was posted. A team that had previously been riddled with chaos and confusion experienced not one major incident the entire year. That first season at South Florida was one of the most gratifying experiences in a long list of wonderful coaching memories. We ended the season 18-11, hosted a first-round NIT game against UConn before 10,259 fans, and won the vote as the Nation's Most Improved Team. I credit the PR system for the turnaround.

Let's look at the system's key components.

Components of the Performance Rating System

The first step to producing accurate statistics is to create a daily performance rating (PR). A daily performance rating is like a daily test score. Each basketball statistic is assigned a weighted value depending on the importance the coach and players place on specific categories. For example, a made free throw counts +1 and a missed free throw –2. An offensive rebound rates +2, but a defensive rebound is only +1. By assigning a value to each category—shooting, rebounding, assists, turnovers, violations, and blocked shots—you can produce a numeric score for each workout and game. The coach should explain the conversion formula to players so that they understand it, accept it as an objective measuring stick of performance, and realize that players with the highest PR scores at each position earn playing time.

This objective system records each player's daily contributions by charting his every move during practices and converting individual production results to a corresponding numbering system. The idea is to have clear guidelines, eliminate misunderstandings, and avoid confusion by assuring that each player has a fair opportunity.

The performance rating system hinges on four factors:

1. Objectivity as the aim
2. Easy implementation
3. Weighted performance criteria
4. Number-based evaluation

Objectivity As the Aim

Changing from an opinion-based evaluation process to an objective process may not be easy, but it's worth the effort to ensure good decisions and reduce player hostilities. Nothing is more important to team morale than fair treatment by the coach. Players know when coaches play favorites and don't treat team members fairly. The result of such behavior is team disintegration. Whether you call it team morale, harmony, or team chemistry, players get along for valid reasons, and effective leadership is one of them. Players grumble, complain, and create dissension when they think that their trust has been violated, and before long they lose confidence in their coach.

An objective evaluation system provides these benefits:

- Provides a useful analytical tool
- Determines a player's weaknesses
- Reflects a player's strengths
- Operates on objective data
- Indicates daily progress
- Eliminates players' concern about fairness
- Provides invaluable data for coach-player discussions
- Offers motivational aid for self-improvement
- Exposes one-dimensional players
- Provides a great system for building team harmony and selecting captains

Easy Implementation

Implementation of the PR system begins with the recruitment of at least 12 volunteer staff from the student body, interns, and student managers. In an orientation meeting, coaches explain the PR system, identify chart responsibilities, and underscore the need for a specific time commitment. The PR system is implemented for practices, home games, and film analysis of road games. The team supplies the minimal required equipment, including charts, pencils, and a written explanation of the fundamentals to be recorded. Training consists of identifying and defining the fundamental that each volunteer keeps—offensive rebounds or defensive rebounds, assists or turnovers, field goals made or missed, and so forth—and showing how to record the results.

The staff of volunteers works directly with the PR director to implement the system and record all the statistics. Here are the roles of key staff and their steps for implementation at a glance.

PR director: Assign a PR director responsible for coordinating the PR system. The director oversees the volunteers and makes daily assignments, keeps accurate daily statistics, and posts the PR daily in a designated place.

Volunteers: The volunteer staff keeps statistics on all five-on-five work that occurs during the practice. The PR director makes sure that all charts are properly administered, recorded, and collected. At the top of the charts, volunteers must fill in the type of work being done that day. After they finish their work, the volunteers sign their worksheets and pass the forms on to the PR director, who tabulates and posts the practice results. The same process applies for games and film analysis.

The second step is to train the staff to divide statistics into the following categories:

- All half-court work
- Controlled full-court work
- Scrimmages
- Practice games and intrasquad games
- Regular season games

In general, volunteers familiar with basketball are better; former high school players make excellent volunteers because they know the game and understand the terminology.

Weighted Performance Criteria

A weighted system for basketball statistics directly reflects the importance the coach places on specific categories within the structure of the game; a weighted evaluation system means that a specific value is assigned to a particular category. For instance, in a raw NCAA box score, any rebound that a player gets during a game counts as simply one rebound. As stated before, however, in my philosophy an offensive rebound weighs more heavily.

Here are the steps to creating weighted performance criteria:

1. Assign a numerical value to each component of the game.
2. Create necessary forms and separate them by different categories—shooting, rebounds, violations, turnovers, assists, and so on. Volunteers record daily statistics on these eight different categories. Before each practice, the PR director passes out folders with forms labeled as follows. Each form has all players listed in alphabetical order.
   a. Shots made and missed (two-point field goals, three-point field goals, free throws)
   b. Rebounds (offensive, defensive)
   c. Assists
   d. Turnovers
   e. Steals
   f. Personal fouls
   g. Blocked shots
   h. Violations
3. Determine a plus (+) and minus (–) value for each category. The point value will vary depending on coach and player perceptions of what is important.

So, how do coaches and players decide what's important? The PR's statistical weighted system is designed to be fair for all. Instead of making the leading scorer the most important player on the team, a weighted system rewards players who rebound, block shots, make assists, get steals, and do the blue-collar work necessary for winning. Some coaches use the NCAA game box to evaluate player performance—I didn't. Instead, I created a weighted evaluation system that included every objective statistic a player could acquire. Following each game, the players might have looked at the box score, but they knew that their PR number more accurately reflected what they did that night. Figure 3.1 provides an example of how to use the weighted system.

Sample Value Sheet

(+ Value)		(− Value)	
Shooting			
Made 2-point field goal	+2	Missed 2-point field goal	(-2)
Made 3-point field goal	+3	Missed 3-point field goal	(-3)
Made free throw	+1	Missed free throw	(-2)
Blocked shot	+1	Shot blocked	(-1)
Rebounding			
Offensive rebound	+2		
Defensive rebound	+1		
Ballhandling			
Assists (pass that leads to the score)	+3	Bad pass / turnover	(-2)
Steal / interception	+2	Traveling / walking	(-2)
Taking the charge	+3	Committed charging foul	(-2)
Violations			
		3 seconds in the lane	(-5)
		Personal fouls	(-1)
		Technical foul	(-5)
		Goaltending	(-3)
		Basket interference	(-3)
		Over and back	(-3)
		Free-throw violation	(-3)
		Jump ball	(-3)
		Out of bounds	(-3)

Notes on the weighted system:
* The makes and misses are weighted the same.
* Free-throw misses cost more than makes, because they are unguarded shots.
* Offensive rebounds +2 / defensive rebounds +1 / offense more difficult to get.
* Penalty violations are all weighted by the coach.
* Any questions concerning personal fouls or turnovers, determined by the coach.
* Always use outside officials for scrimmages.

Figure 3.1 Sample value sheet.

The players believe in the process because they approve of the entire weighted system, fundamental by fundamental. In looking at the weighted numbers, you'll notice that only a few have modifications. A player gets a +2 for an offensive rebound and a +1 for a defensive rebound because an offensive rebound is much more difficult to get. What player would argue with that? None. A made free throw is a +1 and a missed free throw is a –2. Why? Because a free throw is a free shot, taken totally unguarded. Free throws decide all close games. Larry Bird says that hitting free throws requires only two elements—concentration and practice.

Have I ever had a player disagree with +1 and –2 concept? Never. Violations are the thoughtless acts that get teams beat. No player has ever given a good reason why he should be in the lane for three seconds, or why he should get a technical foul, or goal tend, or commit any violation. This system of evaluation is applied equally across the board. That is what players want. The coach can modify the numbers based on his philosophy. My philosophy was to eliminate the mental mistakes that get you beat. I felt that this PR formula did the job.

Number-Based Evaluation

In the performance rating system, players are grouped in a depth chart according to position, 1 through 5. The depth chart reflects the player's daily PR score. This chart is shown in figure 3.2. Another depth chart would reflect cumulative PR ranking.

Depth Chart				
Point guard	2-guard	3-man	Power forward	Postmen
1.	1.	1.	1.	1.
2.	2.	2.	2.	2.
3.	3.	3.	3.	3.

Figure 3.2 Depth chart.

Daily PRs are cumulative and are compiled and posted for each player based on scrimmage and game results. For example, figure 3.3 is a sample box score from the Final Four semifinal game between UNC Charlotte and Marquette. An abbreviated list of categories—field goals, free throws, rebounds, personal fouls, turnovers, assists, blocked shots, and steals—illustrates how to convert a player's game statistics into a player's PR number. With the exception of specific violations, the PR represents the total of his statistical contribution for that day.

Coaches should review box scores before postgame media interviews so that they can offer accurate analysis. The PR can also provide a quick snapshot of player production. Figure 3.4 is a sample PR team rating from the semifinal game that shows that Maxwell (+47 and –18 for +29) had an excellent game; King (+25 and –16 for +9) had a good game; whereas Massey (+26 and –21 for +5) and Kinch (+20 and –16 for +4) had respectable positive production but also had high negative numbers, resulting in low PRs for the game.

Team / Game Sample

NCAA box score / UNC Charlotte vs Marquette

Name	2-pt fg md-att	Free throw md-att	Rebounds of	def	pfs	tos	asts	blks	stls	Points
Massey	7-13	0-0	4	4	1	4	0	0	0	14
King	2-7	0-0	2	3	2	2	4	2	2	4
Maxwell	5-6	7-9	6	6	2	5	2	2	2	17
Watkins	2-4	2-3	0	0	5	2	1	0	0	6
Kinch	1-7	2-2	2	2	2	2	2	2	1	4
Gruber	2-6	0-0	0	0	0	0	0	0	0	4
Scott	0-0	0-0	0	0	0	0	0	0	1	0

Abbreviations: (fg-field goal) (md-made goals) (att-attempted goals) (of-offensive) (def-defensive) (pfs-personal foul) (tos-turnovers) (asts-assists) (blks-blocked shots) (stls-steals)

Performance rating conversion sample, based on game shown above.

	Massey			**King**	
Plus		Minus	Plus		Minus
+14	(2 pt fg)	-12	+4	(2 pt fg)	-10
0	(fts)	0	0	(fts)	0
12	(rbs)	0	+ 7	(rebs)	0
0	(pf)	-1	0	(pf)	-2
0	(tos)	-8	0	(tos)	-4
0	(asts)	0	+8	(asts)	0
0	(blks)	0	+2	(blks)	0
0	(stls)	0	+4	(stls)	0
+26		-21	+25		-16
	PR = (+5)			PR = (+9)	

Figure 3.3 Box score.

Sample PR Team Rating

Date *March 26, 1977*

Performance rating / team ranking

	(PR)		**Total + / -**		**Comment on production**
1.	+29	Maxwell	(+47	-18)	• Excellent PR / shooting / rebounds big plus
2.	+9	King	(+25	-16)	• Does it all / rebounds / asts / only 2-7 fgs
3.	+5	Massey	(+26	-21)	• Depends on shooting / excellent rebounds
4.	+4	Kinch	(+20	-16)	• Gets numbers across the board / fgs 1-7 hurt
5.	+2	Scott	(+2	-0)	• Only played 5 mins / first sub inside
6.	-4	Gruber	(+4	-8)	• Depends on shooting and went 2-6 fgs 7
7.	-6	Watkins	(+9	-15)	• Only 22 mins / 5 pfs / could not get in to it

Figure 3.4 Sample PR team rating.

The Performance Rating System at Work

The performance rating system is based on the hypothesis that as players minimize their weaknesses and improve their strengths, the team automatically improves. This is how it should work:

1. The PR system encourages players to strive for positive results because that is how they get more playing time. When players reduce their individual mistakes, shoot better percentages, and play more effectively, the team has better results. As the positive replaces the negative, team execution improves.

2. The PR system eliminates guessing about who the most effective players are. Practice results are tabulated and posted for all players to see.

3. No one can take advantage of the system because everyone must practice to have a PR number. If a player doesn't practice, he has no PR number. Without a PR number, he sees no game time. Rather than lose a full day of production, players learn to play through sore muscles, nagging irritations, and bad days.

4. Players quickly learn the importance of collecting statistics across the board; the more rounded their game, the better their chance for collecting numbers. Team production goes up as individual execution improves.

5. The system rewards positive play and penalizes poor play. Players pick up on the concept that production precedes playing time. They soon realize a positive score demands work and complete concentration. The PR (shooting only) scale in figure 3.5 provides an example of how to tabulate one player's shooting performance and shows how difficult it is to depend on scoring alone for a PR plus rating.

Individual Sample

PR shooting scale

2-point field goal made	= (+2)		2-point field goal missed	= (-2)
3-point field goal made	= (+3)		3-point field goal missed	= (-3)
Free throw made	= (+1)		Free throw missed	= (-2)

Sample: Shooting statistics from a practice.

Player	2-pt fgs	3-pt fgs	Free throws
Pace	3-6	1-3	4-9

These figures represent Pace's shooting statistics converted into numbers.

PR scoring

			(+)		(-)
2-point field goals	(3-6)	made (3) =	+6	missed (3) =	-6
3-point field goals	(1-3)	made (1) =	+3	missed (2) =	-6
Free throws	(4-9)	made (4) =	+4	missed (5) =	-10
	Totals		+13		-22

PR for workout = (-9)

Figure 3.5 Individual sample.

In the figure 3.5 example, the player hit 50 percent of his two-point field goals, 33 percent of his three-point field goals, but only 44 percent of his free throws. He scored 13 points but was a negative (–9) on the PR system. This example illustrates the fact that seldom do scorers lead the PR rankings. To score a plus in field-goal shooting, a player must shoot better than 50 percent. To be positive in free-throw shooting, he must hit 70 percent on free throws. In digesting the statistics, we see that the player needs to improve his free-throw and three-point shooting. The –9 rating sends a clear message to the player that he must improve his free-throw shooting or he might not get any playing time. In this particular case the emphasis would be on free throws, but in most shooting situations, the concern is shot selection, taking forced shots or out-of-range shots, or failing to finish on drives. A minus indicates a problem. Although 13 points in the box score looks good, this player cannot depend only on shooting for playing time. Of course, shooting is only one category, and players have many opportunities to collect additional positive numbers with rebounds, assists, steals, and all-around good play.

The PR system works as planned. The PR allows players to concentrate on their game and not worry about whether the coaches noticed their rebounds or assists, whether scoring was the only important statistic, or whether the coaches intend to play favorites. When these issues are eliminated, the selection experience becomes a healthy environment in which players and coaches can have friendly conversations in full view of everyone without other players suspecting favoritism. Anyone—player, coach, parent—who has ever competed on a team understands the value of eliminating favoritism, and the PR system does that.

Scrimmage Evaluation Using the Performance Rating System

The PR grading program begins on the first day of practice. Following the normal offensive and defensive fundamental drills and the necessary teaching segments, a 30-minute slot is allotted for scrimmaging in each practice. If the team consists of 15 players, each player has 20 minutes of scrimmage each day. John Wooden, recognized as the greatest collegiate coach ever, was a known proponent of daily scrimmaging. A schedule that would accommodate 15 players might look like this (three teams—A, B, and C—each team scrimmages 20 minutes per day):

10 minutes	A vs. B
10 minutes	A vs. C
10 minutes	B vs. C

Total scrimmage time is 30 minutes. Players will inevitably evaluate their progress against teammates, so it's important to incorporate an all-purpose offense (see chapter 6) that gives each player an equal chance to succeed. Chances are that the offense used for evaluation will not be the primary offense used by the team, but players' positions, ballhandling, and rebounding responsibilities are automatically built in. Therefore, the offense used and the administration of the workouts must have certain basic attributes. The evaluation process eliminates as much ambiguity as possible by incorporating these five requirements:

1. The offense is fair and allows everyone to show his ability.
2. Playing time is the same for everyone. The coach must devise a plan.
3. Players rotate daily to eliminate the assertion that the coach is stacking teams.
4. Hire outside officials from the local association for impartial refereeing.
5. Grade everyone using the same PR system.

This chapter has discussed fair and consistent evaluation procedures, converting statistics into a PR production number, giving players input in policy and rule regulations, emphasizing team success over individual accomplishment, and some of the areas to consider when analyzing and scouting players. The PR system can be one of the best tools for building strong, positive relationships between coaches and players.

CHAPTER 4

Physical Conditioning

E lite basketball players are fascinating to watch. They not only adeptly execute skills and tactics but also give maximum effort throughout each game. Even more amazing is that they make it all look so effortless. Obviously, not every player will perform with the apparent ease of the game's superstars, but with proper physical conditioning a player can improve his output considerably. This chapter presents practical ways to maximize basketball-specific fitness that, in turn, will allow athletes to increase both their minutes played and the quality of those minutes. Specifically, I cover a comprehensive preseason conditioning program that encompasses aerobic and anaerobic training for stamina and endurance, plyometrics for jump training involving rapid stretching and contracting of muscles to increase muscle power, exercises for mobility and flexibility, and weight training for strength.

Total Conditioning

For years, basketball preseason and seasonal training focused solely on developing players' endurance. Athletes were told to run long distances several days a week and play games during the off-season, although there was no evidence that this regimen prepared them for the rigors of the season. Now we know that besides stamina, basketball players need total conditioning to develop strength, quickness, flexibility, and agility.

Total conditioning equips players to perform at a high level throughout an entire game, for an entire season. How players respond to this conditioning challenge is a test of their work ethic, competitiveness, and reliability. From there, conditioning must become part of practice sessions to ensure that teams stay in shape throughout the season.

Base Building

Total conditioning starts with athletes' developing an aerobic and anaerobic base. Think of it as building the foundation for a house. Although we will add stylistic features specific to the dwelling as construction progresses, those elements are unlikely to hold up without a solid base from which to build and sustain them. In this chapter, the foundational movements will be anaerobic and aerobic conditioning, and we'll tailor the stylistic features to the sport-specific movements essential for basketball.

A basic understanding of the types of training is helpful in developing a conditioning program. According to the American Sports Medicine Institute (ASMI), anaerobic training is "activity that lasts from 30 seconds to 2 minutes," and athletes develop it best through interval training. For basketball, effective interval training includes plyometrics, which is characterized by frequent starts and stops, sudden bursts of speed, and bounding movements requiring repeated, rapid flexing and stretching of muscles. Interval training also involves running and calisthenics in intense, limited segments, performed in an exercise-to-rest ratio of 1:2, or, for example, one minute of exercise for every two minutes of rest.

Interval training should make up the major part of anaerobic conditioning. Interval training allows us to experience oxygen debt without feeling exhausted or getting hurt. Oxygen debt is more commonly called "being winded," and recovery from it requires a period of rest. The more fit a player is, the quicker the recovery. Interval training increases lung capacity and oxygen intake, which enhance recovery and endurance. Players must have endurance to maintain performance throughout games and finish strong.

Aerobic conditioning also involves strenuous activity, but it occurs over a longer period. Aerobic exercises may involve running, cycling, swimming, or other activities demanding endurance. Such activities, when well planned and performed at the proper intensity over time, will result in significant improvements in respiration efficiency and heart rate.

Sport-Specific Training

Today we know that expanded training of all physical fitness components—strength, flexibility, agility, speed, power, quickness, and stamina—is essential for top-notch basketball performance. Besides understanding that conditioning is multidimensional, we also know that sport-specific training allows players to perform their best.

Muscles and joints most involved in the skilled and repetitive movements required in basketball must be trained accordingly. The idea that one conditioning program fits all was never effective, and that's even truer for today's specialized athlete. Top athletes at the high school and college levels who compete in more than one sport must adjust their training to fit the demands of the particular in-season activity.

Planning and Preparation

Planning and preparation are the backbone of total conditioning. A plan is important regardless of the level or age of the athlete or the competitive nature of the sport. Plans help form realistic expectations, provide direction, and motivate everyone involved. Preparation means that the players' conditioning should be structured so that it peaks, in both duration and intensity, for the first day of practice. The coach wants to practice hard without having to worry about whether the players can finish. The goal is to have players in such good condition that they can safely complete early practices sessions without fear of breaking down physically.

Three-Phase Conditioning Process

The three-phase conditioning program covered here provides players with a comprehensive program that improves endurance, flexibility, and strength. The program is demanding, yet fair in every way. Competitive players love the daily challenges, and they benefit greatly by completing the sport-specific drills. The program comprises three distinct phases: interval running, agility and plyometric exercises, and competitive play for endurance.

Phase I: Interval Training

In phase I, interval training, the goal is to improve the players' cardiovascular fitness. Here the idea is to reduce the distance that players run and at the same time increase their speed. The way to do this is to focus on the correct muscles. For years, the emphasis in training basketball players was on elongated muscles, muscles that are slender, stretched out, and used for running long distances. In fact, the fast-twitch fibers, those that contract more quickly during shorter periods of high-intensity physical activity, are more important. Interval training, which emphasizes fast-twitch muscle response, is the preferred method for training basketball players.

An interval training program should be conducted in an indoor facility such as a gym or indoor track where administrative props, clock, and stopwatch are constant. The clock serves two major functions—it's visible, reflecting the running time for each interval, and it spurs the players to work harder. The incentive for players is to beat the clock, not teammates, although friendly competition occurs. This motivational aspect of the clock is powerful. With players directing their focus to an inanimate object, the coach does not have to play the role of the bad guy. When using a track, a 94-foot distance must be marked off on one side of the straightaway to replicate a gym floor. It should be noted that an adequate supply of drinking water must always be on hand during training sessions as well as during practices and games.

Here's how to structure the interval training of phase I. Every team member runs one mile, which is divided into intervals of eighths of a mile. This means that each player runs one-eighth of a mile (220 yards) eight times. Required, predetermined times are assigned to the three positions—guards, forwards, and centers. Five years of statistical data on individual players by time and position compiled during preseason conditioning provides the predetermined times for each position. Each player is responsible for running the sprints within that specific period. The goal of each player is to reduce his time daily, thereby increasing his speed.

For example, guards begin the first day by running the eighths in an allowable time of 44 seconds. On the second day the time drops to 43 seconds, on the third day to 42 seconds, and so on. Forwards and centers also work on a position-specific declining time scale (see table 4.1, *a* and *b*).

The interval training involves 10 days of intense, supervised physical training during which all results are recorded. The 10 days are broken into two distinct segments—a Monday-Wednesday-Friday workout and a Tuesday-Thursday workout. The main difference is that on Tuesday and Thursday the interval running distance is a quarter mile, equivalent to 14 trips up and down the court, rather than an eighth of a mile, equal to 7 trips. The longer distance focuses on the elongated muscles to increase endurance and stamina.

Table 4.1, *a* and *b*, offers an example of a 10-day program broken into 6 days for eighth-mile intervals and 4 days for quarter-mile intervals. The tables show the times that players must meet each day.

At the beginning of the interval drill, the clock should be set to 24 minutes to avoid having to reset a stopwatch constantly. The clock runs continually until all three groups (guards, forwards, and centers) finish the mile. Typically, the guards go first. Assistant coaches call and record their times as they cross the finish line. On an eighth-mile day, the forwards follow the guards, beginning at the 23:00 mark. Then the centers move to the starting line and begin their run at 22:00. When the centers finish, the guards start again. The players repeat the process for seven more cycles until everyone completes the mile.

The timing process is the same for the quarters except that two-minute intervals separate the running of the groups. The guards begin at 24:00, the forwards at

Table 4.1a **Sample Workout Schedule**

	First week				
	Monday	**Tuesday**	**Wednesday**	**Thursday**	**Friday**
Distance	(1/8)	(1/4)	(1/8)	(1/4)	(1/8)
Guards	44	1:38	43	1:35	42
Forwards	44	1:38	43	1:35	43
Centers	45	1:42	44	1:41	44

*Times and makeups for the big men should be established in consultation with the player. They are often modified depending on age, weight, and speed.
*Guards and forwards should have no problem making 1st week's times.
*Everyone struggles with breathing in the 1/4s.

Table 4.1b **Sample Workout Schedule**

	Second week				
	Monday	**Tuesday**	**Wednesday**	**Thursday**	**Friday**
Distance	(1/8)	(1/4)	(1/8)	(1/4)	(1/8)
Guards	41	1:33	40	1:33	39
Forwards	42	1:33	41	1:33	40
Centers	44	1:40	43	1:40	42

*Goal is to get the big man down to 1:40.
*Excellent runners make all their times.
*Good runners improve their speed considerably.
*Fair runners noticeably increase their speed.

22:00, and the centers at 20:00. Each group continues in turn until time expires, with each group running four quarters.

If a player misses a time (that is, does not meet his goal), he runs an additional eighth. When making up eighths, 5 seconds is added to the time requirement. A player running the regular eighths in 42 seconds would be allowed 47 seconds for makeups. If the player fails the makeup, he is allowed an extra 10 seconds for the third attempt. For a missed turn when using a court, the penalty is two additional eighths. For the quarters, penalty makeups are 15 seconds on the first miss and individually set thereafter. Following a short rest period, players complete all makeups before beginning the exercises in phase II. Players must touch the end line with their hands on all turns; failure to do so costs an extra interval. The interval begins at the whistle or on the command "Go." The penalty for a false start is an extra eighth.

Whatever the distance, the workouts are challenging. By structuring the sessions so that players are rewarded for reducing their daily times, conditioning supervisors know that everyone comes to practice with a serious, dedicated mind-set. Another great benefit of the eighths conditioning program is the competition that it builds among members. Winning the various heats becomes an issue of pride. Supervisors, assistants, volunteer helpers, and teammates constantly shout encouragement by congratulating those who make their times. Players pull for each other because none of them wants to run that extra interval. In summary, the program prepares the team for practice and builds team rapport.

Phase II: Agility and Plyometrics

Phase II of the preseason conditioning program focuses on muscular endur-ance, agility, mobility, flexibility, balance, strength, and plyometrics for jump training. This work begins directly after the running phase ends. On Monday, Wednesday, and Friday, six basketball-related exercise stations are used. Three exercises—defensive slides, sit-ups, and burpees—emphasize agility, flexibility, and strength. Three exercises focus on plyometric jump training, emphasizing speed jumping, rope jumping, and rebound jumping. On Tuesday and Thursday, following the running, the entire workout consists of plyometric depth jump-ing, a technique that originated in Russia and Eastern Europe in the mid-1960s. The Soviets achieved great success with plyometrics in their training regimen, especially in track and field. Yuri Verhoshansky, a Russian coach whose suc-cess with jumpers is legendary, could be called "the father of plyometrics." He succeeded in increasing his athletes' reactive abilities by adding exercises that involved jumping and leaping and that took advantage of the natural elasticity of muscle tissues.

Agility Drills

The six agility drill stations suggested here are supervised by coaches, trainers, and statisticians, who record each player's results. Each exercise lasts 45 seconds, and a two-minute rest occurs after each activity. The team splits into groups accord-ing to position. Ideally, a team of 15 players consists of three point guards, three scoring guards, three small forwards, three power forwards, and three centers. In that circumstance, players would fall conveniently into five groups, but physical size may be used to balance the groups numerically.

All groups are supervised, and all begin on the same whistle. Each group is assigned a starting drill. Players rotate in an organized manner until they have completed all six drills. With five groups, one station will be free (open) each rotation. The goal each day is determined by the average repetitions set the previous day.

a

Rope jumping—both feet.

ROPE JUMPING

Rope jumping is vital for timing, rhythm, and strengthening the legs and ankles.

The exercise begins by jumping off both feet for 15 seconds. Players then switch to the right leg for 15 seconds and finish with the left leg for 15 seconds.

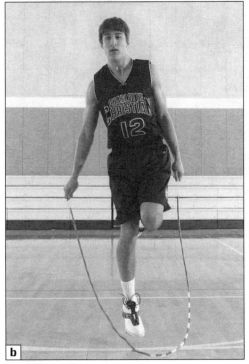

b

Rope jumping—right leg.

c

Rope jumping—left leg.

BURPEE

A burpee, also called a squat thrust, combines multiple exercises and increases strength, mobility, and flexibility.

This drill is especially difficult for large players. The player begins with his feet together. He squats down and places his palms on the floor. The hands should be shoulder-width apart and outside the knees. The player thrusts his legs backward into a front-leaning rest position and touches his chest to the floor. He returns to the bending position, stands erect with the shoulders high, and then repeats the drill. The bending, squat, backward thrust, push-up, and stand-up-straight position make this a physically demanding exercise. From a basketball standpoint, the drill teaches players that they are capable of going on the floor after loose balls and are expected to do so.

a   Squat position.   b   Backward thrust.   c   Push-up.

DEFENSIVE SLIDES

Defensive slides initiate the learning process for proper defensive position with correct footwork.

Slides are great for strengthening the groin, abdominal, and back muscles. Useful props for this exercise are four chairs or orange cones to designate the space needed for sliding. The players move up and back, and side to side. The emphasis is on technique—maintaining low body position and proper balance with the knees bent, the back straight, and the head up during the slides. This defensive slide technique helps prevent groin injury. The drill involves constant movement.

Slide up-and-back position.

Slide-to-side position.

SPEED JUMPING

Speed jumping starts from a standing position. Players jump over a six-inch prop. The exercise improves speed, quickness, endurance, and strength. Players jump over and back in a continuous motion.

A bench or rail six inches in height is needed for this exercise. The emphasis is on speed and quickness, but safety is also a concern because players often tire at the end of the drill. Because of fatigue, players may have to stop momentarily to gather themselves before finishing the drill.

Flat-footed jump.   Flat-footed land and return.

REBOUND JUMPING

Rebound jumping develops strength, rhythm, and explosion off a two-footed jump.

   The drill starts at the free-throw line with a running two-step approach. The player gathers at the backboard and explodes off both feet, slapping the backboard as high as he can with both hands. After returning to the floor, the jumper quickly returns to the free-throw line and repeats the process while the coach counts the jumps. The object is to increase speed, height, and number of touches each day.

a

Pre-position backboard touches.

b

Position at backboard.

SIT-UPS

Sit-ups strengthen the abdominal muscles. Establishing a strong core of abdominal muscles helps prevent strains, tears, and injuries that often take a season to heal.

The exercise begins with the player lying on his back with knees bent, feet flat on the floor, and fingers interlaced behind the head. A teammate holds the feet in place, and the player does curl-ups. A repetition is complete when the elbows touch the knees.

Beginning sit-up position.

Elbows touching knees.

Plyometric Drills

One of the major reasons that young people give for becoming involved in sports programs is the opportunity to improve their skills. Basketball players love to improve their jumping ability, as evidenced by their enthusiasm in first touching the net, then the rim, and ultimately trying to dunk the ball. One of the questions that players ask basketball coaches is whether they can improve their vertical jump. The answer is yes. Players also want to know how many inches they can add to their jump, but a definitive answer to that question requires proper testing.

Jumping involves many factors, some of which the player can control and some of which he cannot. In a 1997 *Los Angeles Times* article, geneticist Hermine Maes stated that two-thirds of a male child's vertical jump ability, two-thirds of his aerobic capacity, and 90 percent of a female child's aerobic capacity are related to heredity. Other studies have shown that higher proportions of fast-twitch muscle fibers in the lower leg are also related to heredity. Recent research, however, has uncovered the fact that specific training can influence fibers—positive news for those willing to work on their jumping.

Because a player cannot control his gene pool, he should select a balanced resistance training program if his goal is to increase his jumping ability. Jump training is one of the proven methods for increasing vertical jump. Plyometrics, which enables a muscle to exert maximal force for a short period, is the method discussed here.

As mentioned early in this chapter, depth jump training evolved from the Russian jump studies that centered on the idea that jumping off a box would increase an athlete's vertical jump. The idea was not universally accepted. Yet some of us coaching in college believed in and experimented with the technique. To apply the depth jump principles, we made our own boxes measuring 12, 18, 24, 30, and 36 inches high with a flat base 36 inches in length and 36 inches in width. These boxes are shown in figure 4.1.

Begin by placing boxes in a row, 24 inches apart, beginning with the smallest and ending with the tallest. A player completes three to six repetitions—right leg, left leg, and then both legs. Remember, plyometric training enhances the tolerance of the muscle for increased stretch loads. A player begins by jumping off the right leg onto the 12-inch box. He immediately jumps down and springs onto the 18-inch box, then quickly jumps down and elevates onto the 24-inch box, and so on. This instant uplift off one leg provides increased tolerance development and efficiency in the stretch-shortening cycle of muscle action. During the stretching, a greater amount of elastic energy is stored in the muscle. The muscle then reuses this elastic energy in the following concentric action to become stronger.

Completing as many boxes as is comfortably safe, the player reverses and returns down the boxes one at a time with the same springing action. After touching the floor, the player immediately begins a cycle off the left leg. He completes the first set of depth jumping with a round using both legs. The second set begins after a two-minute rest.

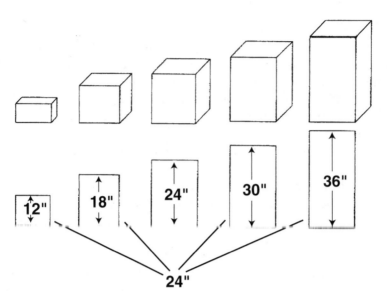

Figure 4.1   Plyometric boxes.

Early in the practices, players might complete only two or three boxes, but as they gain self-confidence and better understanding of balance and jumping technique, they will set higher goals for themselves. I make sure that players work with a qualified instructor and become familiar with correct jumping technique. Players should always perform a good warm-up and cool-down that includes stretching and running exercises. For optimum plyometric training, a resting period of at least two days should occur between workouts.

Determining a player's vertical jump increase requires establishing his exact base and keeping timely documented statistics as he improves jumping performance. To obtain meaningful test results, I suggest using a 12-week period with two to three workouts per week. Although reports indicate that athletes can improve their vertical jump 4 to 8 inches, such factors as genetics, age, and fast-twitch muscle capacity enter into the equation. You cannot realistically expect a jumper with a 10-inch vertical to become a leaper with a 36-inch vertical. Plyometric jump training provides a great plan for mature players who have proper muscular strength and are seeking to improve their vertical jumping. All they need to do is work the plan.

Phase III: Scrimmages

Phase III of the preseason conditioning is full-court work in which players choose the teams and officiate their own games. Veteran players usually keep the younger players in line. The first team to make 10 baskets wins, with winners staying and losers sitting. With 15 players, there are three teams. Each team plays at least two games.

Full-court play helps players develop stamina and endurance. Players are tired, sometimes exhausted, after extending themselves to make their running times in the eighths and doing the sport-specific and plyometric exercises. Therefore, scrimmages are often sloppy and poorly played. To make the necessary progress, individual squad members must push themselves and work their way through the fatigue. Experience shows that after a few days of workouts, players recover more quickly and improve their skills.

Off-Season Fitness

The three-phase conditioning program sets a benchmark for the fitness level of the team. Under the direction and supervision of the coaching staff, players can readily achieve their fitness goals. But in the 21st century, fitness in sports is a year-round proposition. For much of the year, the athlete is away from the practice facility. Planning and setting team goals help effective leaders establish meaningful fitness standards that players take seriously. High school players benefit greatly from open-gym workouts where they have weight-training and scrimmage opportunities. This opportunity may not be available for everyone.

The NBA and the major NCAA programs invest considerable resources in trainers, dietitians, and strength and conditioning coaches to ensure that players have workout programs scheduled throughout the summer. In some cases, strength and conditioning coaches go to the players' hometowns to oversee workouts and make sure that players are meeting summer fitness goals. Others provide a daily workout schedule for each player as he leaves for the summer. Included in the material is a workout form for him to fill out and return. In the NBA, many players hire personal trainers to help them return ready to open camp.

Teams need to establish an acceptable standard of fitness for players to observe during the off-season. Besides maintaining players' overall wellness, such standards reduce leg and ankle injuries and identify potential weight problems.

CHAPTER 5

Offensive Skills and Tactics

In 1982, as cocoach on the USA select team that competed in the 50th Anniversary of the International Basketball Federation (FIBA) games in Geneva, Switzerland, we were fortunate to have Michael Jordan on the team. Then a rising college sophomore, Michael was an extraordinary offensive rebounder, scorer, and open-court player, but what stood out most about him was his cooperative attitude and willingness to work on the fundamentals of the game. Michael was a hard-working leader who understood the importance of passing, pivoting, and screening.

Developing Offensive Fundamentals

Most people automatically praise the player who scored the points without paying any attention to the screener, the passer, the rebounder, or the best defender. Players can also get caught up in the "dunkball" game to the detriment of developing an all-around game. There is a tendency for players to overemphasize shooting the three-point shot and the dunk with little regard for the midrange game. Coaches need to be careful not to fall into a trap here. Don't spend so much time on these skills that you neglect the rest of the game.

An effective offense starts with sound fundamentals—ballhandling, dribbling, pivoting, passing, screening, shooting and rebounding—and then combines those individual skills in offensive sets that best showcase the strengths of the whole. Drill work and one-on-one instruction stressing proper body mechanics and techniques are essential for shoring up any weak links.

Ballhandling drills are best performed in a progression from one-man, to two-man, and eventually to three-man drills. Multiplayer drills emphasize three important components—timing, floor balance, and proper spacing. Coaches should stress proper techniques for passing and receiving the ball, making V-cuts to get open, using speed cuts to the basket, and using proper cutting angles, all of which are necessary for team play. A coach learns a lot about his players during these drills, including their skill levels and ability to learn.

These drills focus primarily on dribbling, making short, quick passes, driving aggressively to the basket, and using proper layup techniques. Drills are run at a fast pace and require quick recognition for effective execution. Good basketball requires players to make split-second decisions, and two-man drills reveal the ability of players to adjust, react, and execute effectively. Run the drills correctly to build a proper foundation.

Dribbling With a Purpose

Explain and emphasize ballhandling and dribbling right from the start. First, explain to each player that when he dribbles, he should do it for a purpose—to take him and the ball to another spot on the court that would be more advantageous for his team.

Here are six situations when the player with the ball is allowed to dribble:

1. Advancing the ball on the fast break
2. Moving the ball in the backcourt against certain presses
3. Following steals when there is a direct line to the basket
4. Attacking the basket off the dribble in the half court
5. Moving to create a better passing angle
6. Eluding a defender

Ball handlers often make the mistake of picking up their dribble without having a passing outlet. We call this "paralyzing oneself," because the player cannot move with the ball after he has ended his dribble. When the player picks up the ball, he invites the defense to employ hard overplays to cut off passing lanes. Successful coaches discriminate between those who are adept at handling the ball and those who are dribble-happy and prone to making turnovers. Nothing is more frustrating to a coach than seeing one of his players pound the ball on the floor at the top of the key with no purpose. All that does is stagnate the offense and discourage player movement. Not much defensive skill is required to stop it.

Position-Specific Requirements

Coaches may use different basic drills, but the fundamentals of dribbling, passing, and shooting remain constant. First, you have to instill in every player the concept that the dribble must take him someplace.

Guards need to be able to take the ball from A to B—from the backcourt against pressure to the frontcourt to set up a half-court offense; from a defensive steal, rebound, or outlet pass to attack the defense in the middle of the court and make good decisions on finishing the fast break; to improve passing angles; and to elude an aggressive defender.

Forwards must clear defensive rebounds on the dribble, and when possible, rebound and take it with a speed dribble to half court. Exceptional ball handlers may go all the way and attack the basket. In the half court, forwards should be able to improve a passing angle and attack the basket from the wing position. It takes excellent ball handlers to elude pressure defense.

Centers, at a minimum, should be able to clear defensive rebounds and outlet the ball. In the half court, they should be able to make their own moves with a one- or two-dribble attack. Although post players are seldom required to dribble, those who can bring a unique asset to their team. They can clear rebounds, ignite the fast break, trail the offense, and swing the ball comfortably. Centers can also step out on high-post sets as passers, be available as an outlet against full-court pressure, and be difficult to defend when they make their own moves to the basket. Being big does not eliminate the need to learn how to be an effective dribbler and ball handler. Developing those skills just takes practice.

Point guards are the primary dribblers for most teams. Some coaches are satisfied to keep the ball in one player's hands, but other coaches work at developing several ball handlers, knowing that a team that dribbles efficiently will have an advantage.

How should players dribble the ball? The preferred dribbler's stance is to have the knees bent and the feet shoulder-width apart, the head up, the eyes forward, and the dribble hand on top of the ball to eliminate palming. The player uses the off arm (nondribbling hand) in a protective mode and dribbles the ball no higher than the knees. Having the hand in a protective mode means that it should be waist high with the elbow bent to ward off any defensive attack. Young players need to work on technique—developing the weak hand, ballhandling control, and change-of-pace action. Coaches should teach these principles, but good ball handlers will seek their own comfort level.

Some great players have different approaches to dribbling. Oscar Robertson, arguably the greatest player ever, said that when he dribbled he liked to get down low, at the same level as his defender. Magic Johnson, on the other hand, was an exception to the standard rule about keeping the dribble low. At 6-9, he liked to bounce it high so that he could see over his defender. For teaching purposes, players should be down as illustrated in the drills following.

Full-Court Dribble Drills

Full-court dribble drills should begin on the first day of practice. The following drills are designed to improve players' ballhandling skills and reduce their weaknesses. The daily repetition of these basic dribble drills provides a solid base and helps immeasurably when players perform more difficult drills that incorporate pivoting and shooting. Building a solid basketball foundation is like building a stairway in a beautiful house. Each step, each fundamental, takes the player closer to the ultimate goal. The first step in this process is learning to dribble correctly, and the second step is combining dribbling with pivoting and layup shooting.

One final note before starting—teaching these fundamental drills becomes more effective when preparation includes specific props to aid execution. Props include a roll of trainer's tape, a set of small orange cones, or some folding chairs. These aids can help the coach point out to players where they should make cuts or set screens, where shots are allowed, or where jab steps are necessary. The props can also be helpful in showing floor balance.

STRAIGHT-LINE DRIBBLE

FOCUS
Execute dribble with right, left, and alternate hands.

PROCEDURE
Players begin on the baseline, three groups of five each. Follow these steps:

1. Form three groups beginning on the baseline with five to a line—guards are group A, forwards are group B, and centers or big men are group C.
2. Players assume proper dribble stance—knees bent, head and eyes up, and hand on top of the ball.
3. On the "Go" command, players dribble full court, wait for each group to finish, and then return.
4. Players use a right-handed dribble on the first trip and a left-handed dribble on the second, and they alternate hands on the third.

5. Group A dribbles full court and stays on the end line. Other groups follow in order.
6. Group B begins when group A gets to midcourt.
7. Group C begins when group B gets to midcourt.
8. When group C gets to the end line, group A begins the return.
9. Group B begins the return when group A gets to midcourt, and group C follows group B.

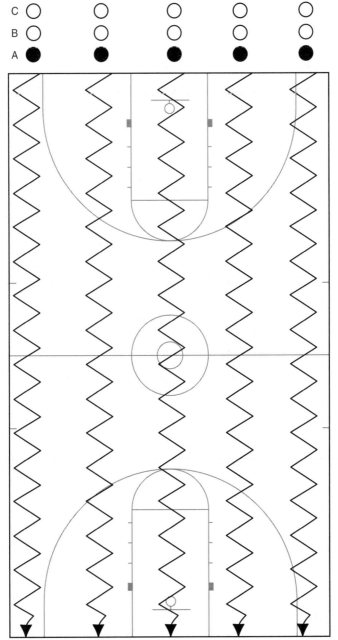

Straight-line dribble.

DRIBBLE PIVOTS

FOCUS

Execute proper pivots while dribbling, alternating between the right and left hand.

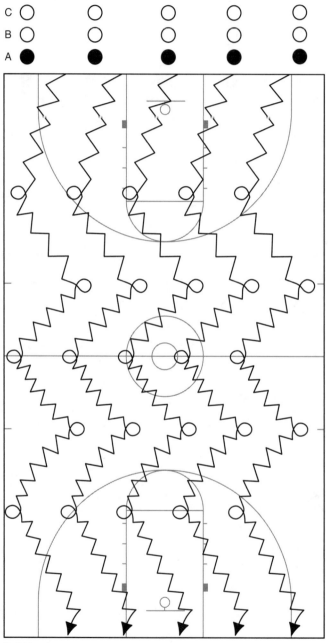

Dribble pivots.

PROCEDURE

Players begin on the baseline, three groups of five each. Follow these steps:

1. Form three groups beginning on the baseline with five to a line—guards are group A, forwards are group B, and centers or big men are group C.

2. Players assume proper dribble stance—knees bent, head and eyes up, and hand on top of the ball.

3. On the "Go" command, the first group dribbles (with the right hand) diagonally toward the right sideline, free-throw line extended, working their way up the court.

4. After three dribbles, players stop, reverse pivot on the left foot while switching from a right-handed to left-handed dribble, and then dribble three times beyond the top of the key.

5. Following the third dribble to the middle, players stop, reverse pivot on the right foot while switching from a left-handed dribble to a right-handed dribble, and head toward the sideline at midcourt. After the third dribble, players reverse pivot on the left foot and continue back and forth until they reach the end line.

6. Group A goes first, dribbles full court, and stays on the end line.

7. Group B begins when group A gets to midcourt.

8. Group C begins when group B gets to midcourt.

9. When group C gets to the end line, group A begins the return.

STOP-AND-GO DRIBBLE

FOCUS

Execute ball control and body balance with the stop-and-go dribble.

PROCEDURE

Players begin on the baseline, three groups of five each. Follow these steps:

1. Form three groups beginning on the baseline with five to a line—guards are group A, forwards are group B, and centers or big men are group C. The coach needs a whistle for this drill.

2. Players assume proper dribble stance—knees bent, head and eyes up, and hand on top of the ball.

3. Players begin a speed dribble on the first whistle and stop on the second whistle, keeping a live dribble. They alternate go and stop on the whistle until they reach the end line.

4. Group A dribbles full court and stays on the end line.

5. Group B begins when group A gets to midcourt.

6. Group C begins when group B gets to midcourt.

7. When group C gets to the end line, group A begins the return. The groups repeat the procedure going back. For a variation, have players alternate hands on each stop. On the stop, have them back up two steps and then sprint forward. On stops, have them back up two steps, alternate hands, and sprint forward. On stops, players can also experiment with behind-the-back and between-the-legs dribbles. They then sprint forward on the whistle.

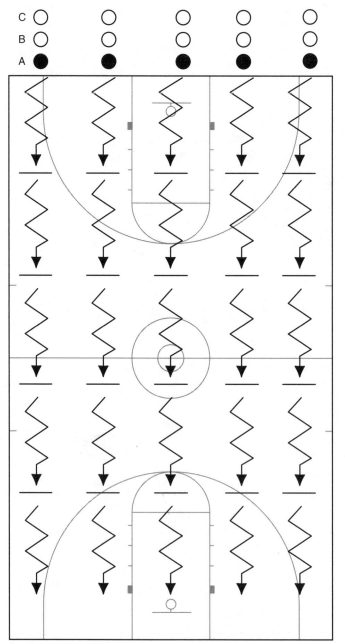

Stop-and-go dribble.

CHANGE OF PACE

FOCUS

Execute ball control and dribble technique with change of pace.

PROCEDURE

Players begin on the baseline, three groups of five each. Follow these steps:

1. Form three groups beginning on the baseline—guards are group A, forwards are group B, and centers or big men are group C.

2. Players assume proper dribble stance—knees bent, head and eyes up, hand on top of the ball.

3. Players begin the change-of-pace dribble by sprinting five quick steps, slowing down and coasting for five steps, and then accelerating and alternating speed to the end line.

4. Group A dribbles full court and stays on the end line.

5. Group B begins when group A gets to midcourt.

6. Group C begins when group B gets to midcourt.

7. When group C gets to the end line, group A begins the return. The groups repeat the procedure going back. Once this drill is mastered, extend the teaching by having players alternate hands.

One-Man Drills: Pivoting

The first step is learning to dribble correctly, and the second is combining dribbling with pivoting and shooting layups. Here are four fundamental drills that develop ballhandling and passing skills. One-man drills for ballhandling and three all-purpose passing drills (discussed later in the chapter) provide a natural progression for building a strong, fundamental basketball base. When practiced daily as warm-up drills, these drills almost guarantee that players will improve. Begin with four one-man drills that focus on dribbling, pivoting, and shooting layups.

SINGLE PIVOT

FOCUS

Execute proper pivot techniques with the dribble-drive single pivot.

PROCEDURE

Players begin at the hash line on the right side and follow these steps:

1. Start with a crossover move, switching from a left-handed dribble to a right-handed dribble.

2. Dribble with the right hand to the free-throw line extended.

3. Reverse pivot off the left foot and dribble twice with the left hand.

4. Attack the basket, exploding with a right-handed layup using the backboard.

5. Retrieve the rebound and go to the left hash line.

6. Repeat the same procedure using the left hand. Prompt players to concentrate and see the ball into the basket.

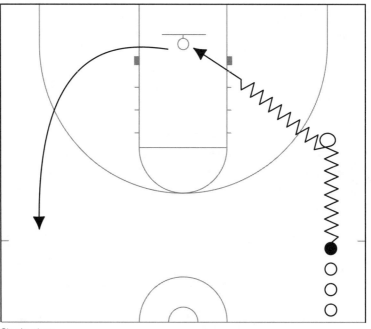

Single pivot.

DOUBLE PIVOT

FOCUS

Execute pivot techniques with a dribble drive and reverse pivots.

PROCEDURE

Players begin at the hash line on the right sideline and follow these steps:

1. Start with a crossover move and a right-handed dribble.

2. Dribble with the right hand to the free-throw line extended.

3. Reverse pivot off the left foot with a left-handed dribble.

4. Dribble with the left hand to the elbow area of the lane.

5. Reverse pivot off the right foot with a right-handed dribble.

6. Drive to the basket and shoot a right-handed layup.

7. Retrieve the rebound and go to the left hash line.
8. Repeat the procedure using the left hand.

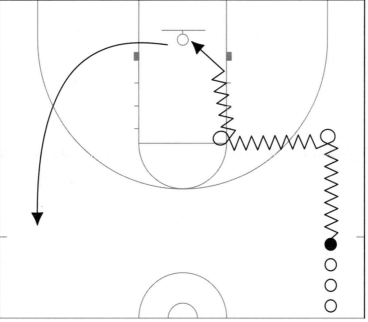

Double pivot.

DIAGONAL

FOCUS

Execute proper dribble, pivot, show ball, and shot.

PROCEDURE

Players begin at the hash line on the right sideline and follow these steps:

1. Start with a crossover dribble, switching from a right-handed to left-handed dribble, in a diagonal to the front of the basket.
2. Come to a complete stop with feet shoulder-width apart and the ball in both hands in front of the chest.
3. Establish balance with the left foot being the pivot foot.
4. Extend the ball upward in the right hand toward the basket with a good ball and head fake.
5. Gather balance and then pivot off the left foot for a layup or short right-handed hook shot.
6. Retrieve the rebound and go to the left hash line.
7. Repeat the same procedure using a right-handed dribble and left-handed shot.

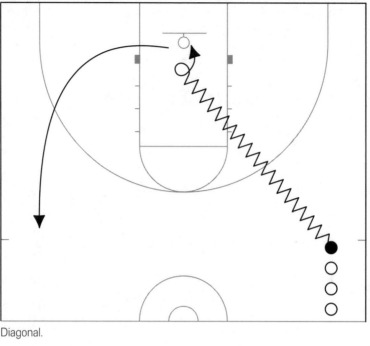

Diagonal.

BASELINE

FOCUS

Execute a baseline drive with dribble, pivot, and layup.

PROCEDURE

Players begin at the hash line on the right sideline and follow these steps:

1. Start with a crossover dribble, switching from the left hand to the right hand, and dribble to the corner.
2. Reverse pivot off the left foot with a left-handed dribble.
3. Attack the basket and shoot a left-handed layup on the right side.
4. On the second time through, shoot a left-handed reverse layup.
5. Retrieve the rebound and go to the left hash line.
6. Repeat the procedure, switching from a right-handed to left-handed crossover dribble—always attacking the basket, exploding up using the backboard, and seeing the ball into the basket on the layup.

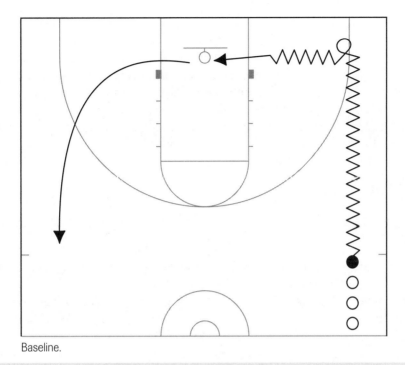

Baseline.

Two Man Drills: Passing

When I was an assistant at the University of Cincinnati, Coach Adolph Rupp from the University of Kentucky was the headliner at our annual Bearcat clinic. Coach Rupp, who won four NCAA championships at Kentucky, made a statement which stuck with me throughout my career. He said that passing was a lost art and that coaches should work diligently to help young players master that skill.

Consistently successful basketball teams pass the ball well, yet passing might be one of the most neglected of the three primary offensive skills (shooting, dribbling, and passing). For example, in the NBA's National Basketball Development League (NBDL) inaugural season in 2000, only one of the eight teams had more assists than turnovers. Turnover differential is a stat that many coaches look at first when evaluating a team's execution.

On the half court, the two-handed chest pass, the overhead two-handed pass, and the bounce pass are the safest and most fundamentally sound. One-handed passes, especially off the dribble, should be discouraged, because the passer cannot hold them back. The passer can hold back a two-handed pass if a defender steps into the passing lane or if the offensive player runs away from the spot. Speed and accuracy are important elements in passing, and bad passes are more often the fault of the passer than the intended receiver. Coaches should emphasize and encourage good habits in this area by implementing sound passing concepts with fundamental passing drills.

Incorporate passing drills into daily practice to work on the two-handed chest pass, the fake-up-and-pass-down maneuver, or the fake-down-and-pass-over technique. Teach passes that your team needs for their particular style of play. Teams need different kinds of passes depending on whether they use the fast-break style or slow it down and run a half-court offense. Teams that fast-break use long outlet passes to players streaking down the court to initiate their attack. A half-court offensive team, on the other hand, emphasizes high-post, mid-post, and low-post entry passes.

The type of pass called for also depends on where the ball is put in play. For example, are you inbounding the ball in the backcourt, on the sideline, or underneath the basket? The type of pass to be used also depends on what's happening in the game at a particular time. Are you executing against strong pressure, against zones, or against presses? Against presses, are you working against a half-court press, three-quarter-court press, or full-court press?

After a thorough study and years of observation, I've concluded that passing depends on skill, instincts, and basketball IQ. Good passers are blessed with peripheral awareness and take great pride in getting the ball to the right player at the right time. Coaches should do what they can to eliminate passing responsibilities for players with poor passing skills.

The following two-man drills incorporate dribbling, passing, layups, timing, and decision-making. All are important, but the key point is on executing a proper pass each time.

INSIDE PASS

FOCUS
Execute two-man passing, dribbling, and shooting.

PROCEDURE
Players begin on the half court and follow these steps:
1. A guard (G) with the ball lines up six feet beyond the top of the key in direct line with the right elbow.
2. A forward (F) lines up three feet inside the sideline, even with the free-throw line extended.
3. The guard makes a two-handed chest pass to the forward and, using an inside jab step, makes a hard speed cut to the basket.
4. The forward prepares to receive the ball by taking a hard jab step toward the baseline and stepping to the passer with both hands up, ready to catch.
5. The forward receives the pass and immediately returns the pass to the guard as he is making his cut to the basket.
6. The guard receives the pass and, depending on his floor position, either dribbles in for the layup or shoots it without the dribble.

7. The forward rebounds and passes it back to the guard. Players then rotate to the left side of the court and repeat the drill.

8. After the guard has shot on both sides of the court, the players change positions, with the forward becoming the shooter and the guard becoming the passer.

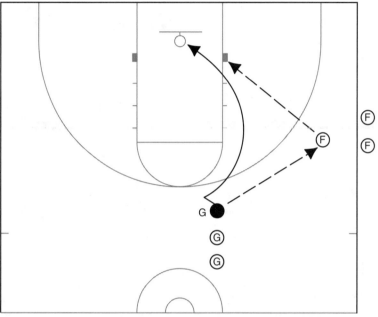

Inside pass.

OUTSIDE PASS

FOCUS

Execute two-man passing, dribbling, and shooting.

PROCEDURE

Players begin on the half court and follow these steps:

1. On the right side, a guard with the ball lines up six feet beyond the top of the key in direct line with the elbow.

2. The forward lines up three feet inside the sideline boundary, even with the free-throw line extended.

3. The guard makes a bounce pass to the outside leg of the forward. The guard follows the pass and receives a return pass from the forward. The guard then attacks the basket with no more than two dribbles and shoots a layup.

4. After passing to the guard, the forward continues to the elbow, executes a reverse pivot off his right leg, and gets the rebound.

5. The forward passes back to the guard, and the players rotate to the left side of the court and repeat the drill.

6. After the guard shoots on both sides of the court, the players exchange positions. The forward becomes the shooter, and the guard becomes the passer.

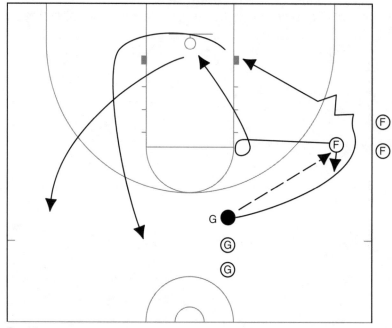

Outside pass.

OUTSIDE DUMP-DOWN PASS

FOCUS

Execute two-man passing, dribbling, and shooting.

PROCEDURE

Players begin on the half court and follow these steps:

1. On the right side, a guard with the ball lines up six feet beyond the top of the key in direct line with the elbow.

2. The forward lines up three feet inside the sideline boundary, even with the free-throw line extended.

3. The guard makes a bounce pass to the outside leg of the forward. The guard follows the pass and receives a return pass from the forward. The guard takes a quick dribble, jumps as if to shoot, and throws a dump-down pass to the forward for a layup.

4. After passing to the guard, the forward continues to the elbow, executes a reverse pivot off the right leg, and goes hard to the basket, where he receives a return pass from the guard and shoots a layup.

5. The guard retrieves the rebound and passes to the forward. The players rotate to the left side of the court and repeat the drill.

FOUR-PASS GIVE-AND-GO

FOCUS

Execute two-man passing, ballhandling, and shooting.

PROCEDURE

Players begin on the half court and follow these steps:

1. On the right side, a guard with the ball lines up six feet beyond the top of the key in direct line with the elbow.

2. A forward lines up three feet inside the sideline boundary, even with the free-throw line extended.

3. The guard makes a chest pass to the outside leg of the forward. He follows the pass and receives a return pass from the forward. He takes a quick dribble and passes to the forward at the mid-post area. The guard continues to the basket, receives a return pass, and shoots a layup.

4. After passing to the guard, the forward continues to the elbow, executes a reverse pivot off the right leg, and receives a return pass from the guard in the mid-post area.

5. The forward retrieves the rebound and passes to the guard. The players rotate to the left side of the court and repeat the drill.

6. After the guard shoots on both sides of the court, the players exchange positions. The forward becomes the shooter, and the guard becomes the passer.

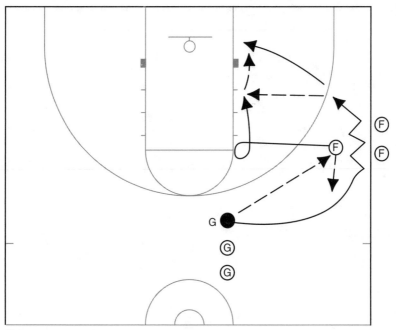

Four-pass give-and-go.

Shooting Pass

Perhaps the most basic passing concept is the shooting pass, a pass from one teammate to another with the receiver catching the ball approximately chest high in a triple-threat position, ready to shoot, pass, or dribble. The shooting pass best prepares the passer's teammate, the shooter, to put the ball in the basket. Coaches should make it clear to players exactly what is expected in the passing game. Bad passes often cease when players learn and accept the concept of the shooting pass.

When players are able to execute the shooting pass, the coach can add drills that are more complicated. Passing drills such as two-man, three-man, and fast-break long pass incorporate passing and movement. Those drills present definite challenges to the passer.

LAYUP PASS

FOCUS

Execute the shooting pass for layups.

PROCEDURE

Players begin on the half court and follow these steps:

1. The guards line up at midcourt. The forwards and the post men line up on the right side at the hash mark, about eight feet in front of the guards. Each drill consists of one participant from each position.

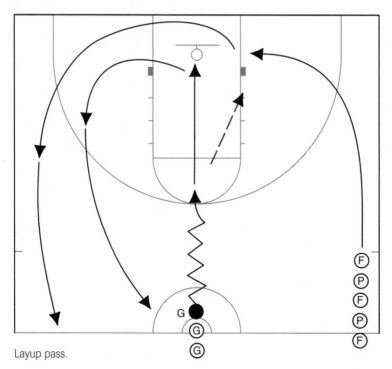

Layup pass.

2. The guard dribbles to the top of the key and delivers a shooting two-handed pass to the wing man as he goes in for a layup.

3. The major coaching emphasis here is on the pass. Define what a shooting pass is and where the receiver should receive the ball.

4. The guard rebounds the ball, and the forward and post man rotate to the left side.

5. After the forwards and post men have done the drill on both sides of the floor, they change positions and execute the shooting pass.

JUMP-SHOT PASS

FOCUS

Execute the shooting pass on the jump shot.

PROCEDURE

Players begin on the half court and follow these steps:

1. The guards line up on the left side at the free-throw line extended, each with a ball. The forwards and post men (P) line up on the right side at the free-throw line extended, facing the guards.

2. A guard begins by making a two-handed chest pass to the forward at the front of the line. After the pass, the guard follows the pass to the middle of the free-throw lane, where the forward makes a shooting pass back to the guard.

3. The guard catches the ball, dribbles once for balance, squares to the basket, and shoots a 10-foot jump shot.

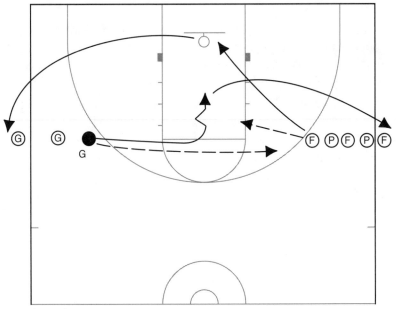

Jump-shot pass.

4. The forward who passed the ball follows his pass, goes to the board, and retrieves the rebound.

5. Players exchange lines; the shooter becomes the passer and vice versa.

LONG PASS

FOCUS

Execute technique on long-pass, fast-break drill.

PROCEDURE

Split the team. Players begin on the end line. Follow these steps:

1. Guards line up on the end line, left of the basket. Forwards and post men line up diagonal to the guards at the far hash line.

2. The drill begins with simultaneous action. The guard throws the ball on the backboard, rebounds, and begins a fast dribble to the opposite basket.

3. As the action begins, the forward breaks toward the hash mark on the side of the floor where he starts the drill. The goal is to touch the hash mark, quickly reverse, stay wide, and sprint to the far free-throw line extended, veering to the basket as if running a fast break. Use chairs or coaches to keep players wide.

4. The guard takes three or four dribbles and sprints up the court, gauging the position and speed of the forward. He then makes a two-handed chest pass to the forward for a layup. The object is to lead the runner to the basket with the pass.

5. The forward catches the ball in full stride, shoots the ball, rebounds it, and quickly dribbles up the court.

6. In the second part of the drill, players reverse roles. The guard who made the first pass continues to run to the hash mark on the same side where he started in the frontcourt. He touches the mark, reverses, and sprints back to the basket where the drill began. The initial passer becomes the receiver leading the fast break.

7. The forward rebounds, takes three or four dribbles, and throws a two-handed chest pass to the guard for a layup. When they complete the drill, the players rotate to the back of their respective lines.

8. The next guard and forward in line step up and perform the drill.

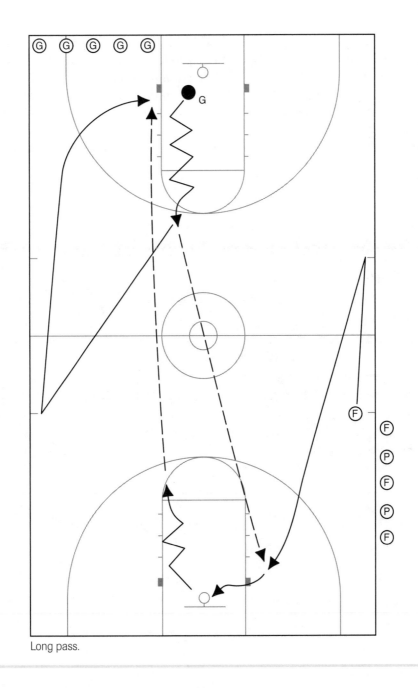

Long pass.

Angles and Vision

A real asset for passers in basketball is good vision. Everyone has heard coaches say of an excellent passer, "He sees the floor well." This means that the player, with his head up so that he can see the court has good passing instincts. Besides good instincts, exceptional passers like John Stockton, the NBA's all-time assist leader, has excellent peripheral awareness. Jeff Meyer, one of my former assistant coaches at Purdue and South Florida put it this way: "Vision on the court is not just for sight, but for insight." Good peripheral vision helps a player see teammates in the outer part of his vision. When running offensive plays, the designated receiver of the pass may often appear to be open, but when the passer delivers the ball, a defender intercepts it. The interception occurs because the passer is focusing only on the receiver, not on the defenders around him. Such a passer has narrow vision; good passers see the receiver and everyone around him.

PASSING ANGLES TO THE LOW POST

FOCUS

Teaching entry-pass technique, being conscious of angles and floor balance.

PROCEDURE

These are the proper angles when passing to the low post:

1. When attempting a direct pass to the low post, having the proper passing angle often eliminates an unforced turnover. Offensive plays should always be designed to eliminate as many defensive obstructions as possible.

2. Trying to pass from the top of the key to a stationary low post is extremely difficult, because a pass from that angle must go through too many defenders with active hands.

3. Instead of passing from the top, the player should dribble to the wing position at the free-throw line extended, clear out a teammate (which eliminates a defensive helper), and then enter the ball from the wing.

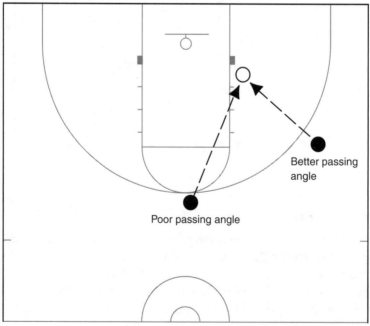

Passing angles to the low post.

4. Designed offensive plays with "slips" and "step-ins" are different because of the deception. Direct passes from the wing, however, are safer and better.

5. Good passers understand three important factors—angles, space, and timing. In considering angles, certain areas of the floor make passes difficult and should be avoided.

Passing Angles in the Middle of the Floor

Another extremely dangerous pass occurs when a team attempts either to reverse the ball or to pass to the top of the key for a shot. The passer puts himself at a tremendous disadvantage when he dribbles too low on the wing, thus permitting the weak-side defender an opportunity to shoot the gap. This play calls for the receiver of the pass to recognize the problem and relocate higher out on the court to ensure the safety of the pass. Coaches must constantly remind players to meet all passes.

PASSING ANGLES TO THE TOP OF THE KEY

FOCUS

Teaching passing angles to the top of the key.

PROCEDURE

Visualize and comprehend proper passing angle.

1. This diagram shows a common occurrence. When there is the possibility of ball reversal off half-court sets, such as pick-and-rolls, horns, zippers, passing

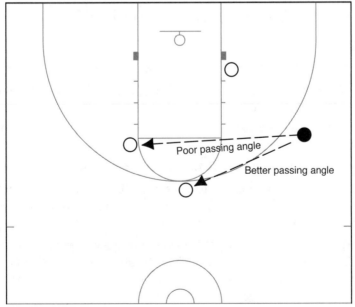

Passing angles to the top of the key.

games, UCLAs, or weak-side pins-downs, players rotate the ball to the top.

2. If there is a poor passing angle, the receiver is giving the defense an opportunity to steal the middle-of-the-floor pass. Instead of stopping, the receiver should continue to the top of the key, or farther if necessary, to receive the pass.

3. The ball handler must remember not to pick up his dribble. He should keep the dribble alive until he has an opportunity to pass.

Three-Man Drills: Screening

The following three-man drills continue to focus on ballhandling, passing, and shooting layups. These drills also highlight proper screening techniques, which are often overlooked. Players must learn these screening techniques: (1) The screener must know the distance restrictions for front, side, and back screens as they apply to the defender being screened, (2) the screener cannot move or lean to cause contact, and (3) proper body position has the feet spread shoulder-width apart, arms and elbows in (not extended), and the body upright. All effective half-court offenses depend on proper screening techniques to avoid committing offensive fouls. Nothing hurts a team more than holding for a last shot at the end of the game and then having a player set an illegal screen to forfeit the opportunity to win. Here are four excellent three-man drills that can build a stronger basketball foundation.

SPLITS: POST PASSER SETS SCREEN

FOCUS
Three-man drill—post splits, screening, passing, and shooting.

PROCEDURE
Players begin on the half court and follow these steps:

1. On the right side, a guard with the ball lines up six feet beyond the top of the key, directly in line with the elbow.

2. A forward lines up three feet inside the sideline boundary, even with the free-throw line extended.

3. The guard makes a direct pass to the post man and sets a screen for the forward.

4. To set up the defender, the forward uses a jab step to the baseline. He cuts to the middle off the screen set by the guard, looking for a pass from the post. This action is commonly known as split action or scissors.

5. In setting the pick, the guard must stop and hold the screen until the forward clears the contact area; otherwise, he commits a moving screen, resulting in an offensive foul. The guard continues to the baseline, looking for a return pass from the post man and the opportunity to score.

6. The post man decides who shoots the ball. He can pass either to the forward cutting down the middle or to the guard on the baseline. The third option is to let both teammates clear the area and then make an individual move.

7. Whoever doesn't shoot becomes the rebounder, and the players return to their respective lines.

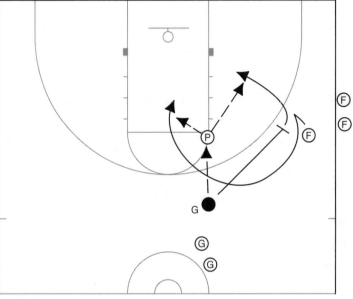

Splits: post passer sets screen.

SPLITS: GUARD REVERSES

FOCUS

Three-man drill—screening, passing, and shooting.

PROCEDURE

Players begin on the half court and follow these steps:

1. On the right side, a guard with the ball lines up six feet beyond the top of the key, directly in line with the elbow.

2. A forward lines up three feet inside the sideline boundary, even with the free-throw line extended.

3. The guard makes a bounce pass to the forward, goes behind the forward, and receives the handoff.

4. The guard makes one or two quick dribbles, stops, executes a left-foot reverse (that is, the left foot is the pivot foot), and passes to the post man at the mid-post area. The guard then sets a screen on the forward's man and cuts to the middle, looking for a return pass and the shot.

5. After the forward hands the ball off to the guard, he takes two steps away from the guard. After the ball goes into the post, the forward cuts baseline off the guard's screen, looking for the ball and a shot.

6. In setting the pick, the guard must stop and hold the screen until the forward clears the contact area; otherwise, he commits a moving screen, which is an offensive foul.

7. The post man decides who will shoot the ball. He can pass either to the forward on the baseline or to the guard cutting down the middle. The third option is to let both teammates clear the area and then make an individual move.

8. Whoever doesn't shoot becomes the rebounder, and the players return to their respective lines.

SPLITS: GUARD IN CORNER

FOCUS
Three-man drill—screening, passing, and shooting.

PROCEDURE
Players begin on the half court and follow these steps:

1. On the right side, a guard with the ball lines up six feet beyond the top of the key, directly in line with the elbow.

2. A forward lines up three feet inside the sideline boundary, even with the free-throw line extended.

3. The guard makes a chest pass to the forward and goes to the ball-side short corner.

4. The forward passes to the guard and takes a couple of steps toward the middle to create space and provide a better passing angle for the guard.

5. The guard then passes to the post man and sets a screen for the forward. After the ball goes to the post, the forward uses a jab step and cuts baseline off the guard's screen, looking for a pass and a shot.

6. In setting the pick, the guard must stop and hold the screen until the forward clears the contact area; otherwise, he commits a moving screen, which is an offensive foul.

7. The post man decides who will shoot the ball. He can pass either to the forward on the baseline or to the guard cutting down the middle. The third option is to let both teammates clear the area and then make an individual move.

8. Whoever doesn't shoot the ball becomes the rebounder, and the players return to their respective lines.

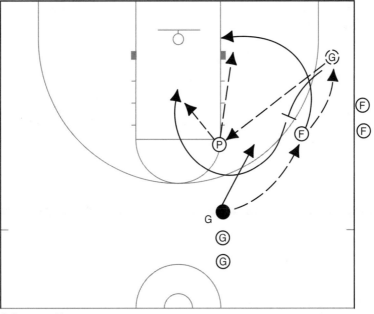

Splits: guard in corner.

SPLITS: FORWARD POST-PASS

FOCUS

Three-man drill—screening, passing, and shooting.

PROCEDURE

Players begin on the half court and follow these steps:

1. On the right side, a guard with the ball lines up six feet beyond the top of the key, directly in line with the elbow.

2. A forward lines up three feet inside the sideline boundary, even with the free-throw line extended.

3. The guard makes a chest pass to the forward and goes to the ball-side short corner.

4. The forward passes to the post man and sets a screen for the guard.

5. In setting the pick, the forward must stop and hold the screen until the guard clears the contact area; otherwise, he commits a moving screen.

6. The forward can step through or use a left-footed reverse pivot and cut to the basket.

7. The post man decides who will shoot the ball. He can pass either to the forward on the baseline or to the guard going to the middle. The third option is to let both teammates clear the area and then make an individual move.

8. Whoever doesn't shoot becomes the rebounder, and the players return to their respective lines.

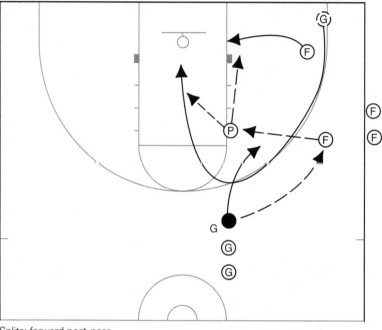

Splits: forward post-pass.

Screens in Half-Court Sets

Screening is one of the most overlooked fundamentals, although it is a teachable maneuver that only takes work and concentration. Players can learn to be good screeners, especially if they are unselfish and team oriented. Many different types of screens are used in basketball. Screening usually involves one player screening another player, but in some offensive sets, two or three players set the screen. The most common screens are cross, down, diagonal, and up screens.

Technique is important, and in most situations the player setting the screen is responsible for establishing a legal screen, which means being stationary at the time of the screen and making sure that the player being screened is permitted distance and proper vision. For example, when a player screens in front or at the side of a stationary opponent, he may be as close as he desires because the man being screened can see him. But if the screen is behind the opponent, the opponent is entitled to take one normal step before contact.

The player using the screen has the responsibility of making sure that the timing is proper; if he moves too soon, an offensive foul occurs. Moving too soon is a fundamental mistake because the player using the screen fails to set up his man properly and moves before the screener can establish a stationary position. Thus, the timing of the screen is a shared responsibility that requires both players to coordinate their movements.

Teaching players how to set and use screens is vitally important to developing an effective offense. To teach proper screening techniques, use a walk-through to show players how to set and use screens. The following drills will help.

DOWN SCREENS

FOCUS
Screening execution for the down screen.

PROCEDURE
Begin on the half court and follow these steps:
1. Split the squad into groups of three and use both ends of the court.
2. Illustrate with no defense and then go live three-on-three—offense to defense, defense off.
3. O1 dribbles to the free-throw line extended and passes to O2.
4. The zipper down screen occurs when O5 at the elbow sets a screen for O2 on the low block on the same side.
5. Down screens are used to free up shooters and passers.
6. To use the screen, the player should jab step in either direction, trying to get his defender between the screen and himself.
7. If the defender does not go with the jab step, the offensive man goes to the top of the key on the inside, closest to the passer.
8. If the defender takes the fake, the offensive man comes up the middle.

WEAK-SIDE PIN-DOWNS

FOCUS
Screening execution and timing for the weak-side pin-down.

PROCEDURE
Begin on half court and follow these steps:
1. Split the squad into groups of three and use both ends of the court.
2. Illustrate with no defense and then go live three-on-three—offense to defense, defense off. Use a coach as the middle passer. On the right side, O1, with the ball, lines up six feet beyond the top of the key in direct line with the elbow. The plan begins when O1 dribbles to the free-throw line extended and passes to the coach at the top of the key.
3. The down screen involves ball reversal for weak-side screens.
4. Weak-side pin-downs can be a single or double screen.
5. The player, O5, or players setting the screen cannot move on the screen.

6. O2, the user of the screen, must run with a purpose. He should read the defense and go away from or eliminate resistance.

7. If the defender blocks the route, the offensive player must find an alternative.

8. When players learn to run their routes with a purpose, the offense becomes fluid.

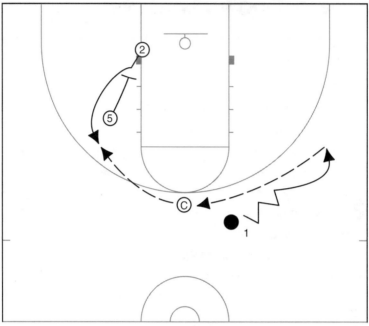

Weak-side pin-downs.

Weak-side screen setup.

CROSS SCREENS

FOCUS

Screening execution and technique for cross screens.

PROCEDURE

Begin on the half court and follow these steps:

1. Split the squad into groups of three and use both ends of the court.

2. Illustrate with no defense and then go live three-on-three—offense to defense, defense off. Play begins on the left side as O1, with the ball, lines up six feet beyond the top of the key in direct line with the elbow. O1 dribbles to the free-throw line extended, three feet from the sideline, and looks to pass inside to O4.

3. Cross screens close to the basket can be extremely physical. Thus, the screener must be prepared for contact, and the big man cannot move early; otherwise, he'll never clear the congested area.

4. The user should wait, move away from resistance, and be quick once he starts. The screener must clear quickly to avoid a three-second violation.

5. Cross screens with a small man screening a big man are excellent for getting the ball on the low post. Defenses seldom switch because of the mismatch.

6. Cross screens are most often used by teams that have good post-up players. Successful teams usually have at least three players capable of posting up.

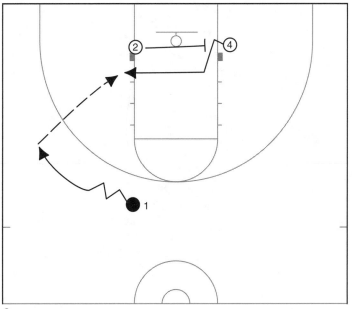

Cross screens.

MULTIPLE SCREENS

FOCUS

Screening execution and timing for cross screen to up screen.

PROCEDURE

Begin on the half court and follow these steps:

1. Split the squad into groups of three and use both ends of the court.

2. Illustrate with no defense and then go live three-on-three—offense to defense, defense off.

3. The pick-the-picker play involves two screens—first, a cross screen, and second, an up screen on the man in the free-throw circle for a lob. O1, with no defender guarding him, positions himself at the free-throw line extended and works on his passing.

4. On the cross screen, the offensive big man takes his man baseline because the screener cannot hold the screen as long because he must turn, get out of the three-second lane, and screen for the man in the free-throw circle for the lob.

5. The lob man must fake his defender with a good jab step left and then look for the lob.

6. The first screen is often a decoy that enables the screener to free up the real target for a shot, lob, or strong-side to weak-side rotation pass.

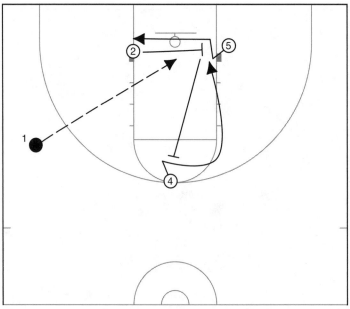

Multiple screens.

DIAGONAL SCREENS

FOCUS

Screening execution and technique for the diagonal screen.

PROCEDURE

Begin on the half court and follow these steps:

1. Split the squad into groups of three and use both ends of the court.
2. Illustrate with no defense and then go live three-on-three—offense to defense, defense off.
3. The purpose of the diagonal screen is to relocate a big man on the low post, as the Utah Jazz did when John Stockton screened for Karl Malone.
4. The diagonal screen is different because it depends on the strength of the person setting the screen and the player's ability to execute leverage.
5. Two factors make this screen difficult to execute: The player being screened sees it coming, and the player setting the screen is usually much smaller than the defender he screens. O1, on the left side with the ball, lines up six feet beyond the top of the key in direct line with the elbow. O1 dribbles toward the sideline free-throw line extended and looks to pass to O4.
6. If the screener doesn't have proper leverage, the big player will power right through.
7. The center or power forward should jab step toward the basket at the point of the screen to establish a good angle for the screener and then make an aggressive cut to the block.

SCREENS ON THE BALL

FOCUS

Communications, techniques, and rules for screening on the ball.

PROCEDURE

Begin on the half court and follow these steps:

1. Split the squad into two even groups and use both ends of the court.
2. The big inside players set the screen, and the perimeter players handle the ball. Divide the time and exchange the positions so that each player learns to set the screen.
3. Illustrate the sideline pick-and-roll with no defense and then go two-on-two—offense to defense, defense off.
4. Screens on the ball present different communication issues and screening adjustments. The player setting the screen must be stationary, and the person with the ball has the responsibility to make that happen.

5.   O1, the ball handler, sees the screen coming, waits until O5, the screener, comes to a complete stop, and then says, "Go" before making a move. This sequence is especially important for sideline, corner, transition, and elbow pick-and-rolls.

6.   In middle pick-and-rolls, the screener is usually set, and the ball handler works off a stationary target.

7.   For sideline and corner sets, the screener should set the pick on the outside shoulder of the defender, straddle the defender's outside leg with his leg, and then reverse pivot and roll to the basket or pop for the jump shot.

8.   The player setting the screen should have his feet shoulder-width apart and his arms down in front of his body with one hand over the other in a protective mode. He cannot lean, extend the elbows or knees, or turn into the defender.

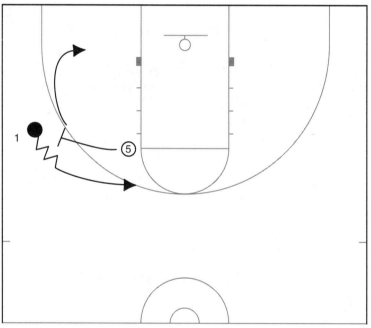

Screens on the ball.

Screen setup for the sideline pick-and-roll.

SINGLE AND DOUBLE SCREENS

FOCUS

Screening execution for running off single and double screens.

PROCEDURE

Begin on the half court and follow these steps:

1. Split the squad into even teams and use both ends of the court.

2. This half-court play requires five position players.

3. Illustrate with no defense and then work the play into the regular half-court offense. With three teams, go offense to defense, defense off.

4. The single-double offensive set gives the player using the screen the option of using a double screen or a single screen.

5. The set uses a tight formation with two screeners, O4 and O5, stacked on one side and O3, a single screener, opposite. O1, in the middle of the court six feet beyond the top of the key, initiates the play by passing to either side.

6. O2 lines up under the rim and first breaks as if he plans to use the single side. After he gets his man moving, he pivots or spins and sprints off the double side, coming as close as possible to the left hip of the first screener and building speed as he rounds the second screen.

7. As the shooter clears both screens, he has three options, depending on the defense: He can curl, fade (if the defender tries to shoot the gap), or pop out for a jump shot.

8. The screeners are stationary because the user of the screens does the work. If O2, the shooter, uses the single side, the screener, O3, after holding his screen, goes off the double-screen side. One big man stays, and one goes opposite to the low block.

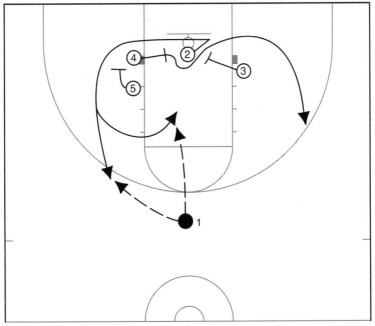

Single and double screens.

BASELINE SCREENS

FOCUS

Screening execution and timing for baseline screens.

PROCEDURE

Begin on the half court and follow these steps:

1. Split the squad into even teams and use both ends of the court.
2. This half-court play set requires five position players.
3. Illustrate with no defense and then work the set into the regular half-court offense. With three teams, go offense to defense, defense off.
4. The baseline screen set is an aspect of the passing game. The formation has two players line up opposite each other just off the low blocks.
5. The large inside players are wide off the elbows and at an angle, in position for a down screen.
6. O2, the low man on the left side, moves across and sets a stationary screen for O3, the opposite low man, who jab steps middle and then uses the screen, takes a couple of running steps, turns, and uses the second screen set by the big man, O5, looking for a catch-and-shoot shot.
7. O2, after setting the first screen, immediately uses O4's big-man screen, opposite side, looking for a jump shot. The emphasis here is getting the angle of the second screen correct and without movement.

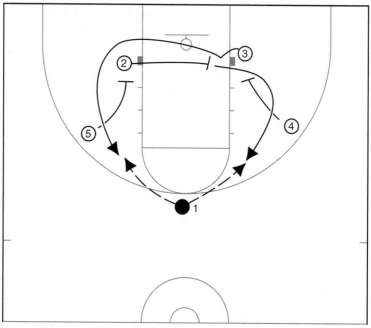

Baseline screens.

Shooting

Shooting should be an integral part of every offensive drill. Players must use proper shooting technique on every shot they take in practice, whether in drills, in half-court work, or in full scrimmages. Let's begin with the three essentials of the jump shot—proper base, visualization, and self-confidence.

Base, Visualization, and Confidence

When shooting, players begin by establishing a solid base with good body balance, feet approximately shoulder-width apart, and shoulders squared to the basket. The ball should rest in the shooting hand, with the fingers on the seams for proper rotation. The shooting elbow should be close to the body, anticipating the lift and shot. Players develop this technique only through long hours of practice. Sometimes, in the heat of action, it is not possible to get the fingers on the seams. With ball support from the off, or nonshooting, hand, the player protects the ball and takes it to a shooting position above and in front of the head. The player should stabilize himself and avoid jerking his head, which would distort his aim. In taking the shot, the player releases the off hand and allows the shooting hand to do all the work.

The arm, wrist, hand, and fingers work cooperatively to release the ball in a smooth, fluid motion. Shooters should understand that the rim is twice the

Free-throw setup.

Free-throw base.

diameter of the ball and that the object is to shoot the ball in an arc, not with flat trajectory or as a line drive, to permit the ball to drop into the basket. A good shooter has his arm, wrist, and fingers all extended on the follow-through. The proper extension involves the wrist being loose, relaxed, and extending forward as though the shooter is picking fruit from a bushel basket above his head. The index finger points directly at the basket as if it's a trigger finger pointing at a target.

Whether catching the ball on the move, off a screen, or pulling up off the dribble, players have to focus on the target as they are preparing to release the ball. Dell Curry, one of the best NBA three-point shooters of all time, said that he always aimed for the hole just beyond the middle flange (the hooks that hold the net) facing him and over the lip of the rim. Great shooters are able to see through the rim and concentrate on the hole between the front and back of the rim as their target. In pregame warm-ups, good shooters begin their workouts close to the basket and work their way out to the three-point line. This approach helps them create an easy, fluid motion for a shot and focuses them visually on the basket.

The third component of shooting involves maintaining confidence. Success in shooting depends on belief in one's abilities. Self-confidence is at the core of sport performance and is based on how one interprets his experiences. When the brain experiences positive input, a positive response is likely. The more shots a player makes, the more confidence he has. Effective leaders understand

c

Free-throw follow through.

d

Jump shot.

that repeated encouragement, confirmation, and support result in positive-in, positive-out experiences. The same experience occurs when a player shoots the ball: The more shots he makes, the more shots he expects to make. Good teachers develop shooting drills that consider the players' strengths and work at building a confident foundation.

Confidence is earned, not ordained. To tell players to play with confidence is wasted energy; you don't hand out confidence as you do water at a practice break. Success, repetition, concentration, competition, and plenty of practice create the environment to develop confidence. Goal-oriented shots during competitive drills that simulate win or lose situations can be great confidence builders. Self-motivating shooting drills that require players to make five shots from one spot, or three in a row, before moving on are highly effective. Such drills have concentration, repetition, and success built in. The addition of a player or group and the declaration of a winner add a competitive element that energizes the experience.

Former Clemson University and Charlotte Hornets' player Elden Campbell, who stood 6-11, shot 47 percent from the field during his NBA career. He had an effective warm-up shooting drill that helped build his confidence. After a few minutes of close-in shooting, Elden would move out to 15 to 18 feet from the basket and shoot from five spots—the baseline, the left elbow, a step inside the top of the key, the right elbow, and the right baseline. He had to make five in a row before he moved to the next spot. After he made five in a row, he would continue shooting to see how many he could make consecutively before moving on. On some nights, he would hit 15 straight, and the drill came easy. On other nights, nothing went in, and only his goal of hitting five straight made him concentrate and complete the task.

Shooting off the Dribble

One of the skills that separates good players from great players is the ability to shoot the pull-up jumper while on the move. Players who can do this have a midrange game, a rare quality in this day of the three-point field goal. Most players can hit the spot-up, long-range jump shot or a driving layup but have difficulty making the in-between 10- to 15-foot shot. Players cannot hit shots in that gap for several reasons: lack of ballhandling skills, poor balance on the pull-up, and lack of body control after beginning the dribble move. Players often resist change, not wanting to move beyond their comfort zone. As a result, they don't work on certain aspects of their game and lack confidence in areas such as dribbling and shooting off the dribble.

Another reason for the scarcity of the midrange game is that coaches don't emphasize it. The best way to approach the issues is to design shooting drills that require all players to dribble and pull up for jump shots, especially midrange shots. The following drills provide an excellent way to develop and improve shooting off the dribble.

SHOOTING OFF THE DRIBBLE, RIGHT HAND

FOCUS

Shooting technique with movement, right hand.

PROCEDURE

Divide the team into two groups of six. Run this drill on both ends of the court simultaneously. Follow these steps:

1. On each side of the court, players divide into two groups of three and line up behind the hash line on each side of the court. Coaches indicate where players take shots. Players begin with a right-handed dribble.

2. Players on the right side use a right-foot pivot, switching from a left-handed to right-handed dribble with a crossover step. They then dribble toward the wing position at the free-throw line extended.

3. Players stay low as they drive middle, using two dribbles before shooting a pull-up jump shot.

4. The shooter follows his shot, retrieves the ball, and rotates to the opposite line.

5. Players on the left side execute the same right-foot pivot technique, switching from a left-handed to right-handed dribble, going middle, and shooting a pull-up jump shot.

6. Each player retrieves his rebound and rotates to the back of the line on the right side. A second crossover dribble to the left hand on the pull-up shot adds more difficulty to the drill.

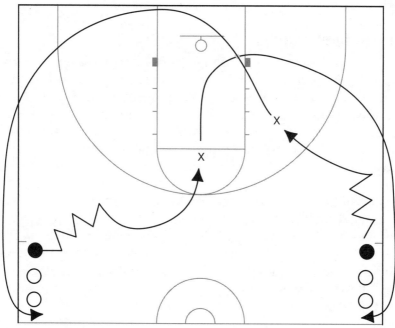

Shooting off the dribble with the right hand.

SHOOTING OFF THE DRIBBLE, LEFT HAND

FOCUS

Shooting technique with movement, left hand.

PROCEDURE

Divide the team into two groups of six. Run this drill on both ends of the court simultaneously. Follow these steps:

1. The drill is like the previous one, except that the left hand initiates the dribble action.

2. On each side of the court, players divide into groups of three and line up behind the hash line on each side of the court. Coaches or chairs indicate where players take shots. Players begin with a left-handed dribble.

3. Players on the left side use a left-foot pivot with a crossover dribble, switching from a right-handed to left-handed dribble, moving toward the wing position at the free-throw line extended. Players should stay low as they drive, taking two dribbles before shooting a pull-up jumper.

4. The shooter follows his shot, retrieves the ball, and rotates to the opposite line.

5. Players on the right side execute the same pivot technique to the middle with a crossover, switching from a right-handed to left-handed dribble and shooting a pull-up jump shot. Each player retrieves his rebound and rotates to the back of the line on the left side. A second crossover dribble increases the degree of difficulty.

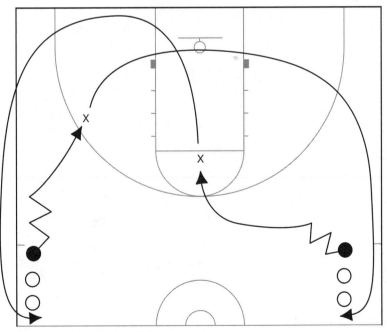

Shooting off the dribble with the left hand.

FULL-COURT SHOOTING DRILL

FOCUS

Shooting technique off the dribble, full court, right-handed dribble, and left-handed dribble.

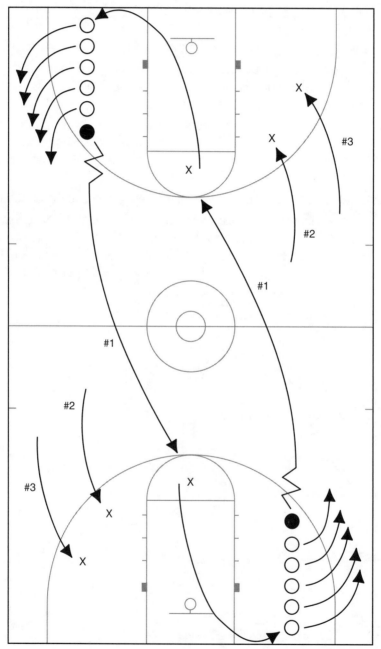

Full-court shooting drill.

PROCEDURE

Divide the squad with six at each end of the court and with each player having a ball. Then follow these steps:

1. This continuous full-court running and shooting drill will improve players' mobility, ballhandling, and ability to shoot off the dribble.

2. The drill is six minutes long. Players use the right-handed dribble for three minutes and the left-handed dribble for three minutes.

3. The emphasis is on ballhandling and shooting with rhythm.

4. Three chairs, marked as Xs on the diagram, are placed at the far end opposite the players, with each chair indicating the shooting spot. Players take the shots in order: first from the middle of the floor, then from the wing, and last from the baseline.

5. The players first in each line start at the same time. The drill is then follow the leader, with a space of two or three dribbles between players. After shooting, players retrieve their own shots and move to the line in the opposite corner from where they started. After this, they return to the corner where they began and repeat the procedure, keeping a continuous flow of motion.

6. On the second trip, they shoot from behind the second chair and so on until they have completed the entire cycle. Should they finish before three minutes are up, they start over at the first spot and continue the drill.

Shooting: Step-Back Move

Every coach looks for the player who has the skills to beat opponents in one-on-one situations. Several skills are associated with good one-on-one moves. Great players possess some, but not necessarily all, of the following skills: a quick first step, an unstoppable crossover, a quick release on the jumper, and a step-back move that creates space between them and the defender. Although Michael Jordan had tremendous skills in all phases of the game, his trademark ability to create space for himself was his most outstanding skill.

Getting the ball at the mid-post, he could go baseline or middle with one dribble, separate from the defender, create space, and get an open look at the basket. During his prime, Hakeem Olajuwon had the same ability. Defenders could be all over him, but with his back to his man, Olajuwon could take one quick step, disengage, and shoot an open shot. In today's NBA, Jamal Mashburn is one of the best at executing this skill. The following drill is helpful in teaching this technique.

SHOOTING WITH STEP-BACK MOVE

FOCUS

Separation moves to create space.

PROCEDURE

Divide the team into two groups of six. Groups work simultaneously on both ends of the court. Players rotate offense to defense, defense off. Follow these steps:

1. Step-back moves can come from anywhere on the court. For teaching purposes, however, the mid-post to low-post area is ideal.

2. The step-back involves good pivoting, footwork, proper balance, and head and shoulder fakes. The offensive player must have a good feel for where the defender is and be able to elevate as he disengages from the defender. Leg strength is important.

3. This drill is a one-on-one in the mid-post on the right side. To emphasize the offensive move, the defender plays behind and permits the entry pass. On the catch, the offensive player gets a feel for the defender. With a preshot head fake, the offensive man determines his route. Quick step-back dribbles help build rhythm.

4. To turn middle, the offensive player must step back into the defender with his right leg to eliminate any space and then use a left-leg power step-away while turning, elevating, and shooting.

5. To turn baseline, the offensive player must step into the defender with his left leg to eliminate any space and then use a right-leg power step-away while turning, elevating, and shooting.

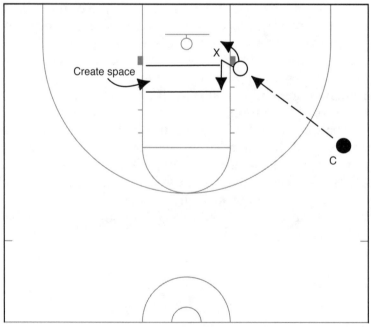

Shooting with the step-back move.

Shooting: Off Draw and Kick

The further a team goes in state competition, NCAA tournaments, or NBA play-offs, the more important it is to be able to shoot the ball off dribble penetration. By the time the regular season ends, sophisticated advance scouting enables teams to know opponent's offensive sets, taking away the first and second options of plays that have been successful throughout the year. Thus, players in the half court must be able to put the ball on the floor either to improve shooting or passing angles or to drive to the basket. In other words, they must be able to improvise if the set is well defended. The three-man draw-and-kick is an excellent drill for teaching dribble penetration while also testing decision making.

DRAW-AND-KICK SHOOTING DRILL

FOCUS

Create shots off dribble penetration.

PROCEDURE

Divide the squad into groups of three and use both ends of the court. Follow these steps:

1. Teams with more than 12 players will go from offense to defense, defense off. Play each possession until the defense captures the ball or the offense scores.

2. The offensive set is a spread, with two wings and one man with the ball in the middle. The object of the drill is to maintain floor balance, with each individual ball handler

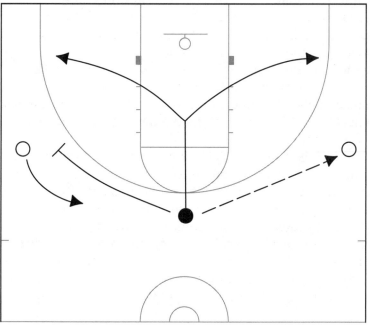

Draw-and-kick shooting drill.

looking to drive to the basket or make a good decision on a shot or a pass to a team-mate. Players must dribble drive, pass, or shoot. They cannot screen on the ball.

3. To eliminate catch-and-shoot situations, in which no dribble precedes the shot, the coach must build in a restriction—loss of ball to the offense. The object is to get players shooting off the dribble.

4. Change players in the drill by having the big man start the play from the middle position.

Position-Specific Shooting Drills

Competitive players working on their shots seldom shoot the ball randomly. They work on things that help them in games. Having a plan tailored to a position helps players improve their shooting efficiency. For example, a perimeter player can work on making a certain number of medium-range jump shots from the left, right, and middle, and then work on making a prescribed number of long-range jumpers from the left, right, and middle. After each series of shots from the different locations, the shooter also hits five free throws. This confidence-building drill requires only a ball, a goal, and a dedicated player willing to execute the plan.

One offensive fundamental that players should practice daily is shooting, in both individual drills and team drills. Individual shooting drills, lasting about 20 minutes, are best performed early in the practice session. Team shooting drills usually come near the end of practice. Colleges and the NBA like to split the squad into two major groups; big men are on one end and guards and small forwards are on the other, with coaches directing prescribed drills that fit position-specific needs. Each player should have a ball so that he can get up as many shots as possible in the allotted time.

Keeping the 20-minute time schedule in mind, here are six different warm-up shooting drills for the big men and the guards. These drills can be incorporated into pregame and shoot-around routines. Guard drills focus on baseline curls, fades, and up-the-middle jumpers, and big men concentrate on low-post shots, spot-ups, and dribble drives.

For shooting drills, split a team of 12 into two equal groups for 20 minutes. The guards and small forwards combine for one group called "the perimeter" or "smalls," and the centers and power forwards make up the other group called "the inside" or "bigs." Players take specific shots, with coaches doing the passing, from designated areas. The first three drills will be for perimeter shots, and the next three are for inside shooting. Competition is built in by setting a goal; either the first side to hit 5 straight wins or the first side to hit a total of 10 shots wins. Then the drill moves to a different spot. The side winning the most spots is the daily winner. Players love this kind of drill.

BASELINE CURLS

FOCUS

Shooting the jump shot, baseline curl, and catch-and-shoot technique.

PROCEDURE

Begin with the guards on the baseline and follow these steps:

1. Divide the players into two groups of three. Players line up under the basket with the first two shooters on the low blocks. The four nonshooters are in line under the basket. Each player has his own ball and gets his own rebound.

2. Coaches are passers and take positions just above the three-point line in line with the free-throw lane extended. The drill begins on the coach's command.

3. The first two players pass to their respective coaches and run a curl cut (similar to a banana curve) about 10 to 12 feet from the basket. For this quick move, the player must be under control and have good balance. He pivots toward the passer with his hands open to receive the pass, squares to the basket, and shoots a fluid jump shot with rhythm and proper follow-through.

4. The shooter retrieves his own rebound and returns to the end of his line, ready for another turn. Players continue to rotate and shoot until one team wins. Then the shot changes or the players switch sides.

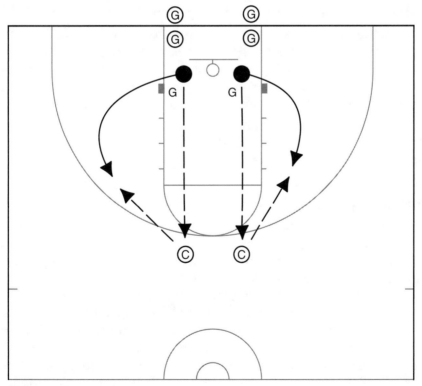

Baseline curls.

Baseline Fade

The baseline fade shot is a countermove to elude a defender who begins to antici-pate the baseline curl by shooting the gap. By shooting the gap, the defender seeks to avoid the offensive screens and runs up the middle of the free-throw lane to reduce the distance between himself and the shooter. The offensive player sees the defender go up the middle, so he fakes as if he is going to curl but instead fades to the corner. This drill teaches the footwork and technique for getting open for the shot.

BASELINE FADE

FOCUS

Shooting, baseline fade, and catch-and-shoot technique.

PROCEDURE

Begin with the guards on the baseline and follow these steps:

1. Divide the players into two groups of three. Players line up under the basket with the first two shooters on the low blocks. The four nonshooters are in a line under the basket. Each player has a ball, rebounds his own shot, and rotates to the end of the line.

2. Coaches are passers and take positions just above the three-point line, in line with the free-throw lane extended. The drill begins on the coach's command.

3. The first two players pass to their respective coaches and begin as if they are going to run a curl. Instead, about five steps into what looks like the curl, the players, while never taking their eyes off the ball, pivot and slide to their respective corners looking for the pass. The player on the right side pivots off his right foot, and the player on the left side pivots off his left foot.

4. On the catch, the player should be square to the basket, under control, balanced, and ready to shoot. The player should always stay within his range, and if necessary, add one dribble to gather himself.

Jump Shot: Up the Middle

The up-the-middle shooting drill is extremely valuable because it offers many variations. Three good options for range and distance are shots from the free-throw line, from the top of the key, and from beyond the three-point arc. All occur in game situations, and players should practice them every day. Up the middle is primarily a catch-and-shoot drill, but beneficial modifications include moves such as a pump fake and one dribble to the right or left, or a quick dribble crossover pull-up. The possibilities are unlimited, depending only on the player's creativity. Players enjoy new challenges, and even minor changes in drills keep them interested and enthused. Effective shooting practice requires proper mechanics, concentration, repetition, and rhythm, working together to help build confidence.

UP THE MIDDLE

FOCUS

Jump shots up the middle, catch-and-shoot technique.

PROCEDURE

Begin with the guards on the baseline and follow these steps:

1. Divide players into two groups of three. Players line up under the basket with the first two shooters on the low blocks. The four nonshooters are in two lines under the basket. Each player has a ball, rebounds his own shot, and rotates to the end of the line.

2. Coaches are passers and take positions just outside the three-point arc in line with the free-throw line. The drill begins on the coach's command.

3. The first two players pass to the coaches, jab step as if they are running a curl pattern, and then run up the middle to the free-throw line. The player on the left side uses a right-foot pivot toward his coach, and the player on the right side uses a left-foot pivot toward his coach.

4. Players need to use the pivot to establish shot preparation by presenting a good target with the hands up, shoulders squared to the basket, and good body balance for a catch-and-shoot attempt. Players always follow their shots.

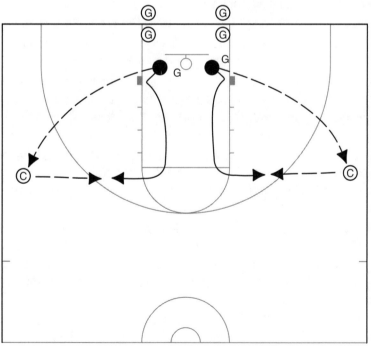

Up the middle.

Shots off Inside Moves

To establish a good low-post attack, you must work with your big people daily. In a 20-minute shooting segment, a big-man routine should consist of low-post power moves, baseline turnaround jumpers over the right shoulder and left shoulder, middle hook shots and jump hook shots, and a mixture of catch, face, and drives from low-, mid-, and high-post areas. Face-up rhythm jump shots from several areas around the horn are always good finishers. Creating competition by having players hit a certain number of shots or hit a certain number in a row builds enthusiasm and creates a more enjoyable work environment.

LOW-POST MOVES

FOCUS

Technique, footwork, balance, and shots for inside players.

PROCEDURE

Begin with inside players on the baseline and follow these steps:

1. Big men, each with a ball, line up on one side of the basket. The coach lines up at the free-throw line extended opposite the players. The first player in line passes to the coach, moves quickly across the free-throw lane, and establishes low-post block position; he may also take a shot at mid-post. From this position, the player executes the shot, gets his own rebound, and rotates to the end of the line.

2. Players execute the following five shots first on the left block and then on the right block. Players reverse all of the maneuvers on the left block:

   a. Drop leg right: The player on the block catches the ball in both hands and leans back into the defender, establishing the right foot as the pivot foot. He takes one dribble and steps toward the middle with the left leg, spins back quickly to the right, dropping the right leg toward the basket, and shoots a power layup.

   b. Step-in right: The player on the block catches the ball with both hands and leans into the defender, establishing the right foot as the pivot foot. He takes one quick dribble toward the baseline and then quickly spins to the middle of the free-throw lane to shoot a right-handed layup or dunk.

   c. Baseline jumper over the right shoulder: The player on the block catches the ball with both hands, dribbles once, and drops left as if to go middle. With his back to the basket and with a right-foot pivot, he takes one long step toward the baseline, jumping in the air and turning around for a right-handed, over-the-right-shoulder jump shot.

   d. Right-handed hook shot: The player on the block catches the ball with both hands and turns quickly with a left-leg step-in and a right-hand dribble. He then moves across the middle of the lane with at least one dribble to shoot a fluid right-handed hook shot.

e. Right-handed jump hook shot: This move is the same as the previous one except that instead of shooting a fluid hook shot, the player comes to a two-footed jump stop and shoots a right-handed jump hook shot.

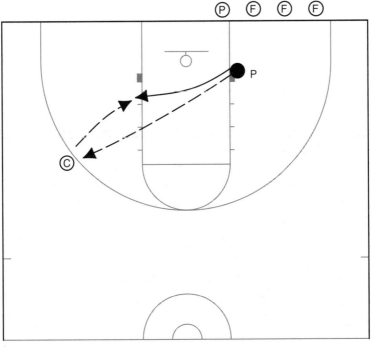

Low post moves.

Post Dribble Drive

Teaching big men to dribble provides both a safeguard against panic and a productive offensive weapon. Having a big man, especially a center, who can handle the ball well is a luxury that allows you to attack the opposing center off the dribble. Most centers aren't able to apply defensive pressure against an opposing center who is playing out on the court. Big men who can attack the basket with dribble penetration are invaluable. The following drill, which incorporates ballhandling and shooting, will improve their skills. Coach Bobby Weiss used it when we coached the San Antonio Spurs in the mid-1980s. The object of the drill is to improve the agility, flexibility, mobility, ballhandling, and shooting skills of big men.

DRIBBLE DRIVE FOR POST PLAYERS

FOCUS

Shooting and drives to the basket for inside players.

PROCEDURE

Begin with post players at the top of the key and follow these steps:

1. Big men, each with a ball, line up in single file between the top of the key and the midcourt line. Coaches line up sideline at the free-throw line extended and serve as passers. When one coach is passing, the other acts as a token defender for the big men to dribble around.

2. The drill begins on the right side with the first big man passing to the offensive coach (C1) and then stepping in the direction of the defensive coach (C2). The player has his arms extended and both hands open, looking for a return pass at the top of the key.

3. The big man establishes his right foot as his pivot foot and immediately breaks down, protecting the ball by bending at the waist and holding the ball in both hands on his right hip away from his defender.

4. The big man straightens up and, using the right foot as his pivot, takes a long stride and uses a left-leg crossover between himself and his defender as he takes one dribble that carries him to the basket for the layup or dunk.

5. The important sequence is to catch, protect, bend, step around, and explode to the basket. Younger players may need two dribbles. On the left side, the player uses a left-handed dribble with a right-leg step through.

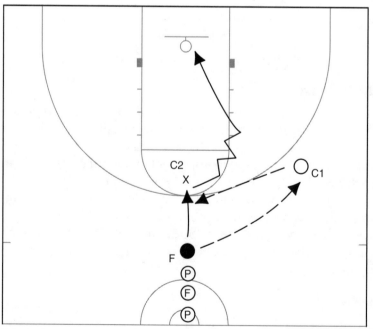

Dribble drive for post players.

Shooting: Spot-Ups for Inside Players

In today's game, power forwards and centers must be able to face up and hit the 15- to 18-foot jump shot. The distance can be increased or reduced depending on the player's range. This excellent drill ensures concentration and competition and creates enthusiasm. Competitive spot shooting has five designated spots marked with tape or cones: (1) left baseline, (2) left elbow extended, (3) top of the key area, (4) right elbow extended, and (5) right baseline. Players compete against each other, building peer pressure into the results.

SPOT-UP SHOTS

FOCUS

Increase range and accuracy in shooting, spot rotations.

PROCEDURE

Begin with inside players on the half court and follow these steps:

1. Coaches, managers, or volunteers rebound, retrieve, and toss the balls back.

2. Two teams of three begin on opposite sides of the floor and compete against each other. Each player has a ball.

3. Players on each team of three line up one behind the other and shoot in order. To advance to the next spot, a team must hit 3, 5, or 10 shots. The coach sets the goal, and assistant coaches keep count. The team on the left rotates 1-2-3-4-5, and the team on the right rotates 5-4-3-2-1.

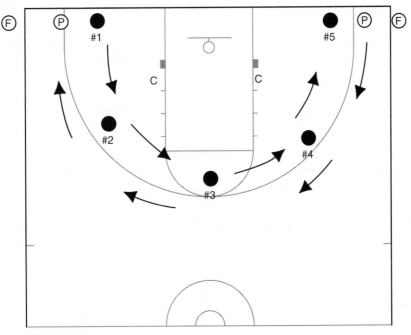

Spot-up shots.

4. The first team to make all its required shots at each spot and then complete the five spots wins.

5. Setting a goal to make three or five consecutive shots is effective with good shooters but will not work with poor shooters.

6. Another option is to use only one ball and have the shooter rebound his shot and pass to the next player in line. This method creates more player movement and emphasizes the shooting pass.

Rebounding

Shooting skills do not always determine the outcome of a basketball game; other factors are crucial. Players need to understand that steals, turnovers, second-chance points, and rebounding play significant roles. Good defense is a major element in successful teams, and rebounding (see chapter 7 for defensive rebounding drills) is central to solid defense.

Successful rebounding is a mind-set. Some gifted players naturally have a knack for coming up with big rebounds, but more often than not, good rebounders are the result of hard work and concentration. For players who want to excel in rebounding, the following list may be helpful:

- **Anticipation.** Players need to recognize that NBA teams, with the best players in the world, shoot between 44 and 46 percent. This means that more than 50 percent of all shots taken present rebound possibilities. Shooting percentage drops off at the college and high school level, presenting an even greater need for rebounding proficiency.

- **Aggressiveness.** Rebounders compete in the physical dimension of basketball, down where the push and shove confrontation is a test of will. The trenches are the place where bodies bang, leapers explode, and the physical power of the game achieves respect. Rebounding is not for the meek. This is a place where physical players who love contact excel.

- **Timing.** An essential requisite for effective rebounding is timing. Rope jumping, backboard touches, and power jumping drills all increase jumping skills and develop the rhythm necessary for good timing. Players with good timing don't always have to jump high; they just need to get good position and jump at the right time.

- **Position.** Defensive rebounders need to maintain contact with the opponent when a shot is taken, either by stepping back with a reverse pivot or by using the step-through technique, which takes them toward the player they are guarding. The body should be in a crouched position with hands and palms up, arms spread and lifted to shoulder height, and legs shoulder-width apart for good balance.

- **Boxing out.** The art of boxing out is a great asset when used properly. Good defensive rebounders are either great jumpers who have excellent timing skills or players who have perfected the art of boxing out. Ask any basketball player about box-out artists, and you'll understand how frustrating it is to play against them. A player who will put his butt in your belly or knees consistently is one dreaded player. Boxing out requires no magic—just concentration, hard work, and consistency (see chapter 7).

- **Offensive rebounds.** When constructing an offense, the coach needs to build in a triangle concept of putting three players, one being the shooter, on the offensive boards. Teams scoring off offensive rebounds and second-chance points soon find themselves winning games.

- **Rims.** Smart players always check the rim of the basket before the game. Some rims are lively and provide more bounce to the ball, whereas others tend to soften ball reaction and cause it to hang on the rim longer. Lighting and floor surface are not identical in all arenas, and players should factor in the effect of those elements on rebounding.

Many factors, including size, strength, hands, timing, body control, balance, aggressiveness, physical stamina, and jumping ability, are important to rebounding effectiveness. Players willing to concentrate and learn the technique of boxing out are important to every team. Rebounding in the trenches is blue-collar work. Any dyed-in-the-wool player willing to devote himself to the fundamentals of rebounding can improve and make a spot for himself.

One reason that great players are difficult to defend is because they move without the ball by setting screens, crashing the backboard, running pick-and-pop action, and setting up flares for a throw-over. Great players understand that when they set a back pick and one player dives toward the basket while the other pops out, one of them will get open. Also, when two players are involved in a screen and both move, defenders usually hesitate or switch, which allows someone to get open.

The best offensive rebounders depend on movement, which makes it hard for defenders to stay in touch and box them off the glass. Dennis Rodman, one of the most effective offensive rebounders in NBA history, was so good at moving and getting to the offensive boards that his team ran no specific plays for him. He was more valuable to the team when turned loose on the boards. The following drills are basic half-court, low-post split plays. In the first drill, players are stationary. In the second, movement is built in to make sure that certain players go to the boards.

TEAM ALIGNMENT WITH NO MOVEMENT

FOCUS

Alignment showing a lack of movement on post-up.

PROCEDURE

Begin with players on the half court and follow these steps:

1. Position one team in a direct post-up overload set.

2. Show a stationary set by placing the ball on the low post and spotting up the other four players around the perimeter of the three-point line.

3. Illustrate with no defense. Then work the set into the regular half-court offense with three teams. Rotate offense to defense, defense off.

4. Players should recognize that this alignment requires a low-post player who demands being double-teamed and is surrounded by excellent spot-up shooters. Otherwise, it's one-and-done basketball.

5. This attack offers little opportunity for an offensive rebound because no one is working to get to the basket.

6. The next drill illustrates how to modify this play by incorporating movement and putting rebounders at the boards.

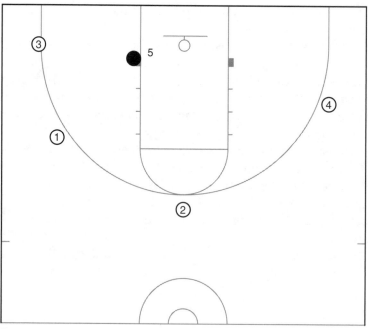

Team alignment with no movement.

BUILD IN OFFENSIVE MOVEMENT

FOCUS

Alignment showing movement to the basket created out of existing offensive sets.

PROCEDURE

Begin with players on the half court and follow these steps:

1. Position one team in a direct post overload set.

2. Build in designed screens, basket cuts, and rolls to the basket by placing rebounders at the basket. Here's how:

    a. Once the ball gets to the low post, O1 sets a down screen for O3 and cuts baseline to the basket. O3 comes off O1's screen and attacks the basket from the wing.

    b. O4, who usually works his way to the boards, sets a back screen for O2, who runs a flare and continues to the board.

    c. O4 can spot up or dive down the lane for a rebound.

3. Illustrate this with no defense and then work the set into the regular half-court schedule. With three teams, rotate offense to defense, defense off.

4. The coach must designate someone to be back for defense, but everyone else is an offensive rebounder.

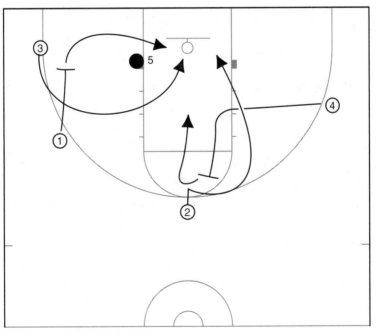

Building in offensive movement.

Four All-Purpose Team Drills

Choosing team dribble and passing drills that emphasize several fundamentals is an excellent way to teach a variety of skills. Both of these four-corner passing drills bring together dribbling, pivoting, and passing in a spirited team activity. All players must focus as they rotate from one position to another, because proper timing is an essential element. Any lapse, such as an errant pass, a lazy runner, or poor execution at the pivot point, will cause the whole drill to break down. Another effective passing drill is the three-person ball fake-and-pass drill (called "man in the middle"). The object of this drill is either to fake down and pass over the defender or to fake up and pass the ball under or around the defender. The drill challenges players to make good decisions and deliver a good pass while facing defensive pressure. All four of these drills—four-corners middle, four-corners long pass, ball fake, and motion movement—help develop well-rounded players.

FOUR-CORNERS PASSING

FOCUS

Concentrate on proper execution for the dribble, pivot, and pass drill.

PROCEDURE

Players form four equal groups in the corners on the half court. Each group has a ball and should follow these steps:

1. This is a dribble, pivot, and pass drill synchronized with a whistle or oral command by one of the players.

2. Before starting the drill, the coach will call for either a right-foot pivot or a left-foot pivot.

3. On the command to start the drill, the players in the front of each line dribble to the middle and stop just outside the free-throw circle. They continue dribbling until the whistle blows or the command to pivot is announced.

4. The players, in unison, pivot and pass a two-handed chest pass to the player in the next line. The players follow the pass and rotate to the next line.

5. The player receiving the pass must show a target by opening both palms to the passer.

6. The coach can call, "Reverse!" to change the direction of the pivot at any time to keep the players alert and involved in the drill.

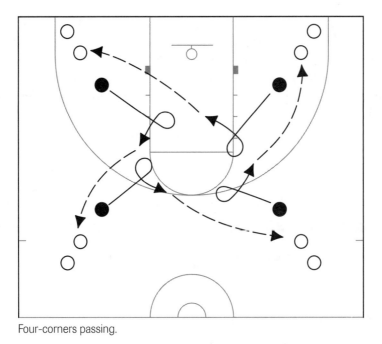

Four-corners passing.

Four-Corners Long Pass

The long pass demands great timing, a longer distance to run, and a flip pass and a quick pivot. Because timing is so important, players must work together. The drill depends on the accuracy of the long pass and the speed of the players. One mishandled pass or one player who runs too fast can disrupt the drill. Players must be alert and stay together.

FOUR-CORNERS LONG PASS

FOCUS

Concentrate on proper execution for all-purpose passing, pivoting, and the dribble drill.

PROCEDURE

In a half-court setting, players form equal groups, with at least three in a group, and line up in the four corners. Each group has a ball and should follow these steps:

1. This is a dribble, pivot, and pass drill that is synchronized and done in unison.

2. Before starting the drill, the coach calls for either a right-foot pivot or left-foot pivot to indicate the direction of the drill.

3. On the command to start, the player in the front of the line dribbles once and makes a long, two-handed chest pass to the person inside the boundary. The receiver has his palms up, ready to receive the pass. The passer follows his pass.

4. The passer continues running and stays to the inside of the receiver. A return flip pass brings the runner to a two-foot jump stop. At this point, the player executes the pivot and returns a short flip pass to the initial receiver.

5. The receiver of the first long pass now becomes the player who rotates to the next corner with the same procedure—a quick dribble and a long two-handed chest pass to the next player in line.

6. The player follows the pass and stays to the inside of the receiver. A return flip pass brings the runner to a two-foot jump stop. Again, the player executes the pivot and returns a short flip pass as the rotation continues. A variation is to run at half speed and come to a complete stop for the pivot with the knees bent and the body low. Spin on the pivot and give the continuing player an inside-handoff flip pass. and returns a short flip pass as the rotation continues. A variation is to run at half speed and come to a complete stop for the pivot with the knees bent and the body low. Spin on the pivot and give the continuing player an inside-handoff flip pass.

Passing: Man in the Middle

One of the most difficult passes to make occurs when a defender gets between the passer and the receiver. As teams build their half-court offense and entry passes to the low post are needed, this drill becomes necessary. Passers must learn to square up to the defender and execute the pass without the ball being deflected or intercepted. The passer must learn to read the defender and know whether to fake down and throw over, or fake up and pass under. To be an effective passer to the low post a player must understand the fundamentals of squaring up, pivoting properly, and finessing the defender.

THREE-LINES FAKE-AND-PASS

FOCUS

Execute passing and pivoting techniques with the fake-and-pass drill.

PROCEDURE

Begin with players in groups of three and follow these steps:

1. On the half court, align players in groups of three, each group with a ball.

2. Two offensive players are about 12 feet apart with one defender in the middle. Passing the ball to a teammate when a defender is between the two takes good judgment, a brisk pass, and finesse.

3. The drill begins with the defender in the middle passing the ball to an offensive player. The defender then tries to keep that player from passing the ball to his partner.

4. The offensive player with the ball can use only one dribble to attack or escape the defender and pass the ball to the partner.

5. Players exchange positions on deflections and steals. The drill is a form of keep-away, except that high, over-the-head passes are not permitted.

6. The object is for the passer to pivot or dribble to improve the passing angle and make a good pass.

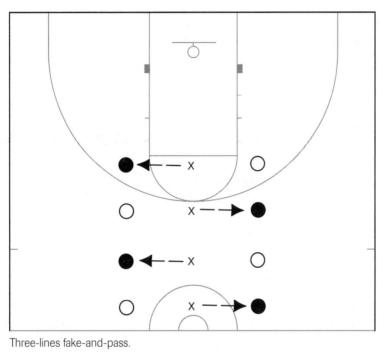

Three-lines fake-and-pass.

A shock awaits most high school stars when they arrive for college basketball: All of their teammates were also the stars of their high school teams. Players need to develop a new mind-set. They must learn to move without the ball and understand the importance of floor spacing and balance if they are to reach their full potential as college players.

A good college coach understands the strengths and weaknesses of each player on his team. Smart players are receptive to hearing what these are. If they're open to helpful criticism, players will soon understand that they need to improve parts of their game, such as playing effectively with the off hand, being able to score with a medium-range jump shot, and passing the ball rather than stagnating the offense with pointless dribbling.

Move Without the Ball

If you've been to a basketball game, you've probably heard the coach yell, "Move the ball!" to his players. The admonition usually comes when the team has stopped running the fast break, when a player has stopped running the offense, or when players are not cutting to the basket or moving to receive passes. Fatigue is the enemy. When it strikes, players tend to stop cutting and slashing and begin to stand around. The rule in basketball is never to rest on defense, so the only time that players can catch their breath is when they are not directly involved in the offense. Consequently, coaches attempt to counter fatigue with their offensive structure. The easiest way to do this is with some type of motion.

The kind of movement needed to be successful in basketball is spontaneous. The best players are quick to read an on-court situation and react to it. Their play is instinctive, not something they have to stop and think about. In any field, the great ones don't paint by numbers; a flow accompanies talent. A few players understand the importance of movement early on, but most acquire the skill through training. The following drill teaches players the concepts of movement, spacing, and floor balance.

MOTION MOVEMENT

FOCUS
Teaching players to move by setting screens and basket cuts.

PROCEDURE
Begin with players three-on-three in the half court and follow these steps:

1. Divide the team and work both ends. This drill works well with nine players.
2. Players rotate offense to defense based on the outcome of each possession.
3. Allow no dribbling or offensive screening on the ball. Players must work their way to the basket by passing and cutting.
4. The ball begins in the middle of the court. O1 can pass either way, and he then has these options: pass to O2 and screen away for O3 or pass to O2 and dive to the basket. If there is no return pass, he goes to the strong-side or weak-side corner.
5. O2 has these options: pass to O1 for a layup, pass to O1 in the strong-side corner, or pass to O3 at the top of the key.
6. Following O1's move, players may
   a. backdoor anytime,
   b. dive to the basket after passing and go strong side or weak side,
   c. come off a screen and catch and shoot if open,
   d. replace or fill the vacancy one pass away if not involved in passing or receiving, but
   e. may not screen on the ball.
7. To encourage more movement, the coach can demand three or four passes before the shot.
8. Using these guidelines, the four-on-four motion offense is also a good drill.

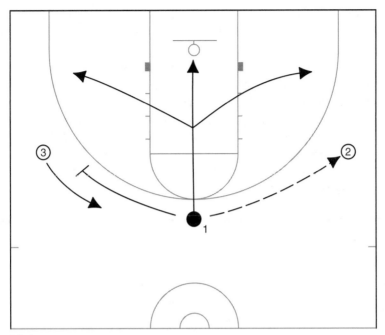

Motion movement.

Offense three-on-three pass and cut.

The passing game is popular in high school and college basketball because player and ball movement are built into the pattern. NBA teams, on the other hand, depend more on individual matchups and one-on-one strategy; therefore, they run more isolation plays with less ball and player movement. Still, at all three levels, teams use continuity offenses to keep the ball and players moving.

These six fundamentals—dribbling, pivoting, passing, screening, shooting, and rebounding—are essential for total player development. Players can do only four things with a basketball—dribble it, pass it, shoot it, or hold it. These fundamentals teach players the proper way to execute each action. Next, we examine four important player tools, describe two full-court drills, and build an all-purpose half-court offense with the LA offensive pattern.

CHAPTER 6

Individual and Team Offense

B asketball players come in all shapes and sizes. The only requirement for making any squad, regardless of level, is that you bring some skill that the team needs. No rule stipulates that you be large or small, short or tall, heavy or thin, fast or slow, because it takes all types of physical skills and character traits to assemble a team. Furthermore, it's what you do with what you've got that matters. For example, though small by conventional standards, point guards Earl Boykins at 5-5, Tyrone Bogues at 5-3, and Spud Webb at 5-6 all parlayed ballhandling skills and uncommon quickness into excellent NBA careers.

Players bring different levels of skill to the court. The coach's goal is to help players develop their skills to the highest level possible. The status quo is rare in basketball, because players usually improve or fall back in each practice. No magic is involved; each player must seize the opportunity through hard work. Pragmatically, the important thing for players is to be confident in their game and positive in their approach when they receive constructive criticism.

Most players enjoy fast-paced offenses, and the wise ones soon realize that scoring is a by-product of executing sound fundamentals. Basketball teams that insist on player and ball movement on offense are extremely hard to guard because the constant movement can cause a defense to break down, thus creating excellent scoring opportunities. Good offensive players spend hours practicing such skills as ballhandling, passing, screening, and shooting. In addition, they learn to balance the court and use good spacing to make themselves and their teammates more difficult to guard. Add the important element of good decision making, and chances are that players will be on the right track toward improvement.

Even if a player doesn't have all the skills, he should never give up. For instance, a player who is big but not fast can find a place if he has good instincts, knows how to set screens, and has passing skills. An athletic rebounder with good speed who doesn't shoot well can complement team defense. A small guard who has limited rebounding or low-post defensive ability but who is able to make good playmaking decisions is ideal on a pressing team. Coaches need be flexible when considering players and positions, especially when it comes to scoring. Regardless of size, shooters are always in demand. Remember, the stereotypical pieces sometimes don't fit, and on most levels of play below the professional level, you work with the skills that your players have.

Let's examine the skill areas of speed, soft hands, and jumping and then add decision making, that all-important intuitive quality, as we work our way to completing the process by building an offense.

Athletic Tools

Many factors go into determining athletic success—talent, genetics, mental attitude and desire, and even access to facilities and training. To a large degree, genetics determines some part of success in many sports. Jockeys are small, and sumo wrestlers are large. The average female gymnast is 4-9 and weighs 83 pounds. Sprinters have the high ratio of fast-twitch to slow-twitch muscles, a composition needed for explosive power. In contrast, marathon runners have 85 percent slow-twitch muscles so that they can sustain long periods of energy production. The average height of an NBA player in 1995 was over 6-7, and research shows that only 1.7 percent of American men between the ages of 25 and 34 were over 6-3. Of course, training can shape body type. For example, marathon runners become leaner over time, weight lifters bulk up and gain definition, and speed skaters develop massive legs.

Genetic factors are not set in concrete, and one cannot categorically say that something or another is in the genes and that nothing can be done. Many coaches and athletes believe that speed, quickness, and jumping cannot be improved, but that is a myth. The fact is that players can improve all three of these factors through proper techniques and training.

Speed

Players can improve their speed with the eighths program explained in chapter 4. Basketball players intent on increasing their speed need to start early with strength and weight-training programs. Research tells us that an athlete's muscular power largely determines his speed; an athlete cannot develop his highest level of speed without developing peak power performance. A physiological perspective suggests that an athlete can improve speed in two major ways: by increasing the frequency of the stride or by increasing the length of the stride. Both occur when the player trains the body beyond its normal capacity, that is, by applying the overload theory.

Overload training depends on implementing a concentrated program including warm-ups, strength, power, endurance, flexibility, and speed techniques. Today's college and professional teams support their coaching staffs with weight training and conditioning coaches. High school coaches looking for the best results should explore recent trends and research in speed training.

Players need to understand that speed is a great asset for any team. When coaches have the opportunity to select players with speed, they will. Teams with speed have unlimited possibilities on offense and defense. A fast, well-conditioned offensive team can keep the pressure on an opponent's defense by pushing the ball on every possession. On defense, speed permits a team to press, overplay, and create turnovers, which they can turn into easy baskets.

Quickness may separate two players with equal speed. Good quickness enables a player to create space or blow by a defender. It gives the player a chance to break down the opponent's overall defense. In addition, when a defender learns that he's at a quickness disadvantage versus his opponent, a demoralizing factor enters the equation. A quickness advantage allows the offensive player to change sides of the court to initiate the offense without being vulnerable to a five-second count or the possibility that he will have to pick up his dribble. Developing a playmaker with size (to see over defenders) and quickness (to elude defenders) is sound basketball strategy. For some, this drill will provide convincing proof that they should seek a speed-running program.

SPEED WITH THE BALL

FOCUS

Teaching players to create space with ballhandling.

PROCEDURE

Players begin at the left-side hash line. Follow these steps:

1. The coach is the passer. O1 starts on the left-side hash line, closely guarded by X1. O1 dribbles with speed and quickness toward the sideline, free-throw line extended. While continuing to dribble, O1 must create space between himself and X1 by quickly backing up or sliding to one side.

2. After O1 sheds the defensive pressure, he reverses the floor and establishes a new position on the right side of the court to begin the offense.

3. This drill concerns ballhandling, foot speed, and the ability to elude a defender and take the ball to a different position on the court. It's an excellent drill for evaluating ball handlers.

The diagram shows the drill on the half court, but it is also an excellent full-court drill.

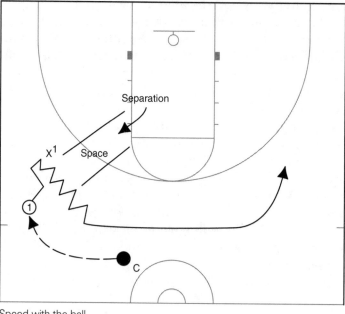

Speed with the ball.

Hands

Another valuable attribute, especially for inside players, is soft hands, or the ability to catch the ball in traffic. Being big and strong can make a player a prospect, but if he can't catch the ball, his basketball future is limited, and so is the coach's inside attack. Colleges desperately looking for big men sometimes gamble that they can develop big players who have weak hands. To varying degrees, improvement is possible. One way to accomplish this is by doing daily hand and finger ball drills and by squeezing a rubber ball for finger flexibility. Three major factors—motivation, concentration, and practice—are necessary for improvement.

Soft hands in this context refers to the player's ability to catch the ball without bobbling it, mishandling it, or turning it over. Having soft hands also means that not every pass must be perfect for him to receive it. Then there's the distinction between catching the ball while stationary, such as in direct post-ups, and catching the ball while on the move or in traffic. In a half-court offense, cross screens, pin-downs, slips, step-ins, and pick-and-rolls all necessitate movement. Executing these techniques can be difficult for players with poor catching skills.

Early in the developmental phase of a young player's career, the coach can determine whether the player needs to be stationary on post-entry passes. If a player must use two hands to catch the ball, the passer needs to be deliberate and exact. The passer should use the receiver's chest as the target for pass entry, and the receiver should have both arms up, shoulder high, elbows extended, and hands open to receive when calling for the ball. Teams trying to establish an inside attack know the importance of having post-up players with soft hands.

SOFT HANDS

FOCUS

Improve the ability to catch the ball and develop soft hands.

PROCEDURE

Players begin on the half court. Follow these steps:

1. The purpose of this drill is to improve catching, passing, and handling the basketball.
2. This drill requires a coach, three players, and two balls.
3. O1 lines up under the net with a ball, O2 lines up on the left elbow without a ball, and O3 lines up on the right elbow with a ball.
4. Players fire two-handed chest passes back and forth as quickly as possible for 15 seconds without dropping the ball. On all misses, they start over.
5. O1 is on the hot spot and must keep two balls going. As O1 passes to O2, O3 passes to O1. O1 returns O3's pass, catches a pass from O2, and immediately passes back to O2. This cycle continues until the drill is completed. This drill is excellent for improving hand-eye coordination.
6. After completing the chest pass, players practice the two-handed bounce pass, the overhead two-handed pass, and right- and left-handed passes.
7. As players become proficient, the coach should move to some one-on-one drills.

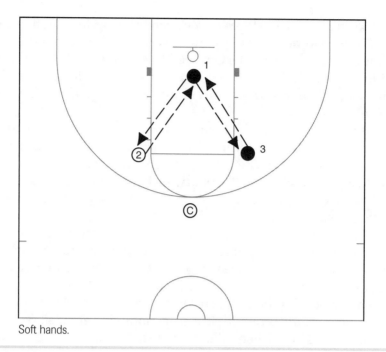

Soft hands.

Jumping

The ability to jump is one of the most important components of a basketball player's set of skills. We have seen in chapter 4, "Physical Conditioning," that a player can increase vertical jumping ability through improved techniques, desire, and a strenuous plyometric jump-training program. But the significance of being able to jump is another matter. Basketball is a game that is all about jumping.

Players with pronounced jumping skills can have a dynamic effect on many aspects of the game. Jumping shot blockers shock opponents by swatting away what look like guaranteed layups. Dominating offensive rebounders explode with thunderous dunks as they punctuate their power. Three-point shooters who fluidly stop, rise, and sink a 25-footer over a tightly guarding defender make the game special. Successful coaches understand that developing a player's jumping ability allows him to elevate quicker and go get rebounds, to intimidate shooters and change the direction of a shot even without blocking it, and to have a greater effect on the game.

The benefits of working on jumping include more that just attaining greater height; timing is also important. Players who can anticipate, accelerate, and elevate in a timely manner are a step ahead of the competition. Top coaches understand how a jump-training program helps maximize players' skills. Players with amazing jumping ability find basketball a natural fit. In the NBA, an outstanding example is Eddie Robinson, formerly of the Charlotte Hornets and Chicago Bulls. A 6-7 small forward, Robinson scored higher than any Hornet on fitness tests. He could tip out at 12 feet, 4 inches, had a standing vertical of 31 inches, a one-step vertical of 36 inches, and a running vertical of a phenomenal

43 inches. Eddie combined world-class speed with great jumping ability and was one of the most exciting players in the league when running the wing on the fast break looking for a lob.

JUMPING TO IMPROVE TIMING

FOCUS

Increase strength, explosion, and timing.

PROCEDURE

Players line up under the backboard and follow these steps:

1. Players end practice with this jumping drill.
2. The player extends both arms above the head, bends at the waist, jumps, and slaps both hands on the backboard.
3. The player lands on the balls of both feet and immediately explodes, repeating the jump while keeping the arms and hands extended. He does all this in a continuous motion. The player is not allowed to stop, gather, and then jump.

Establishing balance for the power jump.   Exploding off the floor.

4. The player continues this process for 30 seconds with a coach and a recorder. Only two-hand touches count.

5. Players develop stamina and improve their timing. For high school players unable to touch the backboard with both hands, a piece of tape on the wall measured in inches will serve the same purpose.

In summary, players can improve three extremely important attributes—speed, soft hands, and jumping ability. The amount of improvement depends on motivation, dedication, and the coach's innovation. Finding the right training programs for players lacking speed, jumping ability, or the ability to catch the ball is up to the coach and the player.

Accelerated Drills

A natural progression occurs in learning the game of basketball from middle school, high school, and college on into professional ball. Adjusting to the next level is not always easy because everything accelerates. From the shot clock to the midcourt time line and the backcourt to frontcourt rule, the game speeds up considerably. Players grow bigger, stronger, quicker, faster, and they become better shooters. Everyone is trying to make the team at the next level. These next two drills, two-touches and thru, speed up the physical and mental demands. The two-touches drill is a full-court, warm-up drill. Players should warm up and stretch before running. The thru drill, also a full-court drill, is a secondary break offense used in transition.

TWO TOUCHES: OPTION 1

FOCUS
Running hard and making those important layups.

PROCEDURE
Players form three lines on the end line and follow these steps:

1. The two-touches drill has two options. The first diagram, option 1, shows the beginning of the drill through the first layup. Option 2 shows the turnaround and the second-shot finish.

2. Players should be warmed up and loose for this full-court fast-break drill.

3. Have an even number of players in the three lines with the ballhandling guards in the middle. Centers, forwards, and big guards run the outside lanes.

4. Teach the drill with a one-dribble allowance for the first couple of days and then eliminate dribbling altogether. Two-handed chest passes are recommended.

5. O1, with the ball, begins at the free-throw line with O2 and O3 on the end line occupying the running lanes. As O1 throws the ball on the backboard, O2 and O3 sprint toward the opposite goal, staying wide in their lanes.

6. O1 throws a lead pass to O2, who catches the ball in full stride and throws a two-handed lead pass to O3, who catches and shoots the layup.

7. O1 must sprint to the basket and catch the ball before O3's layup hits the floor. O2 changes sides of the court by cutting across the top of the circle and taking the opposite lane. O3 shoots the layup and continues running to the opposite lane, looking for a short outlet pass from O1.

8. Option 2 picks up the drill from this point.

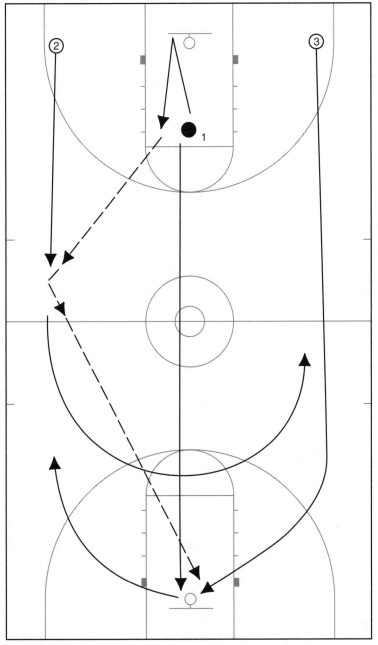

Two touches: option 1.

TWO TOUCHES: OPTION 2

FOCUS

Running the lanes correctly, making good passes, and hitting the layup.

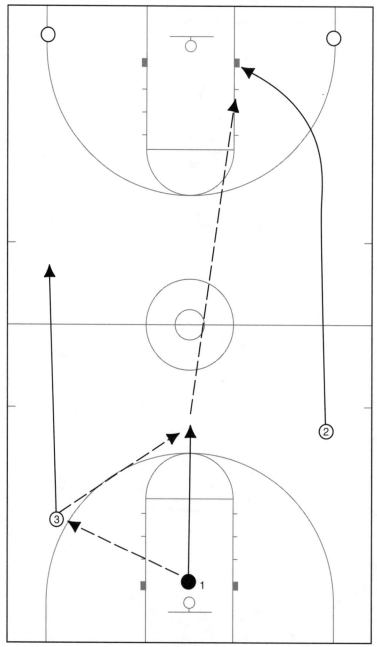

Two touches: option 2.

PROCEDURE

Continuation of two touches with the second layup. Follow these steps:

1. O1 rebounds the made layup and, without dribbling, passes to O3, who clears the area after making the first layup.

2. O2 has changed sides of the court and begins his sprint toward the opposite basket as O1 rebounds and passes to O3.

3. O3 catches the pass and, without dribbling, passes back to O1, who is cutting up the middle.

4. O1 catches on the dead run and, without breaking stride, makes a two-handed chest pass to O2, who is streaking to the basket for a layup. All passes in this drill are lead passes.

5. The next three players in line begin as O2 is shooting the layup. The guard in the middle gets the rebound out of the net and, without dribbling, throws a lead pass almost to midcourt to the wing runner, and the drill continues. All players must be alert and ready to run when their time comes.

6. After any missed layups, the group runs again.

7. This drill builds with repetition. Begin with one, then two, and eventually three times up and down the court for each group. Layups become important, especially when players are running two and three times.

Besides using demanding warm-up drills, professional teams use the entire 94 feet when they go on the offensive attack. Teams call the secondary break different names, such as early, turnout, thru, or quick, but the strategy is the same: Enter the frontcourt with a scoring plan. On steals, long rebounds, or bustouts, players automatically attack the basket. The difference is that on normal rebounds, when a big man rebounds and outlets to a guard, most teams have a specific strategy. As the defense retreats in transition, the offense has a planned attack, looking for mismatches, early post-ups, and catch-and-shoot scoring opportunities.

A major benefit of the secondary break is player and ball movement. The offense creates a faster pace and puts the onus on players to make good decisions. In situations in which teaching time is limited, such as the Chicago Predraft Camp, summer leagues, or the Portsmouth Invitational Tournament, the thru secondary pattern is perfect because it's not complicated and players can learn it quickly.

The thru set is an excellent offense for coaches to use in evaluating overall player skills. The guards must pass the ball ahead, the inside players must run, screens are designed to free players for shots, pick-and-roll options are built in, and good decision making is essential. The inside big players must run from block to block, so that coaches can evaluate how quickly they run in the open court and how fast they can change ends. The thru secondary break has two options.

THRU: OPTION 1

FOCUS

Proper alignment off the rebound.

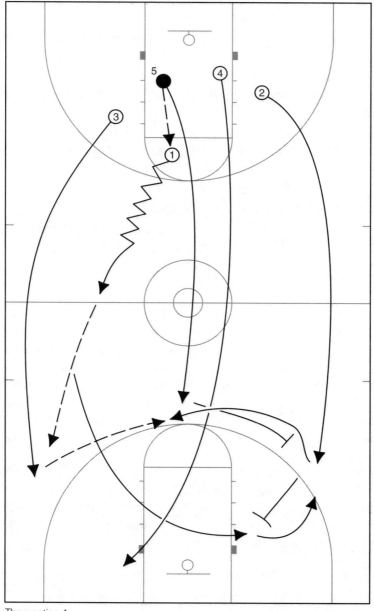

Thru: option 1.

PROCEDURE

One team begins on the half court. Follow these steps:

1. Start by defining the routes and roles for each player. O1 handles the ball, O2 and O3 run the wide lanes, and the bigs, O4 and O5, either run to the block or rebound and trail.

2. When O2 or O3 receives the pass, he can drive to the basket, pass to the low post, or pass to the top of the key for ball reversal.

3. Begin the play with O5 rebounding and passing to O1. O1 uses a sideline pass ahead to the open wing man, O3, and cuts through to the low block on the weak side.

4. The first big down the court, O4 in this case, goes to the block on the strong side for a post-up.

5. The second big, O5, becomes the trailer and goes to the top of the key as an outlet. If there is no low-post pass, he screens for O2 coming to the top of the key and then pins down on O1.

6. Option 2 picks up with the ball at the top of the key.

THRU: OPTION 2

FOCUS

Execution of proper space and floor balance.

PROCEDURE

Continue play from option 1 by following these steps:

1. Begin with O2 catching the ball at the top of the key.

2. O1 pops out off O5's pin-down and looks for an O5 post-up or calls O5 out for a sideline pick-and-roll.

3. O4 sets an up screen for O2, who cuts to the basket looking for the lob. If there is no pass, O2 continues out the weak side and runs off a staggered double screen by O3 and O4, looking for a catch-and-shoot pass from O1.

4. Thru is a continuity pattern run in transition. The pattern has constant movement with post-up opportunities on both sides, up and down screens, and a pick-and-roll and catch-and-shoot option at the end. The pattern requires making decisions on the run and offers an excellent situation for analyzing player skills.

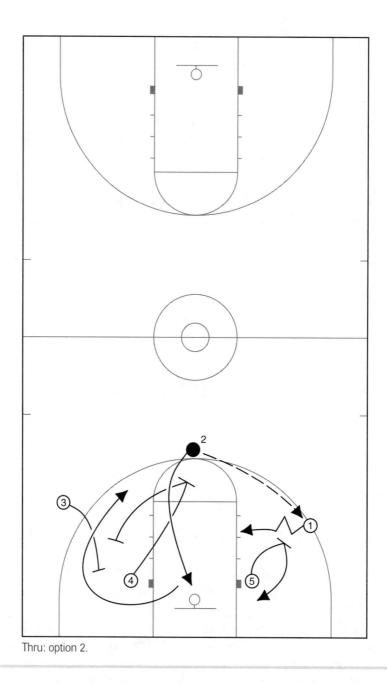

Thru: option 2.

As players move up the competitive ladder, they must adjust to spending a lot of energy in a lengthy shooting warm-up before their games. They must expect a seriousness of purpose in this warm-up. Coaches go on the floor, especially in pro ball, and work with players during these warm-up sessions. In the NBA, teams require players to be on the floor at a designated time, usually 90 minutes before game time, to participate in group shooting drills. Group shooting drills follow along the lines of the next drill.

PREGAME WARM-UP SHOOTING

FOCUS

Jump-shot shooting techniques.

PROCEDURE

Each player has a ball. Follow these steps:

1.   Divide the team evenly into two groups. One group begins on the left baseline, and the other begins at the hash line on the right side. The coach is the passer.

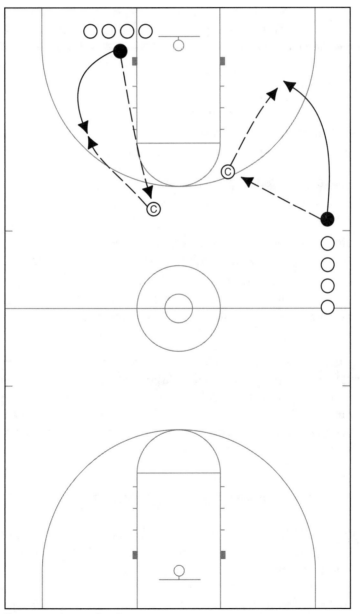

Pregame warm-up shooting.

2. Players follow their shots, get their own rebounds, and return to the end of their lines.

3. The baseline shooters work on the following shots:
    a. Curl: two- and three-point shot attempts
    b. Fade: two- and three-point shot attempts
    c. Up the middle: shot at the free-throw line
    d. Up the middle: shot inside the three-point line
    e. Up the middle: three-point shot

4. The perimeter shooters on the right side, with a right-handed dribble, work on the following shots inside the three-point arc (when they switch to the left side, they dribble with the left hand):
    a. Catch-and-shoot with no dribble
    b. Catch-and-shoot with one dribble
    c. Catch-and-shoot with one dribble, bank shot
    d. Catch-and-shoot with two dribbles
    e. Catch-and-shoot with one dribble crossover

The perimeter players then repeat the sequence for three-point shots.

5. Coaches have players shoot both inside and perimeter shots on one side and then switch sides of the court.

6. After both sides have finished, the players split up and focus on position-specific shots. One coach works with the inside players on post-up moves.

7. The coach moves to the free-throw line extended and works on perimeter shooting. The players, each with a ball, begin at midcourt and pass to the coach, using the drill sequence they used for the catch and shoot on the sideline.

The two-pass full-court layup drill, the transition offense, and the pregame shooting drills are all designed to help players adjust to the speed of the game, adjust to transition possibilities, and develop good shooting habits. Developing proper shooting mechanics with the right form, base, and follow-through is a matter of concentration and practice. Coaches at each level work constantly with players to improve their shooting skills.

Mental Approach

Basketball players with the right mental fundamentals come to the team with a positive attitude. They are eager to participate and willing to work unselfishly. They agree to support team rules and policies, accept the challenge to improve, and compete in a sportsmanlike manner. As for the game itself, no one is perfect, so players must commit to their best effort and welcome constructive criticism.

Coaches analyze players' assets and put them in situations where they can succeed. The fewer mistakes a player makes, the greater his playing opportunities become. Just as their skill levels differ, so does their comprehension of the game. When talent exceeds understanding, the coach must be assertive.

Decision Making

A player who consistently makes the right decisions has a high basketball IQ. What does making a good decision mean? For basketball, it means doing the right thing at the right time. Coaches who demand discipline, concentration, and focus usually have teams that make fewer mistakes. This concept is not complicated. To avoid making mistakes, players must thoroughly understand the game. They must know when to dribble, pass, or shoot, and they must play fundamentally sound defense when the opponent has the ball.

Coaches and players must exert a concerted effort to eliminate areas where decision making is a liability. Ill-advised acts such as the following can hurt the team: committing charging fouls, making careless passes, overdribbling or dribbling into traps, forcing shots, failing to box out, fouling jump shooters, permitting coast-to-coast layups, fouling in the backcourt, and gambling at the wrong time.

On the flip side of the coin, success-oriented players don't just beat you in one way; they beat you in many ways. They will do whatever it takes. Smart players get the rebound, block the key shot, dive for the loose ball, and make the big defensive stop. They make the right play at the right time.

The question then becomes whether you can teach players to make good decisions. Coaches can, for example, help passers by providing learning situations such as three-on-two, two-on-one, three-on-three with no dribbles, the UCLA balance and space drill, or through any drill that puts players in decision-making situations. Yes, players can improve their basketball IQ if they pay attention and absorb what they're taught. But if they don't have natural instincts, peripheral awareness, and the concept of unselfishness, chances are slim that they will make consistently good basketball decisions. For players trying to learn whether to set the screen or use the screen, the UCLA balance and space drill is an excellent aid.

UCLA for Balance and Space

When teaching players about balance and spacing, it helps to break down the game into smaller areas. To underscore the significance of having three on one side and two on the other, the UCLA set serves as a great example. When running the initial cut for the layup or the post-up, balance and spacing are crucial. Players need to be able to read the defense and respond with the correct offensive strategy. In the UCLA set, if the defensive center drops off to help defend the guard, the post man will be open. If the defensive center plays the post tight, the guard is a post-up option. Following the wing pass to the high post and the pin-down, if the play doesn't end with O1's jump shot, many teaching opportunities are available. The UCLA strong-side options provide an excellent drill for teaching balance, spacing, and timing.

UCLA MOVEMENT

FOCUS

Execute movement, screening, spacing, and timing.

PROCEDURE

Begin with three-on-three and follow these steps:

1. Divide the team and run at both ends.
2. Players rotate from offense to defense based on the outcome of each possession.
3. Allow no dribbling or offensive screening on the ball. Players work their way to the basket by executing proper balance and spacing with good screens and passes.
4. The offense must make five passes before taking a shot, unless they shoot a layup.
5. Begin play with O1 passing to O2 on the wing. O1 rubs off O3's stationary screen, looking to get a layup or quick post-up.
6. After O3 sets the screen, he takes two steps toward midcourt and receives O2's pass.
7. O2 sets a down screen for O1, who curls middle or wide looking for a pass from O3.
8. Players have made only three passes, and this is where the teaching kicks in.
9. When O1 receives O3's pass, O2 must either up screen for O3, or O3 must down screen for O2. This is the decision that assures continuity, movement, and learning.

UCLA movement.

Players who understand floor balance and spacing avoid dribbling into congested areas or passing into tight quarters where space and vision are limited. Del Harris, with whom I worked in Milwaukee at the Bucks, called it "dead baseline" if a ball handler tried to attack the basket while a teammate was on the low block on the same side. He gave it that name because the man on the low block had nowhere to go. This common mistake shouldn't happen, and it is easily corrected.

The three-point shot improves floor balance, because the three-point arc gives coaches a marker that players recognize. Players are instructed to clear to the three-point line when running cuts and setting screens. This spacing gives the offensive player room to maneuver when driving to the basket or dribbling to improve a passing angle.

Offensive flow improves when players understand the importance of floor balance and spacing, which are important keys in making effective entry passes to the low post. If a defender drops off the passer into the lap of the intended receiver, a smart player will dribble quickly to establish a better passing angle or pass to a teammate who has better spacing for an entry pass. Players with basketball savvy know not to force the ball into areas where a turnover could easily occur.

Coaches need to design sets that emphasize proper floor balance and spacing and constantly emphasize their importance. The players must then execute the plan and know when to pass and when not to pass. The concept of "sight and insight" is a determining factor for many coaches, and they work to reduce the passing responsibilities of players who can't grasp the concept.

LA Offense

The most enjoyable strategic and tactical aspects of basketball don't involve the separate offensive options, such as backdoors, splits, pop-outs, post-ups, give-and-goes, cross screens, pick-and-rolls, or UCLA variations. Putting those components into a continuity pattern is what makes an offense effective. This pattern should not be complicated or overemphasize one player or position. In the early evaluation process, the goal is to adopt an offensive style that is fair, quickly taught, and effectively evaluated.

The LA, or all-purpose offense, is one that I designed by combining offensive concepts, plays, and drills from clinics and books by John Wooden, Adolph Rupp, and Dean Smith, all winners of NCAA championships. The idea is to take a play from one coach, a drill from another, a strategy from yet another, and put them together into a continuity offense.

The LA set is a combination of some of the best plays in basketball. The offense requires guards to handle the ball, attack the basket, pass to designated shooters, and make good decisions. Forwards must set good screens, hit the perimeter jump shot, pass to moving targets, and maintain half-court balance with proper spacing.

The center will play both the low post, with his back to the basket, and the high post, facing the basket where he has passing and shooting opportunities.

The beauty of the LA set begins by identifying three passes. Each pass requires a spontaneous and different set of offensive maneuvers. The three passes are guard-to-forward, guard-to-guard, and guard-to-center.

Guard-to-Forward Pass

As the guard enters the ball into the frontcourt, the forward, at the strong-side free-throw line extended, works to get open. The forward should receive the ball and establish a right-foot pivot.

GUARD-TO-FORWARD PASS: OPTION 1

FOCUS

All-purpose offense, guard-to-forward pass.

PROCEDURE

Players begin on the half court. Follow these steps:

1. The guard to forward pass has four different options.

2. Players set up this offense with a two-guard front. The two wing players are at the free-throw line extended, and the center plays a high post.

3. When the guard enters into frontcourt, he can make three basic passes—to the

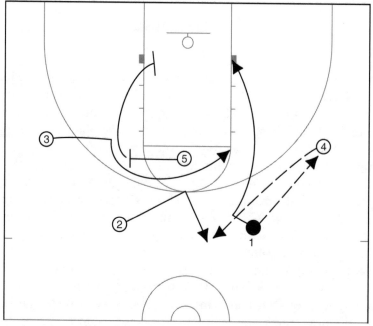

Guard-to-forward pass: option 1.

opposite guard, to the forward on his side, and to the high-post center. We start with the guard-to-forward pass.

4. O1 passes to O4, takes a hard jab step to the middle, and tries to get his head and shoulder around his man for an inside ball cut. If he's open, he gets a quick return pass. If he's not, he continues to the low block on the strong side.

5. As O1 cuts, O5 turns and screens for O3, who relocates to the strong-side elbow looking for a pass and a possible shot.

6. O2 V-cuts to the top of the key and gets a pass from O4.

7. O5 relocates to thc low post on the weak side. (Option 2 picks up here.)

GUARD-TO-FORWARD PASS: OPTION 2

1. O2 takes one or, at most, two dribbles, looking to reverse the ball.

2. As O2 receives the pass, O1 turns out off O5's baseline screen. O3 continues toward the basket and relocates to the low block opposite O5.

3. After O4 passes to O2, he pins down on O3's man and O3 pops out. This puts O4 at the basket for the rebound.

4. O2 passes to O1, who can shoot, pass to O5, or call O5 out for a sideline pick-and-roll.

5. After O2 passes to O1, he turns and screens for O3, who is coming off O4's down screen.

6. The guard-to-forward option 3 has various options.

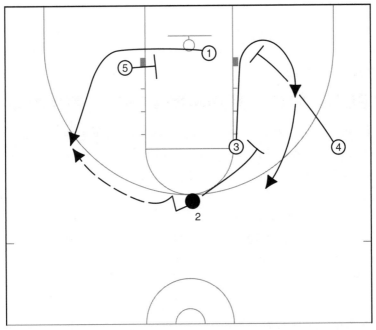

Guard-to-forward pass: option 2.

GUARD-TO-FORWARD PASS: OPTION 3

1. Play begins with O2 catching the ball at the top of the key.
2. O4 screens down on O3, and O1 turns out off O5.
3. O2 has the option of starting toward O1, reversing his dribble, and passing to O3.
4. If he reverses and dribbles toward O3, O5 steps into the middle, looking to post X5.
5. This effective counterplay can be called at a time-out.

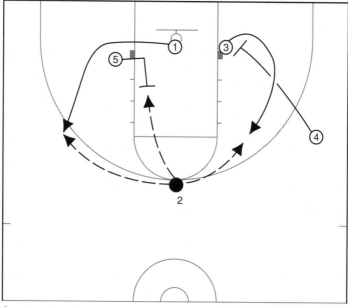

Guard-to-forward pass: option 3.

GUARD-TO-FORWARD PASS: OPTION 4

1. Another option has O2 with the ball at the top rotating the ball to O1.
2. O2 then reverses and sets a staggered double screen with O4 for O3.
3. O3 works off the screens, looking for a catch-and-shoot.
4. If the pass goes to O1, O5 is a post-up option. O1 can also run a pick-and-roll with O5 or look for O3 coming off the double stagger.
5. Either guard can start the play to either side.
6. In this scenario, the shooting options went to O1, O3, and O5. If O2 starts the play to O3's side, the scoring options go to O2, O4, and O5.

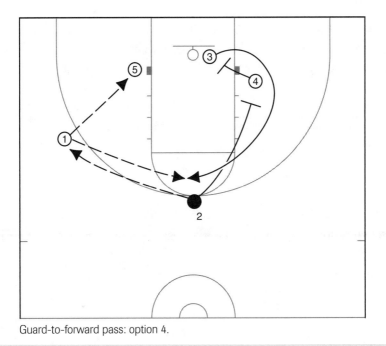

Guard-to-forward pass: option 4.

Guard-to-Guard Pass

As the guard enters the ball into the frontcourt, the opposite guard gets parallel, 15 feet away, with hands up to receive a pass.

GUARD-TO-GUARD PASS: OPTION 1

1. The guard-to-guard pass option has three different options.

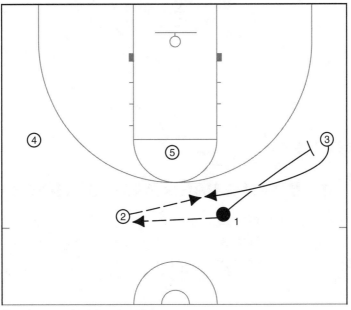

Guard-to-guard pass: option 1.

2. In the LA offensive set, either guard can start the play on either side.
3. O1 passes to O2 and sets an inside screen for O3.
4. O3 exchanges position with O1 and receives a direct pass from O2.

GUARD-TO-GUARD PASS: OPTION 2

1. O3 passes to O1.
2. Using a jab step, O3 tries to get an inside ball cut as he dives to the block on the strong side.
3. O2 dives to the block on the weak side when he sees O3 pass to O1.
4. O5 watches both O3 and O2 clear the post area and then pops out to receive the pass from O1.
5. O5, after receiving the pass, turns and faces the defender, always protecting the ball.

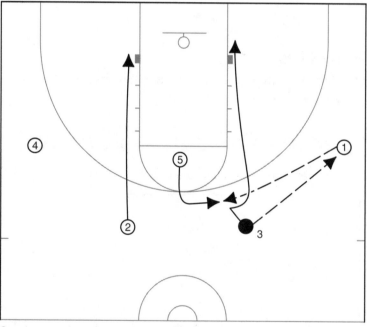

Guard-to-guard pass: option 2.

GUARD-TO-GUARD PASS: OPTION 3

1. O5 now becomes the passer.
2. As O1 passes to O5, O3 steps up and sets a back pick on O1's man.
3. An inside cut to the basket is preferred because X3 must loosen up and help should X1 get screened.

4. If O1 is open, that's O5's first pass option.

5. After setting the back screen, O3 takes two steps and opens to the ball, looking for a catch-and-shoot jump shot.

6. On the weak side, O4 pins down on O2, who comes off looking for a catch-and-shoot or a curl to the basket.

7. If O2 pops and catches, he also has a good opportunity for a two-man game with O4. O4 can post up or run a sideline pick-and-roll.

8. After O5 receives the ball, he has these passing options:

   a. Pass to O1 on a back screen

   b. Pass to O3 on a turn-in

   c. Pass to O2 on a turn-out or curl

9. O5 must keep his dribble available in case he has to use a dribble handoff to get out of trouble.

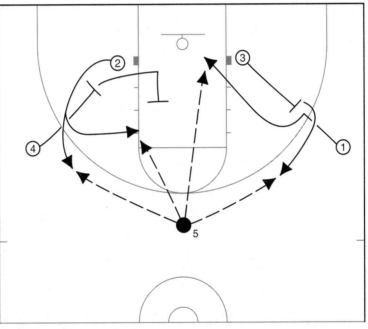

Guard-to-guard pass: option 3.

Guard-to-Center Pass

As the guard brings the ball up the court, the center establishes a high-post position with his hands up and legs shoulder-width apart, looking for a pass. Anytime there is pressure on the guards, the center must be ready to step out to meet the pass and be an outlet while continuing the pattern.

GUARD-TO-CENTER PASS: OPTION 1

1. The guard-to-center pass has three different options.

2. The guard-to-center pass can be initiated any time the offense is set.

3. When the defense applies pressure, the play can start from the midcourt area, especially when defensive forwards overplay their men.

4. This diagram shows the post pass, with the strong-side forward making a backdoor cut and the passer setting a screen for the opposite guard.

5. The backdoor cut, the first option, is an automatic timing play that is very effective against pressure defense.

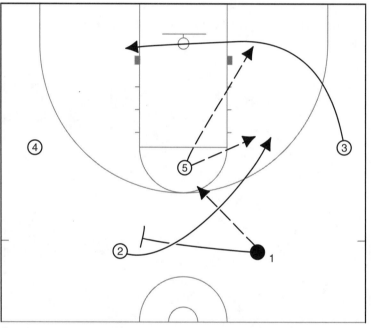

Guard-to-center pass: option 1.

GUARD-TO-CENTER PASS: OPTION 2

1. After looking for the backdoor cut, O5 looks to see whether O1's screen frees up O2.

2. If O2 is open, O5 passes to him for a jump shot or a drive.

3. O2 has the entire side of the court to work one-on-one against his man.

4. If O2 is not open, O3, the third option, uses the double-stack screen set by O4 and O1, looking for a catch-and-shoot jump shot.

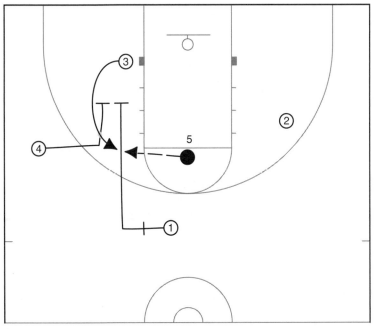

Guard-to-center pass: option 2.

GUARD-TO-CENTER PASS: OPTION 3

All offensive patterns should include releases or escapes. In the event the basic options bog down, the coach should present alternatives. If for some reason the forward backdoor cut, the guard-around, or the turn-out off the double stack all fail, here are suggested releases:

a. When O5 cannot pass to O3, he immediately uses a dribble handoff as O3 keeps coming to the ball.

b. O4 dives to the middle off O1, who has the inside lane.

c. Third, O5 may choose to pass the ball to O2, who has now relocated on the sideline, free-throw line extended, and run a pick-and-roll.

Remember, in all half-court offensive sets, the coach must designate one player to rotate back to protect the basket and another to contain the ball by slowing down the opponent's outlet pass and dribble penetration.

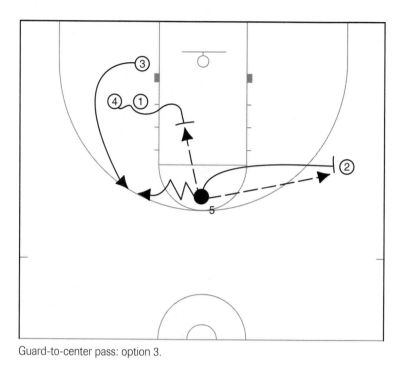

Guard-to-center pass: option 3.

An idiom often expressed at basketball clinics and workshops states: "Players don't go to the park without a ball to work on their defensive skills." Check it out: Players of all ages go to the park or gym to shoot. Young players grow up thinking that they need a ball to work on their game. But there's much more, and these past two chapters have provided drills for individual improvement that go beyond just catching and shooting. Defense requires not only a different mind-set, but also another person with whom to work on such things as contain, close out, and contest. Chapters 7 and 8 will explore these and many other concepts.

CHAPTER 7

Defensive Skills and Tactics

B asketball is a game in which divergent talents and skills collide. It's a game of finesse versus strength, a game in which athleticism, quickness, and strength can disrupt the flow and rhythm of a silky smooth finesse team blessed with pure shooters. Putting points on the board and defending are equally important to the outcome of games, but those tasks demand different skills. People often say that offensive players are born, not made. The same is not true of defenders. Most players naturally gravitate to scoring and shooting, whereas they must be taught team and individual defensive fundamentals.

Defensive Philosophy

Regardless of body characteristics, good defenders have several identifiable qualities. They are athletic and quick. They enjoy physical contact, anticipate well, play with reckless abandon, love to take the challenge, and are usually good team players. They will sacrifice their bodies by taking the charge, boxing out, and defending bigger, stronger opponents. They have a focused mind-set. Defensive-minded players respond well to predetermined goals, for both the team and the individual, and they love to hold teams under their per-game field-goal percentages and keep opponents' star players under their scoring averages.

Defenders are usually well built and are seldom heavy or overweight. They are well proportioned and strong. Good defenders anticipate well, are quick to the ball, and are always thinking one pass ahead. By combining quickness and anticipation, defenders have the ability to show an open area and then close it off before the dribbler can get to it. Another important characteristic of a good defender is aggressiveness. A good defender will attack the offensive player to make him change direction, and the best defenders are able to stay in front of their opponents and deny dribble penetration. Defensive-minded players play hard and get through screens, front opponents, and deny passes one man away.

Defense, when played right, can be consistent every night. Coaches love to say that defense travels, meaning that when the offense fails on the road, the defense will be there to keep the team in the game. Good defensive coaches understand the importance of selling defense. Lip service will not work. Defense is the emotional part of basketball. Coaches teach players to execute basic individual defensive principles that complement team strategy. Executing the following individual principles is integral to a team defensive philosophy:

Individual Defensive Fundamentals on the Half Court

In precise terms, the object of a good defensive team is to reduce opponents' field-goal percentage, free-throw attempts, and second-shot opportunities. The following 16 fundamentals, consistently implemented, provide the foundation for a sound defensive philosophy. The fundamentals are listed alphabetically, not in order of importance.

1. **Activate the passer:** Anytime the offensive player picks up his dribble, the defender should apply pressure, looking for a deflection or a steal. By picking up his dribble, the ball handler has essentially paralyzed himself. When his defender applies pressure, all defenders who are one pass away should immediately overplay and be in a denial position. The defender on the ball should call out, "Deny" or "Up," communicating to teammates that pressure defense has been activated.

2. **Ball-you-man theory:** This defensive concept applies to the position of the defensive man guarding on the weak side. The concept involves three players: the man with the ball, you in the middle, and the man you are guarding. The

idea is for the weak-side defender (you) to position himself at the point of the triangle where he sees the man with the ball and the man he's defending. The size or angle of the triangle will vary depending on the position of the man with the ball. The weak-side defender should always be in a position of support. This theory reinforces the importance of seeing the ball and teaches players proper weak-side position when providing weak-side help and checking cutters going from weak side to strong side. Ball-you-man is an excellent tool for teaching defensive awareness, body positioning, and player alertness.

3. **Box out:** The defender can capture rebounds in three distinct ways: box out with a reverse pivot, box out with a step-through pivot, or disregard his man and attempt to outjump opponents for the ball. Two of these methods, the reverse pivot and the step-through pivot, depend on teaching and repetition. The third, outjumping opponents, depends on instinct and the player's ability to elevate. The safest and surest method for most rebounders is the step-through because the defender maintains eye contact longer. But today's players are so athletic that they prefer to just go for the ball. Coaches should expose players to all three methods, determine which one suits them best, and help them develop their technique.

4. **Close out under control:** When an offensive player has the ball within a scoring area and the defender rotates out, it's called "close-out." The two key aspects to closing out properly are staying down so that the ball handler can't penetrate to the basket and being under control in order to direct the offensive player in a predetermined direction, whether to the middle or the baseline.

5. **Communicate:** Nothing is more important than communicating on defense. Teammates must let each other know, for example, which way to drive an opponent, middle or baseline. Or, on pick-and-rolls, they must yell, "Over," "Under," "Switch," and so on, so that the player getting screened knows how to play the situation. Without an oral call, the person getting screened is vulnerable. Designing a communication drill in which players must yell a command is much more important than you might think.

6. **Contain the dribbler:** The object is to stay in front of the ball to keep the offensive player from penetrating. The proper stance—bent knees, being balanced, and being prepared to slide or run—is critical. Players must learn to assess their own speed and quickness as compared to that of their opponent. If the defender perceives his man to be quicker, he'll have to back up a step because the goal is not to be beaten off the dribble. Fundamentally sound defenders do not gamble and reach, thereby putting their teammates at a disadvantage.

7. **Contest each shot:** According to one NBA statistical analyst, there is a 12 percent difference between a guarded shot and an open shot. Therefore, defenders should contest every shot. The technique is to get the arms up and extended to obstruct the shooter's vision. The defender should use the same-side hand for the blocking procedure. If the shooter is right-handed, the defender's left hand should be to the ball side. If the shooter is left-handed, the right hand should be to the ball side. When low-post defenders find themselves directly behind an offensive

opponent, with knees locked and at a definite disadvantage, the important goal is to avoid fouling. Instead, the defender extends both arms as high as possible and maintains vertical position. This situation often occurs when the defender is rotating to help or when an offensive player gets a put-back.

8. **Do not foul jump shooters:** Good defenders are aggressive in containing the dribbler, closing out, and contesting shots. But sometimes they are too aggressive, resulting in fouls on the jump shooter. That is not acceptable, especially on three-point attempts. When practicing close-out techniques, players must stay down with the hands up. If they jump off the floor, they are far more likely to foul the shooter. As the defender runs out to cover an open shooter and closes the distance to the offensive man, he takes smaller steps, drops his body lower, and becomes more under control. This action enables him to have complete body balance for contesting the shot or preventing dribble penetration.

9. **Fake at the dribbler:** This maneuver occurs in full-court and half-court situations when two offensive players with the ball attack one defender at the basket. When the defender is caught in a two-on-one situation, he must lower his body, fake a jab step at the ball handler, and slide toward the opponent without the ball, looking to deflect or steal the pass. If no pass is made, the defender then challenges the attacking offensive player.

10. **Follow your man:** Teams run various baseline action plays with pin-downs, screens, pop-outs, and turnouts. The defender's responsibility is to follow the offensive man as closely as possible (*shadow*) by trailing on his outside hip and running step for step with him. The defender does not attempt to shoot the gap or avoid the screen by going up the middle.

11. **Overplay and pressure wing passes:** The defender should force receivers out on the floor to start their offense. After the opponent receives the pass, the defender uses his body angle to dictate the offensive man's direction. The game plan determines middle or baseline direction. When the offensive man cannot get the entry pass and decides to reverse on the baseline, the defender stays focused on his man, does not open up, and looks for the cutter's reaction to the ball with the intent to deflect or steal the pass.

12. **Promote hustle plays:** Hustle plays have a way of inspiring players and exciting the fans. Coaches need to encourage plays such as taking charges, going to the floor for the ball, and hitting the offensive boards. Each of these reflects alertness, desire, and all-out hustle—and hustle is contagious. Phil Scott, when a freshman at UNC Charlotte, once blocked three consecutive shots during a single possession and received a standing ovation. That play inspired everyone in the arena—especially everyone pulling for UNC Charlotte!

13. **Protect the basket:** Giving up an easy basket is against team objectives. This concept takes root by establishing that each player is responsible for protecting the basket. Players get caught on the weak side and must give support to the low post. If defenders are beaten, teammates must rotate to prevent a layup. Regardless of the situation, players must always give support and protect the basket.

14. **Provide weak-side help defense:** Good defensive teams understand the concept of giving support and help, from both the weak side and the strong side. Playing good defense is about sacrifice and willingness to help a teammate in trouble. Whether it's double teaming, protecting the basket, picking up an open cutter, drawing a change, rotating to an open shooter, or giving a foul when necessary, players must be willing to give support. A defense that forces an offense to make the extra pass or throw to a poor shooter is an effective defense.

15. **See the ball:** Unless instructed to deny and overplay an opponent, defenders should always be able to see the ball. Not keeping the ball in view is one of the most important but most frequently violated defensive principles. Communicating this principle during the game is a full-time assignment for an assistant coach. Seeing the ball requires players to turn their bodies constantly to get into proper defensive position. A common bad habit occurs when a player retreats on defense to midcourt and beyond before trying to see the ball. In practice, constant encouragement, repetition, and sometimes penalties (like running an eighth) are needed to get the point across.

16. **Step toward the receiver:** Teams that have excellent shooters at the 2 and 3 positions like to run them off screens for catch-and-shoot jump shots. When teams are running curls and pin-downs, the defender on the passer should step toward the receiver each time, hoping to disrupt the timing of the play. By stepping with the pass, the defender may distract the receiver for just an instant, giving his defender an opportunity to catch up. He also positions himself as a help-side defender should the offensive man decide to drive the ball middle.

Individual Skills and Team Objectives

Incorporating these 16 individual fundamentals into a team concept brings the coach's half-court defensive philosophy into full play and gets to the heart of team defense. Here is where the coach must have a master plan, goals to accomplish the plan, and the ability to execute the plan to achieve the goals.

Specifically, coaches must design a defensive plan that covers ways to influence the ball handler, pick-and-roll coverage, rotations out of low-post double teams, where weak-side defense help comes from, and a multitude of defensive strategies that teams employ. Successful coaches reduce these myriad defensive techniques to the smallest common denominator to promote better understanding and eliminate confusion for players and coaches. A descriptive concept for the defense presented here might be "eliminating ball penetration." In this proactive, full-throttle defense, coaches continually applaud and encourage deflections, steals, rebounds, taking charges, proper footwork, body angles, and any play that shows hustle.

A defense that eliminates ball penetration breaks down into five key team defensive objectives. Coaches must identify these objectives and apply them from the beginning of practice or training camp. Here then are the five key half-court team objectives, the foundation for an effective overall defense:

1. Keep the ball out of the middle.
2. Allow no middle-dribble penetration.
3. Permit no ball-side cuts.
4. Allow no second shots.
5. Contest all layups.

These objectives all lead back to the underlying goals of playing good defense: Keep the ball out of the middle, eliminate ball penetration, and force opponents to shoot from the outside. Coaches and players soon discover that these five team defensive objectives incorporate three important features:

1. They are easily understood by players and coaches.
2. They offer consistent objectives with teachable techniques.
3. They apply equally to man-to-man and zone coverages.

Objective 1: Keep the Ball Out of the Middle

The two major strategies that this defensive system combats are getting the ball into the middle of the court and reversing the ball quickly to the weak side. The key is preventing post-entry passes, whether it's to the high-, mid-, or low-post area. Is this difficult? You bet. Impossible? No, but it takes a lot of work and concentration. The following drills focus on the three post areas and offer the strategies for keeping the ball out of the middle. We will break the concept down by looking at each defender on the floor.

Defender Guarding the Post Man

The position this defender takes is determined by where the ball is. He needs to be ball side in a three-quarter defensive position. The arm closer to the ball is up in a denial position, and the leg to the ball side is slightly in front of the offensive player, almost in a hugging position. The opposite arm is bent at the elbow with the palm open, maintaining contact with the opponent's hip. This contact permits the defender to know when the offensive player attempts to reverse to the basket. No excuse is acceptable for failing to execute the proper stance. Proper footwork is critical, and working individually with players so that they can find a comfort zone is helpful.

DEFENDING THE HIGH POST

FOCUS

Keeping the ball out of the middle while defending the high post.

PROCEDURE

Players begin five-on-five on the half court. Follow these steps:

1. A coach or one of the guards begins the drill by passing to either O3 or O4, who set up at the free-throw line extended on the wings.

2. X3 has his hands up to discourage a post pass and his body down, preparing to force baseline.

3. X5 is in a three-quarter denial defensive position, with the left arm on the ball side and his legs straddling O5's leg to the strong side. X5's primary function is to keep the ball out of the middle. X4 has basket-protection responsibility.

4. X1, one pass away, drops to the lap of O5 to discourage a pass.

5. X2, two passes away, drops two steps toward the free-throw line and two steps to the ball to support weak side. X2 takes X4's position if X4 goes to trap.

6. X4, three passes away, is in a weak-side support position with basket-protection responsibilities.

7. If O3, with the ball, drives baseline, X4 rotates to the strong-side block and stops dribble penetration. X2 drops (sinks and fills) with the responsibility of keeping O4 off the boards. X1 drops to the middle as O3 drives baseline, looking to intercept a pass to the middle, or rotates out and covers the first pass out if a double team occurs.

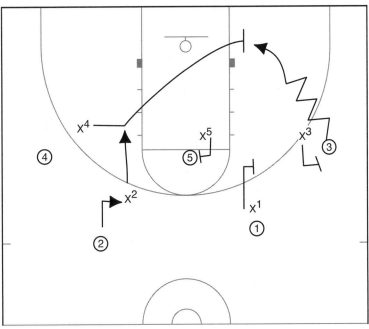

Defending the high post.

DEFENDING THE MID-POST

FOCUS

Keeping the ball out of the middle while defending the mid-post.

PROCEDURE

Players begin five-on-five on the half court. Follow these steps:

1. O3 has the ball at the free-throw line extended, by dribble or pass. X3 has his arms extended to deflect a pass and straddles O3's outside leg, forcing the baseline drive.

2. O1 (or any offensive player) occupies the strong-side corner. X1, one pass away, drops a full step to the middle, in support position for X3, and looks for the charge or a pass to the corner.

3. X5 is in a three-quarter deny defensive position with the left arm ball side and his legs straddling O5's leg to the strong side. X4 protects the basket.

4. X2, one pass away at the top of the key, drops to discourage a post pass and supports X3 in case of a middle drive. As the ball drops toward the basket, so does X2, sinking, filling, and looking for rebounds. O2, normally a spot-up shooter, is X2's primary concern. If O2 cuts to the basket or moves away, X2 maintains distance and vision to contain a pass or contest his shot.

5. X4, two passes away, is in total support mode, has basket-protection responsibility, and must guard against all lobs to O5.

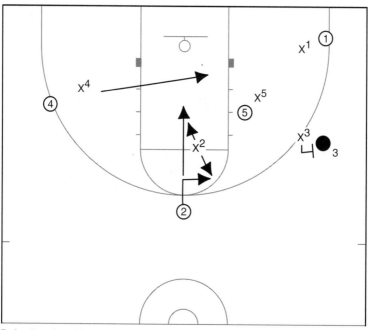

Defending the mid-post.

DEFENDING THE LOW POST

FOCUS

Keeping the ball out of the middle with the low-post defender.

PROCEDURE

Players begin five-on-five on the half court. Follow these steps:

1. Low post-ups come off direct passes to the post and after turnouts, which occur when O2 and O3 curl off O4 and O5, who have established low-post position.

2. O1 makes an entry pass to either O2 or O3, then cuts diagonally to the far corner or makes a shallow cut to the weak side.

3. Defensively, X2 keeps the ball on the side by forcing his man baseline with an exaggerated overplay, straddling the outside leg of O2. X2 must maintain ball pressure, with hands up, to eliminate an easy lob to O5. X5 plays three-quarter topside.

4. X3, at the top of the key, steps toward the ball and provides weak-side support. If the ball rotates to O3, X3 closes out under control and applies pressure to eliminate a lock-and-lob to O5.

5. X1 is now the primary weak-side supporter and has the responsibility of protecting the basket, including guarding against the lob to O5.

6. X4, two passes away, must sink and fill as X1 vacates and must be alert for O4's flash to the post area or flare screen for O3.

7. All five defensive players have rebound responsibilities.

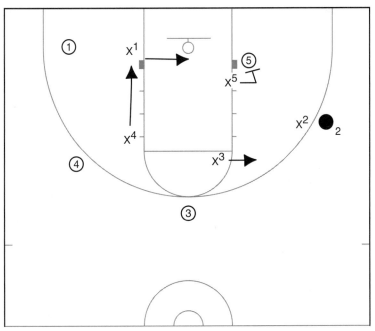

Defending the low post.

Defender on the Ball Handler

The defender on the ball handler plays a major role in keeping the ball out of the middle. He is the first line of defense. When the ball handler picks up his dribble, the defender plays a cat-and-mouse game—first closing and then retreating with arms up and hands extended, trying to deflect, discourage, or steal the pass. Will the guard get an open look at the basket when the defender retreats? Possibly. But by knowing the tendencies of the opponents' personnel, you can better gauge how far the defender should be from the offensive player. The policy here is to prevent inside passes; it's better to give up a three-point attempt.

DEFENDING THE POST

FOCUS

Keeping the ball out of the middle when the ball handler picks up his dribble.

PROCEDURE

Divide the squad evenly and work on both ends of the court. Follow these steps:

1. The defensive philosophy is to defend the inside first. Make every effort to prevent the ball from getting to the post.

2. If the defense must give up a shot, play the percentages and make opponents hit the outside shot.

3. On the right side, O5 is at mid-post when the ball handler picks up the dribble. X2 must defend with the in-and-out technique. Alternate players at various positions.

4. X2 is tight defensively until the ball handler picks up the ball. X2 then retreats immediately, with hands and arms up, dropping directly to the lap of the center.

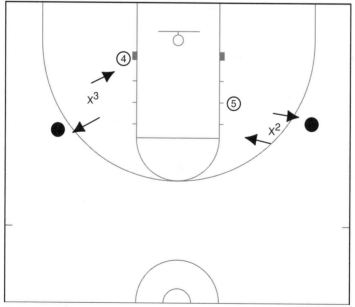

Defending the post.

5. On the left side, O4 is on the low post when the ball handler picks up the dribble. X3 must defend with the in-and-out technique.

6. X3 is tight defensively until the ball handler picks up the ball. X3 then retreats immediately, with hands and arms up. X3 drops a couple of steps toward the low post but makes sure that he can get back and contest the offensive threat.

Weak-Side Defenders

Players on the weak side provide support and must always be aware of lobs to the low post and mid-post. They are also responsible for weak-side rebounding and, in most situations, have basket-protection responsibilities on baseline drives. The defender positioned on the weak side below the free-throw line, in the low corner and farthest from the basket, drops to the paint, looking to help with steals, deflections, charges, or rebounds. To communicate his support to the post defenders, he is drilled to call out, "I've got the basket," or simply, "Basket."

DEFENDING THE LOW POST

FOCUS

Keeping the ball out of the middle, weak-side defender, low post.

PROCEDURE

Players begin five-on-five on the half court. Follow these steps:

1. The major concerns are the lock-and-lob from the side or the top of the key and the direct pass from the wing. X5 plays three-quarter topside aggressive.

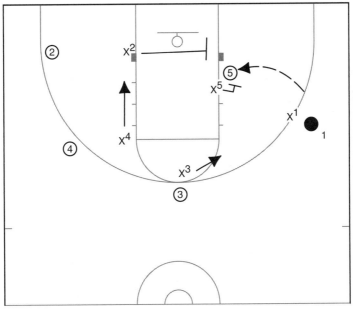

Defending the low post.

2. X1 forces his man baseline or drops down to disrupt O5's dribble. When he goes to help, he still has responsibility for O1. X5 must be in a three-quarter topside or front position.

3. X3, at the top of key and one pass away, provides help against the middle drive and drops to discourage a weak-side flash post. He also has rebounding responsibilities at the free-throw line.

4. X2, three passes away, has basket-protection responsibilities. His area extends across the free-throw lane to the opposite block to stop spin drives and lob passes.

5. X4, two passes away, drops to the ball and into the weak-side paint, ready to relocate and replace X2 if he vacates. He also has weak-side rebounding responsibilities.

Defender Ball Side, One Pass Away

The defender one pass away will constantly change as the ball moves from player to player. Players should understand that once the ball enters one side of the floor, they should make a supreme effort to keep it on that side. Defenders must constantly work to push the ball to a wing position and then establish an angle that will force the ball handler baseline.

DEFENDING THE POST, BALL SIDE

FOCUS

Keeping the ball out of the middle on the ball side, one pass away.

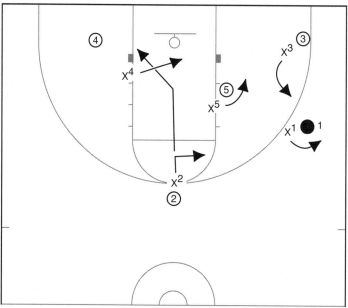

Defending the post on the ball side.

PROCEDURE

Players begin five-on-five on the half court. Follow these steps:

1. With the ball on the wing, two players are one pass away—one at the top of the key and one in the strong-side corner.

2. The principle, to stop dribble penetration and keep the ball out of the middle, equally affects the wings, corner, and the player at the top of the key.

3. To discourage penetrating passes and give support on middle or baseline drives, X2 and X3 should move two steps from their opponents and slide one step to the post player, if there is a post player. Depending on their quickness, X2 and X3 could move closer or farther away from their opponents. X4 must keep O4 in his line of vision and be ready for a lob or baseline drive by O5. X2 keys off X4 and should be ready to rotate and screen out O4 if X4 goes to help X5.

4. The goals here are to prevent middle drives, keep the ball out of the post, prevent a weak-side flash post, and force the dribbler baseline, where weak-side help is waiting.

Defending the Ball in the Middle of the Court

The issue is team support when the ball is in the middle of the court, at the top of the key, in a 1-4 spread offense with no post player. In this open offensive set, the defense is at risk because of the one-on-one dribble action. The team goal is to eliminate drives to the basket and stop dribble penetration. A drive to the hoop leaves the defense vulnerable to the draw-and-kick perimeter jump shot. Here's where run-and-jump defensive principles can maintain pressure on the shooter. Let's look at the defensive alignment and coverages when the ball is entered into the frontcourt from the top of the key.

DEFENDING 1-4 SPREAD OFFENSE

FOCUS

Keeping the ball out of the middle against a 1-4 spread or open set.

PROCEDURE

Players begin five-on-five on the half court. Follow these steps:

1. X1 must contain O1 and not permit a dribble drive. After O1 passes to a wing player, X1 drops toward the basket and looks to support. If O1 passes and screens away, then X1 drops and follows or switches on a predetermined call.

2. If O1 passes the ball to O3, X2 immediately drops a step and slides to the middle for support. Should O1 and O2 exchange positions, X2 reads the situation and adjusts. If no switch occurs, X2 goes with his opponent while being conscious of middle support.

3. X3 straddles O3's outside leg and forces baseline with help from X5.

4. X5 supports X3 by dropping two steps to the middle, preventing a dribble drive. Should O5 vacate the corner, X5 calls, "Clear" and trails O5, always watching O3 and ready to double-team if O3 attacks the basket.

5. X4, two passes away, has basket-protection responsibilities and watches O3, anticipating a drive. X4 rotates across the lane looking for a charge, deflection, or steal.

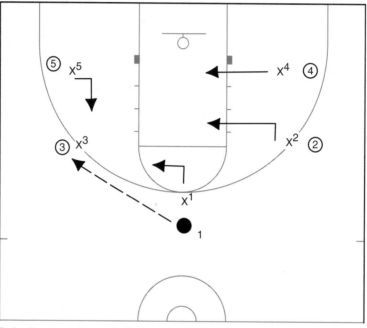

Defending the 1-4 spread offense.

Objective 2: No Middle-Dribble Penetration

Most defensive objectives discussed thus far can be readily accepted, but the issue of keeping the dribbler out of the middle is not often practiced, much less subscribed to. This philosophy is contrary to the commonly held notion that the dribbler should be forced to the middle rather than to the baseline. The no-middle-dribble-penetration defense is a system designed to direct the offense rather than allow the offense to dictate the flow of the game. This aggressive defense acts on predetermined principles rather than reacting to a multitude of offensive sets. To teach this concept, begin with the most basic drills and build on them daily.

IDENTIFYING FLOOR AREAS

FOCUS

Defining no-middle-drive areas.

PROCEDURE

The diagram defines areas and player responsibilities.

1. The court is divided into six basic areas, with players' responsibilities defined by the position on the floor.

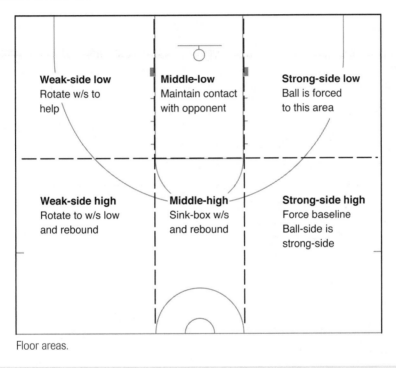

Floor areas.

No Middle Drives

To eliminate middle drives, guards should funnel or, as coaches like to say, influence the ball handler to the side court as the ball enters the frontcourt. Once the ball handler declares a side, the defender must keep him on that side. The defender must understand angles, the relative speed and quickness of his opponent, and positioning.

When drilling this concept, three important teaching techniques come into play. First, players must learn to cut the angle so that the dribbler cannot get to the middle. Second, the defenders must understand the proper close-out technique when a ball reversal or long offensive rebound necessitates a run-out to cover an open opponent. Third, players must become effective in rotating to help, that is, helping from the weak side on baseline drives.

PROPER ANGLE TECHNIQUE

FOCUS

Techniques on how to cut the angle and prevent middle penetration.

PROCEDURE

Players begin on the half court. Follow these steps:

1. A coach is the passer. Players rotate from offense to defense. After they play defense, they step off the court to the rear of the line.

2. O, the offensive player, makes a V-cut to get open and faces X, the defender, with a live dribble.

3. X permits the catch and cuts the angle to prevent the middle drive. X straddles O's body with his outside leg closer to midcourt. X's body position has his back at an angle slightly toward midcourt and at a safe distance, disallowing a blow-by.

4. O attempts to drive middle as X contains and overplays. X forces O baseline with X trying to catch up and cut off the baseline drive. The idea is to show baseline and then beat the dribbler to it and cut him off.

5. O attacks the basket or pulls up for a jump shot, as X defends through the possession.

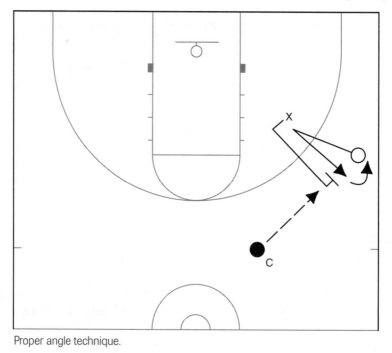

Proper angle technique.

No Middle Drives: Close Out

When an open opponent has the ball, the defender must close out (run out), typically over a distance of 12 to 30 feet, to contest the shot. The key here is control. The defender should sprint for about three-quarters of the distance and then drop, bend down, and take short, choppy steps, making sure that he's well balanced with his arms at shoulder height as he approaches the ball handler. The defender must avoid taking the ball fake and jumping off the floor, which permits the ball handler to blow by and get to the basket. Thus, the sequence is close out under control, contain the offensive player, and contest the shot.

Because our goal is to prevent the middle drive, we must add other elements. The defender must execute the close-out technique and get the angle that forces the ball handler baseline. The concern is not to block the shot but to be under complete control and give the offensive player only one option—to drive the ball baseline where help is waiting. In this drill, the defender cannot foul, jump to block a shot, or permit the offensive player to blow by for a dribble drive. If the defender does any of these three, he has failed. Besides the close-out and the force baseline, a third and forth option are factored in. Here we begin working on the team concept by building in a weak-side baseline rotation. A third person may be added to the drill to cover the basket, which has been vacated by the rotation. This player is in a sink-and-fill support position, looking to protect the basket and rebound weak side. In this no-middle defensive design, all parts are interchangeable. Therefore, everyone learns the procedures and drills from all spots. In general, this is a solid drill for reinforcing the four "Cs" of individual defense. These four factors come into play each time the defender guards the man with the ball. When a defender moves out on the floor to challenge an opponent with the ball, this is the proper sequencing:

1. Close out under control.
2. Contain by staying in front of dribbler.
3. Contest by getting the hand on the ball side up.
4. Clear the rebound aggressively.

CLOSE OUT PROPERLY

FOCUS

Closing out so that no middle penetration occurs.

PROCEDURE

Players begin on the half court. Follow these steps:

1. Split the team into two even groups. Players rotate offense to defense, defense to offense.
2. The objective of the drill is to teach the defender how to get the correct angle and force a baseline drive.
3. Begin with the understanding that the offensive player has the advantage because the defensive player is going to close out to the high side.
4. Relative distance, speed, and size put the responsibility of getting to the offensive player in time to contest a shot squarely on the defender.

5. To start the drill, a coach can pass the ball to O. Alternatively, X, starting under the net, can speed roll the ball to O.

6. X should get to O in time to contest (not block) a jump shot, be down and under control to prevent a middle drive, and in proper position to force a baseline drive. Coaches must constantly emphasize good footwork.

7. X begins in an all-out sprint and then slows down for control, balance, and proper close-out angle. X is not giving up the baseline but rather is driving O with pressure, looking to block any jump-shot attempt. As players learn to close out properly, adding a come-from-behind, shot-blocking feature enhances the drill.

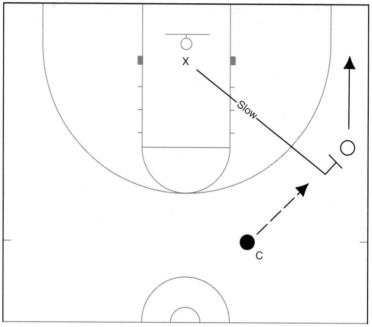

Close out properly.

Close out under control.

CLOSE, CONTAIN, AND CONTEST

FOCUS

No-middle emphasis for close-out, contest, and contain techniques.

PROCEDURE

Players begin three-on-three. Follow these steps:

1. The emphasis in this drill is on technique, spacing, communication, weak-side rotations, basket-protection responsibility, and weak-side rebounding.

2. In this multiplayer drill, defenders rotate and play all three positions. After they've completed the cycle, another group of three steps in.

3. A coach begins the drill by passing to O2. X2 yells loudly, "I've got ball!" as he rotates to close out and force O2 baseline.

4. X4, defending low on the weak side, must read, anticipate, and yell (so that all can hear), "I've got baseline!" He then sprints across the free-throw lane, clearing it, and establishes position with both feet on the opposite block. X4's call tells X2 that he has support. X4 looks to double-team the driver, block a shot attempt, or get the charge.

5. X3, defending at the top of the key, sees the drive and then yells, "Basket!" as he sinks and fills, telling everyone that the basket is protected. If O2 shoots a quick baseline shot, X3 must zone up and go for the weak-side rebound.

6. The drill continues until the offense scores, the defense steals the ball or captures the rebound, or the ball goes out of bounds. On defensive fouls, the offense retains the ball and repeats the drill. On offensive fouls, teams exchange positions.

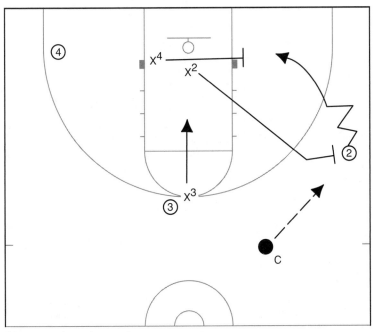

Close, contain, and contest.

Objective 3: No Ball-Side Cuts

A ball-side cut is any cut by an offensive player that puts him between the defender and a teammate who has the ball. A good ball-side cut results in a layup for the offense or establishes a good low-post position for a player coming from weak side to strong side. Properly defended ball-side cuts prevent straight-line layups and weak-side post flashes to the elbow and low block. The concept of eliminating ball-side cuts, the third objective of a five-part defensive philosophy, ties in with the goal of keeping the ball out of the middle. Not defending ball-side cuts, a seemingly simple offensive maneuver, will cost you easy baskets. The defensive technique is first taught in two- and three-man drills and demands concentration, alertness, anticipation, quickness, and strength. The following diagrams illustrate the ball-side cut areas.

DENY BALL-SIDE CUT

FOCUS

Preventing problems created when permitting ball-side cuts.

PROCEDURE

Players begin on the half court. Split the squad and follow these steps:

1. O1 passes to O2 and makes a ball-side cut. If O1 gets to the inside of X1 (meaning closer to O2 and the ball), then O1 has beaten X1, the defender.

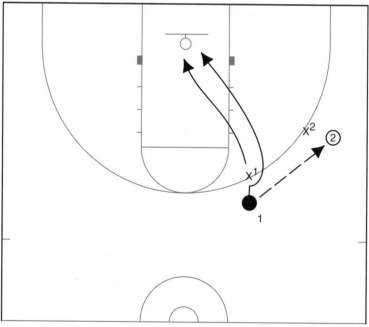

Deny ball-side cut.

2. If X1 permits O1 to get ball side, he puts himself in jeopardy for two major mistakes. First, he is vulnerable to being scored on because O1 can get his head and shoulders in front of X1, where a good pass by O2 produces a layup. Second, even if O1 does not score but catches the pass, X1's only alternative is to foul and prevent the easy basket. Even worse, O1 can make the basket and draw a foul.

3. The previous diagram clearly shows O1 getting ball side and X1 defending from a disadvantaged position.

4. In the next diagram, we learn the defensive techniques that help eliminate this problem.

Guard, No Ball-Side Cut

This drill shows the offensive guard's pass and cut to the basket with an explanation of the defender's position. The following diagram provides a visual of the defensive guard's position as O1 makes a basket cut on the strong side of the court.

GUARD, DENY BALL-SIDE CUT

FOCUS

Footwork execution and jump-to-the-ball techniques.

PROCEDURE

Players begin two-on-two on the half court. Follow these steps:

1. Split the team into equal groups and then go two-on-two, offense to defense, defense off.

2. The purpose of this drill is to teach X1 to slide—some call it jump to the ball—two steps to prevent O1 from getting an inside cut.

3. In most cases when X1 slides to the ball and O1 makes the cut, incidental contact will occur as X1 denies O1 an easy route inside.

4. X1 begins the drill in a normal guarding position, indicated by the dotted-circle X. After sliding to the ball on the pass, the defender relocates inside O1 and shadows him on the cut to the basket.

5. X1 should have his arms up to discourage a pass and should focus on O1's eyes, anticipating a pass as they clear through the free-throw lane area.

6. After O1 clears the rim, X1 turns and finds the ball.

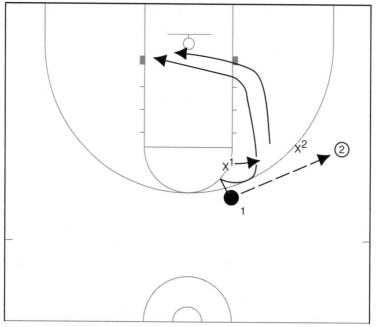

Guard denying ball-side cut.

Ball-side cut.

Forward, No Ball-Side Cut

A quick post flash from the weak side is one of the most difficult moves to defend in basketball. Even fundamentally solid defensive teams have difficulty guarding this move, because, besides defending the flash, they have two other key weak-side responsibilities—protecting the basket and boxing out. To execute all three coverages simultaneously requires total concentration; thus, working on this drill is mentally demanding. If the offensive player gets his head and shoulders in front of the defender, the defender is beaten. Ideally, the defender should be a step off the offensive man and shading two steps to the middle in a normal weak-side defensive position. The player is bent in a crouching position, with arms at shoulder height, focusing on the ball-you-man theory and anticipating a cut to the basket.

FORWARD, DENY BALL-SIDE CUT

FOCUS

Technique to defend the weak-side flash.

PROCEDURE

Players begin on the half court. Split the team equally and follow these steps:

1. O1 passes to O2 and cuts behind O2 to the corner.
2. O3 makes a ball-side cut from the weak side to the strong side.
3. To defend, X3 must be positioned to the middle and able to see O3 making the ball-side cut.
4. X3 steps in front of O3, makes contact at the elbow, and reroutes O3 down the middle of the free-throw lane. X3 has his hands up and watches O3's eyes for a possible pass from the strong side.

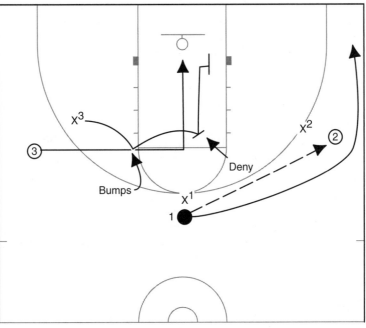

Forward denying ball-side cut.

DEFEND LOW-POST BALL-SIDE CUT

FOCUS

Denying the ball-side cut in the low-post position.

PROCEDURE

Players begin three-on-three on the half court. Follow these steps:

1. Divide the squad equally for this three-on-three drill. Go offense to defense, defense off.
2. O1 passes to O2.
3. O5 makes a ball-side cut from the weak side to the strong side.
4. To defend, X5 is off O5, shading two steps to the ball.
5. As O5 moves across the lane, X5's job is to deny the cut, the position, and the ball.
6. X5 steps in and makes contact with his hips and lower body, with his arms up to discourage a pass.
7. The drill teaches low-post footwork and positioning to prevent O5 from getting the low-post, strong-side position.

Objective 4: No Second Shots

One of the hardest things a coach has to deal with is watching his team play solid defense throughout a possession but then give up an offensive put-back because someone failed to block out. All that hard work of keeping the ball out of the middle, eliminating weak-side flashes, denying weak-side cuts, and keeping the ball on the side goes for naught if someone fails to block out. Coaches must emphasize the importance of defensive rebounding by using box-out drills and giving regular reminders. They may find this a difficult job because many players would rather use their jumping skills to rebound instead of putting a body on the opponent.

Players are willing to work on their shooting skills and ballhandling, but they neglect the art of boxing out. Not surprisingly, players often fail to check out, and the result is that their teams lose games. Nothing is more demoralizing than watching an opponent get an offensive rebound off a missed free throw and convert it into a basket. Teaching the correct box-out techniques should begin early, in junior high school at the latest, and coaches should constantly reinforce the techniques at all levels. Regardless of their jumping ability, all players should learn two basic box-out techniques—the reverse pivot and the step-through. Let's look at these techniques.

Box Out With a Reverse Pivot Technique

Players box out for a simple reason: to reduce the number of shot attempts by the opponent. Permitting the offense to get tip-ins, put-backs, and second-chance points is a surefire way of losing the game. Teaching proper box-out techniques should be a high priority and come early in the teaching phase of practice. Coaches must worry about two categories of offensive players—shooters and nonshooters. Boxing out the shooter is easy because he is concentrating on the shot and the defender is within touching distance. On the other hand, a defender on a nonshooter is generally several steps away from his opponent, looking to give support, which makes the job more difficult. The box-out technique is the same for shooters and nonshooters, with pivoting as the basic move.

BOX OUT WITH THE REVERSE PIVOT

FOCUS

Reverse pivot technique on the box out.

PROCEDURE

Players begin three-on-three on the half court. Follow these steps:

1. After the coach explains the technique, three offensive and three defensive players pair off approximately 15 feet from the basket.

2. The drill begins with the coach passing to one of the three offensive players, who shoots the ball. The defenders must execute the reverse pivot, box out, and capture the rebound. If the offense gets the rebound, the defense stays on the court. The coach determines how many stops the defense has to get before the next group participates.

3. The technique is as follows: The defender must make contact with the offensive player as soon as possible after the shot. The defender is down in a crouch, with arms extended and hands up, face high, and ready to rebound.

4. If the offensive player goes to the defender's right, the defender pivots on the left foot into the offensive player's stomach. The defender is in a crouched position, bent at the waist, elbows shoulder high, arms up, legs at least shoulder-width apart, and solidly balanced.

5. If the offensive player goes to his left, the defensive player pivots on the right foot into the offensive player's belly (using the body mechanics in step 4).

6. The biggest issue that most players and coaches have with this technique is the fact that the defender loses sight of the ball when executing the pivot. Executed properly, however, this technique neutralizes the offensive player.

a

b

Beginning of the reverse pivot—bending the knees and staying low.

Holding the position.

Box Out With a Step-Through Technique

The major difference between the step-through and the reverse pivot box-out technique is footwork; in the step-through the defender never loses sight of the offensive player. The step-through, or front pivot, is a classic case of face guarding; the player may lose sight of the ball but never the man because his only responsibility is keeping the offensive player off the boards. This technique is often successful in keeping great offensive rebounders in check. When the offensive man moves to the basket, the defender steps in front, makes contact, and impedes his movement. When the offensive player is far from the basket, the step-through is the most effective maneuver. The reverse pivot is more effective closer to the basket. Thus, coaches must teach both techniques. Inside players can quickly pivot, maintain contact, and keep the opponent away from the ball. Out on the court, however, defenders must use the step-through, with visual contact, to keep athletic players from using a running start to crash the boards from the weak side.

BOX OUT WITH A STEP-THROUGH

FOCUS

Step-through rebound technique and footwork on box outs.

PROCEDURE

Players begin three-on-three on the half court. Follow these steps:

1. As in the previous drill, three offensive and three defensive players pair off approximately 15 feet from the basket. The defender maintains eye contact with the opponent. When the shot is taken, the defender steps out, initiating contact with a front pivot.

2. If the offensive man goes to the defender's right, the defender, while maintaining visual contact, pivots on his right leg and steps in front of the offensive man with his left leg and shoulders blocking the offensive man's path to the basket.

3. If the offensive man goes to the defender's left, the defender, while maintaining visual contact, pivots on his left leg and steps in front of the offensive man with his right leg and shoulders blocking the offensive man's path to the basket.

4. The step-through technique leaves the defender vulnerable to air balls.

Seeing the man.

Using a reverse step-through pivot.

Never losing sight of your man.

Objective 5: Contest All Layups

The fifth objective of a hard-nosed defense is to prevent easy layups. Fouling a player who is shooting a layup means that the player must hit two free throws from 15 feet to earn those two points. A smart defensive team will focus on using fouls only in the paint area, calling this approach "fouling for profit." Teams that foul out on the court or in backcourt are not playing smart basketball. Players will have plenty of opportunities to use fouls in an intelligent, constructive way. Anytime a player drives for an open layup or an offensive player gets an offensive rebound and is looking at a point-blank dunk, giving a foul makes sense.

Easy scores off layups should be hard to come by. The best way to eliminate them is to stress their importance by keeping a statistic demonstrating the differences between how many layups your team gets and how many your opponent gets. This statistic is one that coaches think about but that you won't hear or read about. Keeping account of layups and whom they were scored against can be extremely useful in certain game situations. Team and individual charts showing game-to-game totals can be a tremendous motivator. This drill teaches proper fouling techniques when trying to prevent layups.

CONTEST ALL LAYUPS

FOCUS
Giving a foul at the basket.

PROCEDURE
Players begin on the half court. Follow these steps:

1. Divide the team into two groups and run the drill on both ends.
2. X is the defender, the coach makes the pass, and O is the shooter.
3. Os form a single line just beyond the three-point arc. The distance may vary depending on the speed of the players. After X defends three attempts, he rotates out and an O takes his place.
4. The drill begins with the coach passing to the first player in the O line. O must attack the basket and shoot a layup.

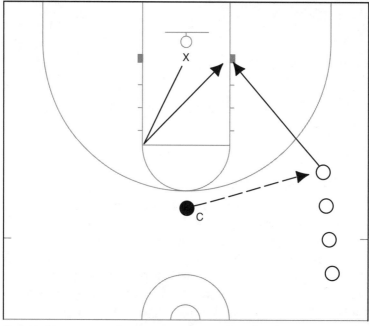

Contest all layups.

5. X, the defender, begins under the basket. On the coach's pass, he sprints and touches the intersection of the free-throw lane and the free-throw line with his foot. He then turns and sprints back to prevent a layup by O.

6. The idea is to go for the ball first (to block the shot) and the offensive man's wrist second before he gets airborne. This foul should not be a hard foul, but an intelligent foul. The idea is to teach players how to foul properly, using the same strategy as giving a foul when the clock is short and pressure is on the offense to score.

This chapter is a road map for both coach and player, offering a thorough explanation of what it takes to play good half-court defense. The 16 half-court individual defensive fundamentals provide greater appreciation of what it takes to play man-to-man defense. Coaches looking for a sound half-court defensive system can profit by implementing the five basic objectives discussed in the no-middle defensive strategy. The next step is to put the individual fundamentals and no-middle objectives together to build an effective half-court defense. Chapter 8 does just that.

Team Defense

I n chapter 7, we learned that defense is about dissecting team concepts into comprehensible, individual units called defensive fundamentals. Players must work at understanding these 16 fundamentals and be able to execute their techniques proficiently. Once they accomplish that, the parts become integral components of a complete defensive system that has five major objectives. Defense depends on emotion and intensity, but it must be channeled uniformly and intelligently to produce positive results. Chapter 7 identified those five objectives, and chapter 8 shows how to use each component as a building block in a well-defined, effective defensive system. Let's begin by stating that these five objectives—keeping the ball out of the middle, allowing no middle-dribble penetration, permitting no ball-side cuts, allowing no second shots, and contesting all layups—provide the foundation for an effective defensive philosophy.

These objectives apply to man-to-man and zone defenses. The best way to teach these concepts is through the shell drill because it incorporates all the fundamental defensive tools needed for effective teaching. The shell drill also provides the perfect opportunity to work against opponents' offensive sets and decide how best to defend them.

Defense As a Coordinated Unit

Good defense is produced when players are alert, active, aggressive and constantly anticipating the next move from the offense. Translated, this means players are constantly moving their heads, their feet, arms, and body position depending on where the ball is. A defender guarding one pass away could be assigned to deny the ball, push the man out to receive the pass, or play soft and off. Players two passes away must recognize and either drop two steps toward the basket, or adjust by moving to a closer support position. No one is ever static on defense.

The shell drill is an active defense taught on the half court using four players on defense in a box set—two guards out front (called "perimeter players") and two big men (called bigs or "inside players") who slide from the baseline (deep and wide) to the elbow area, free-throw line extended. Shell work begins with a review of footwork, spacing, proper angles on close-outs, floor alignment for support, and body movement as the ball is passed.

For the purpose of this drill, players will be designated as Xs and Os rather than by position, because all positions are interchangeable in this drill. Shell work features two passing drills—around the horn and diagonal. Begin the drill with a dummy defense or no defense, just slides. The coach determines when to initiate live action.

Shell Drills

Teams play good defense when players are alert, active, and aggressive and when they are constantly anticipating the next move from the offense. Players constantly move their heads, feet, arms, and bodies, depending on where the ball is. A defender guarding one pass away could be assigned to deny the ball, push the man out to receive the pass, or play soft and off. Players two passes away must recognize this and either drop two steps toward the basket or adjust by moving to a closer support position. No one is ever static on defense.

Shell Drill: Passing Around the Horn

This drill begins with the coach defining the body angle, stance, slide, and support responsibilities for all four defenders as the offense moves the ball from the right corner to the right wing, from the right wing across to the left wing, and from the left wing to the left corner. The defender rotating to check the offensive man receiving the pass must execute the proper close-out technique. To save time and confusion, have at least three teams with different colored scrimmage vests.

PASSING AROUND THE HORN

FOCUS

Around-the-horn passing for defensive slide techniques and stance.

PROCEDURE

Players begin in the half-court, four-man shell set. Follow these steps:

1. Begin in a box set. Two perimeter players are at the elbow extended, beyond the three-point line. The two big men are wide and deep on the baseline.

2. On a pass from perimeter to baseline, all four defenders move in unison with slides and close-out techniques. The object is to teach proper positioning and support assignments.

3. X1, guarding the ball, drops down two steps and slides one step toward the ball, protecting against the middle drive. X2 drops to the middle of the free-throw line, discouraging middle passes.

4. X3 closes out under control, influencing the shooter baseline. X4, in the weak-side corner, rotates to the block, looking to help. If an offensive player drives baseline, X4 continues to the strong-side block for a double team.

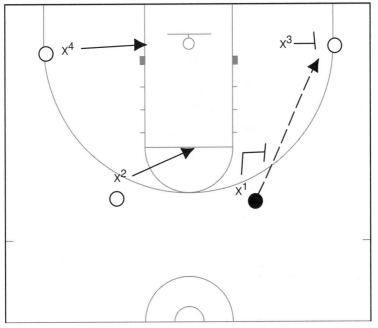

Passing around the horn.

AROUND THE HORN CONTINUED

FOCUS
Around-the-horn passing and slide techniques.

PROCEDURE
Players begin in a four-man shell set. Follow these steps:

1. This drill is a continuation of around the horn with the ball in the corner.
2. After the four defenders make their slides, the offense should pass the ball out to the strong-side perimeter player, who passes to the weak-side perimeter player. He then passes to the weak-side corner player.
3. At each passing interval, the defensive players slide and rotate either to cover the ball or to be in a help position.
4. The drill ends when the ball rotates from one corner to the opposite corner and back. The offense then goes to defense, the defense steps off, and four additional offensive players come to the court.

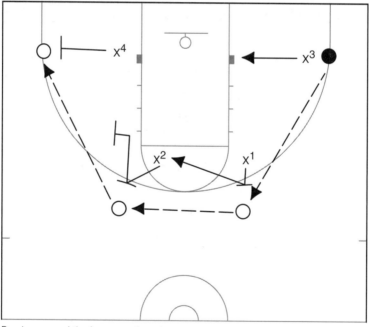

Passing around the horn, continued.

Shell Drill: Passing Diagonal

The diagonal passing entry into the shell drill adds three important new coverages to defend—longer passes, the skip pass, and live offensive sets. Begin the drill by explaining each defender's shifting position as the ball moves from player to player. To initiate the drill, the passing sequence begins with the perimeter player throwing a long diagonal pass to the corner. The corner passes to the opposite corner, and then that receiver passes out diagonally to the opposite perimeter player. All four players have touched the ball, and live action can begin. To teach proper player defensive coverage, the drill uses four-man play sets.

As the ball moves from player to player, coaches should stress the ball-you-man concept and emphasize coverage area, proper spacing, and close-out techniques. After the drill becomes live, the coach has an opportunity to evaluate the players' defensive abilities, speed, anticipation, and comprehension.

DIAGONAL PASS

FOCUS
Diagonal pass drill passing and sliding techniques.

PROCEDURE
Players begin in the half-court shell set. Follow these steps:

1. Players practice the same defensive slides that they used in around the horn.

2. Players close out under control, and perimeter players sink and fill, according to the position of the ball and their positions on the floor.

3. The offense makes three passes before the drill becomes live. The first pass goes from the perimeter to the far corner, the second pass goes baseline to baseline, and the third pass goes from the baseline diagonally to the perimeter. Before the defensive players begin their slides, the offensive players should practice the passing routine. After they have done that, add defensive slides and player movement as the ball rotates.

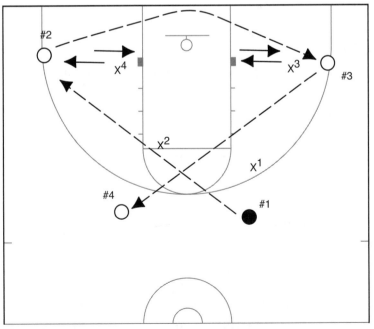

Diagonal pass.

4. To start, the defender on the ball is up on his man in normal defensive position. The other guard defender is in help position, denying the middle drive.

5. The defenders guarding the big men on the baseline start at the free-throw lane and rotate in a close-out stance to contain and influence baseline.

6. The weak-side big man rotates to the free-throw lane, protecting against the drive. When one big man protects the lane, the other big man is out guarding his man. They work in tandem, as though tied together at the waist with a rope. In theory, when one goes out, he pulls the other to the free-throw lane.

Defense Against Six Half-Court Plays and Full-Court Transition

Teaching the shell drill using only four players opens up the court and eliminates congestion in the low post. With a fifth player, the defense becomes sluggish and play soon becomes a half-court scrimmage. Coaches should remind players daily that the focus of the shell drill is playing intense defense. For identification purposes, here are the seven key areas that we will cover, including some options:

1. **Baseline screens:** single, double, and triple picks
2. **Pick-and-rolls:** sideline, corner, middle, elbow, double, step-ups, and drags
3. **Cross screens:**
    a. A guard covers a big man.
    b. A big man covers a guard.
    c. A guard diagonal screens for the big man.
4. **Post-ups:** turnouts, splits action, and on direct pass to the post
5. **Isolations:** low post, wing, middle, and end-of-quarter spread
6. **Motion offense:** several post variations
7. **Full-court transition:**
    a. Generates 50 percent of the offense.
    b. Fewer fast-break opportunities.
    c. Teams tend to be more conservative.
    d. Fewer rebounds.
    e. More accurate shooting.

The coach must explain each of those seven situations to eliminate any confusion in the minds of the players. The shell drill gives the coach an opportunity to teach proper defensive techniques while running specific offensive sets against the defense. Let's start by covering screens.

Play 1: Defending Baseline Screens

Baseline screens are off-the-ball screens so that a team's best shooters can curl off a big man for a catch-and-shoot. The range of the shooters, as well as their individual skills, determines the route that they take. The defender must know his opponent's strengths and weaknesses to defend him effectively. A whole range of individual player tendencies is available from scouting reports, game films, and scouting services. Does the offensive man prefer to come out off the screen left or right? Is the offensive man right-handed or left-handed? Does the offensive man like to dribble before he shoots? Does he like to curl tight off the screen and attack the basket? Does he like to fade? If crowded, will he put it on the floor or look to pass? Does he like to catch, measure his defender, and shoot, drive, or pass? Does he favor going right or left? Coaches have access to this kind of information as it relates to all the drills explained in this chapter, but the information is effective only if used. A single screen occurs when an offensive player rubs his defender off a stationary teammate (the screener) to get open for a shot. An inside big man on the low post usually sets the screen. The shell drill begins with the diagonal or the around-the-horn passing drill to teach sliding techniques and area responsibilities.

SHELL DRILL VERSUS SINGLE SCREENS

FOCUS

Defending play 1 baseline, single screen.

PROCEDURE

Players begin in the half-court shell set. Follow these steps:

1. The action begins when the ball returns to a perimeter player.
2. A perimeter player, O1, dribbles to the top of the key, and O2 moves to the middle of the free-throw lane, looking to curl off either of the big men for a jump shot.
3. Both big men move on the catch by O1 to their respective low-post blocks to set a screen for O2.
4. As O2 begins to move into position for the screen, X2 positions his body to give O2 only one direction to run. This action establishes the route that O2 takes and tells X2 where the screen is located.
5. X2 gets to the outside hip of O2, bends low, and sprints to shadow O2 and evade the screen.
6. At the moment of contact with the screener, X2 needs to be in contact with O2 to create some space and stay step for step with O2.
7. After O2 and X2 clear the screen and O2 catches the ball, X2 needs to be close enough to O2 to close out, contest the shot, and box out.
8. X2 cannot dodge the screener, avoid contact, or shoot the gap up the middle.

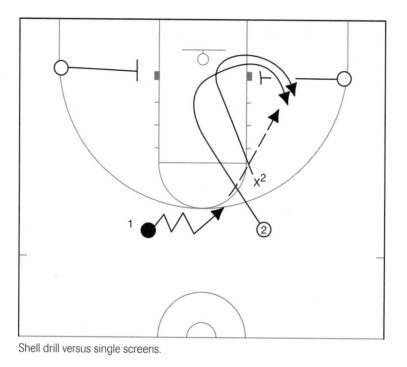

Shell drill versus single screens.

Play 1: Baseline Double Screen

A double screen occurs where two offensive players come together in tandem (side by side) or in staggered fashion (one behind the other) to free a teammate for a jump shot. Teams use staggered doubles in single-double sets and on crossing action in which O2 and O3 cross under the basket (either may be designated as the screener) and then curl off the inside big on the opposite side.

SHELL DRILL VERSUS DOUBLE SCREENS

FOCUS

Defending play 1 baseline, double screens.

PROCEDURE

Players begin in the half-court shell set. Follow these steps:

1. The shell drill starts with a diagonal or around-the-horn passing drill.
2. The action begins after the ball returns to a perimeter player, in this case O1.
3. In a double screen, O4 and O5 must relocate and set the staggered double screen.
4. In this diagram, O5 relocates across the free-throw lane to the opposite block. O4 moves from the corner about six feet behind O5 and becomes the second screener in the set.

5. As O2 moves to the free-throw lane, X2 jumps or slides to the ball and eliminates a ball-side cut. X2 also positions his body in such a way that O2 has only one direction to run, thus indicating to X2 where the screens are.

6. X2 gets to the outside hip of O2, bends low, and sprints to shadow O2 and evade the screens. X2 trails hard and does not shoot the gap.

7. At the moment of contact with the screener, X2 needs to be in contact with O2. A major point to emphasize here is that X2 must not let O2 get a running start off screens. If that happens, X2 will never catch up. X2 must maintain contact and know that he must evade two screens.

8. After O2 and X2 clear the screens and O2 catches the ball, X2 needs to be close enough to O2 to close out, contest the shot, and then box out. If O2 curls and goes to the basket, X4, the last screener, must hedge or switch, discouraging the pass and protecting against the middle drive. Hedging, that is, stepping out and showing, will buy some time and permit X2 to catch up.

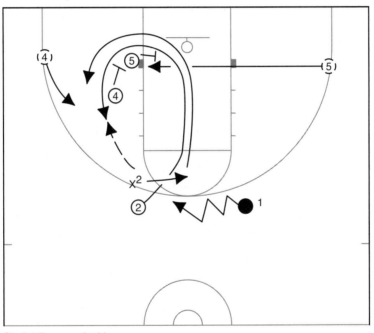

Shell drill versus double screens.

Play 2: Defending the Pick-and-Roll

The pick-and-roll screen on the ball is one of the most frequent and effective offensive sets in basketball, often separating the good players from the great ones. In the NBA, a guard can sink or swim based on his ability to run the pick-and-roll. John Stockton is the all-time NBA assists leader, primarily because of his success in running the pick-and-roll with Karl Malone.

The pick-and-roll is a direct attack on guards who can't get over screens, post men who will not step out with the screener, and weak-side defenders who go to sleep on good jump shooters. After you have determined your defensive scheme, the shell drill is the best way to teach it.

Because offensive schemes have many ways of getting into the pick-and-roll, it's imperative for coaches to have a well-developed plan of attack. Offenses can use the sideline version, the step-up, the corner, middle pick-and-rolls, variations off the break (drags), and other variations in which the pick-and-roll is merely a decoy for weak-side movement involving double-stack action.

Many teams use a weak-side run into the sideline pick-and-roll because of the deceptive possibilities. For all these pick-and-rolls, the defense must decide either to go over, go under, go into and under, switch, hedge, show and follow, force down, trap and rotate, or zone. The method employed depends on talent, team speed and quickness, the ability to anticipate, and the opponent's effectiveness in running pick-and-rolls. Regardless of where on the floor the offense runs the pick-and-roll, the defender should use three important tools: (1) He must communicate by talking and letting his teammate know that the pick is coming, (2) he must not let the offensive guard split him and the defender on the screener, and (3) if he decides to trap, he must stay in it until the guard passes the ball.

Let's look at the sideline, the double high elbow, and middle pick-and-rolls to get an idea about the variety of coverage needed and how to implement the shell drill effectively.

Play 2: Defending the Sideline Pick-and-Roll

The most important decision in defending the sideline pick-and-roll concerns how to play the guard with the ball. The defense must know the guard's tendencies. If he turns the corner and gets into the lane, will he pull up and take a jumper, drive for a layup, or draw and kick to an open teammate?

Determining the best defensive strategy depends on the skill of the ball handler. Going over the screen would make good sense against a good jump shooter, whereas going under is recommended against a player who likes to attack the basket. Once the defense makes a decision about how to defend the ball handler, the focus is on what happens when a screen is set. What the defense does on the point of the screen dictates the action that follows. When O5 sets the screen for O1, X1 and X5 must know player tendencies and communicate their predetermined instructions. Any confusion here gives the offense the advantage.

SHELL DRILL VERSUS SIDELINE PICK-AND-ROLL

FOCUS

Execution, communication, and technique versus sideline pick-and-roll.

PROCEDURE

Players begin in a half-court shell set. Follow these steps:

1. The shell drill begins with a diagonal or around-the-horn passing drill.
2. When the ball returns to O1, a perimeter player, O1 dribbles to the free-throw line

extended as O5 relocates from the same-side corner to set a pick-and-roll screen for O1.

3. In this drill, O1 gets to the middle and has the following options:
   a. He can shoot the jump shot.
   b. He can pass to O5, who has popped to the corner.
   c. He can pass to O2 for the jump shot or drive and dish to O4.
4. The first decision comes on the point of the screen from O1 and O5.
5. If O1 gets to the middle, the interior defense has to scramble.
6. The defense must predetermine its technique: stay with the man, go under, fight over, switch, or trap to create a team rotation process.
7. If X2 stops O1, O2 has an open shot. If the defense traps, O2 must sink and find O4, should X4 rotate to cover O5.

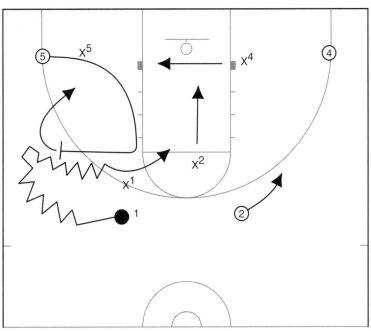

Shell drill versus sideline pick-and-roll.

Setting your man up for the screen.

Play 2: Defending the Middle Pick-and-Roll

The middle pick-and-roll is difficult to defend because the screener is typically a big man who screens and then rolls to the basket. Alternatively, the big man may be a good perimeter shooter who pops out for the medium-range jumper. Defending these sets takes lots of practice and team coordination. The all-important defensive decision comes at the point of the screen, with O4 screening X1.

Coverage options may vary, but maintaining close defensive presence on both the ball handler and the screener is the goal. The defense can't give the ball handler an open look and must be ready to rotate and pick up the screener on the roll to the basket or on the pop-out action. In the following drill, the opposite perimeter player slides to a wing position, and the weak-side corner slides to the block and rotates high as the screener rolls to the basket.

SHELL DRILL VERSUS MIDDLE PICK-AND-ROLL

FOCUS

Execution, communication, and technique versus middle pick-and-roll.

PROCEDURE

Players begin in the half-court shell set. Follow these steps:

1. The shell drill begins with a diagonal or around-the-horn passing drill.
2. When O1, a perimeter player, receives the last pass, O2 slides to the wing position at the free-throw line extended.

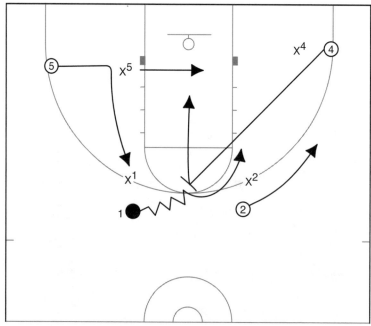

Shell drill versus middle pick-and-roll.

3. O4 rotates to the top of key and sets a screen for O1.

4. O5 slides toward the low block and rotates high for a jump shot as O4 rolls to the basket.

5. X1 and X4 must defend the screen with a trap, a hard show with X1 going over or under, a switch, or some combination of those available options.

6. X5 has the responsibility of checking O4 on the roll. Important strategy develops here as X5 must rotate to O4 and X4 rotates to O5. Everything revolves around how the screen is defended.

7. To eliminate rotations, a team can zone, switch, or attack the ball handler to force him away from the screen.

Play 2: Defending the Pick-and-Roll in the Double High Set

The double high pick-and-roll set involves two screens set at the respective elbows. Unlike in the sideline or the middle pick-and-roll (in which the positions of the offensive players are well defined), the guard has the option of using either screen in the double high. This complicates coverage because the screener will often dive to the basket and the opposite post player (weak side, in this case) will rotate to the top of the key for a medium-range jump shot, a maneuver that is especially effective when the shooter is matched against a bigger defender.

SHELL DRILL VERSUS DOUBLE HIGH PICK-AND-ROLL

FOCUS
Execution, communication, and technique versus double high pick-and-roll.

PROCEDURE
Players begin in a half-court shell set. Follow these steps:

1. The shell drill begins with a diagonal or around-the-horn passing drill.

2. When O1, a perimeter player, receives the last drill pass, O4 and O5 relocate at the elbows, on the same side on which they started.

3. O2 slides to the sideline and relocates in the corner.

4. Communication on the point of the pick, between X1 and X4 or X5, is essential. For example, if O4 sets the pick and rolls to the basket, X5, because of a switch, will have to pick up O4. In this case, who rotates to O5 at the top of the key?

5. If X1 rotates backward and picks up O5, then X4 stays on O1.

6. If X4 shows hard and rotates to O5, X1 must be able to catch up with O1, which is difficult to do.

7. Whatever is done on the point of the screen determines the defensive rotations.

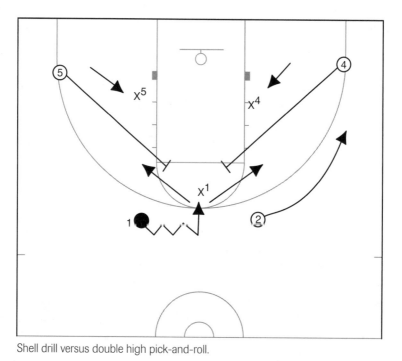

Shell drill versus double high pick-and-roll.

Play 3: Defending Screens—Cross, Up, Down, and Diagonal Screens

The four most commonly used screens are the cross, up, down, and diagonal. Teams normally use screens to get a better position for a player, whether to free up a shooter for a good shot or to enable a passer to rotate the ball to the weak side.

Each type of screen requires a different defensive technique. Cross screens usually occur in the block area, with a smaller player setting a screen on a big to get better post position for the bigger player. The most common cross screens are O1 or O2 screening for O5 or O4, and O3 screening for O2 (or vice versa) to initiate the baseline pin-down action (see chapter 5).

Determining the best defensive technique for your team can be a process of trial and error. On cross screens, switching is usually not a good option because a post-up player is coming to the ball, and the screener is generally a guard. The defense can use two techniques here: X2 should attempt to slow down the screener by bumping O5 in the crossing action, and X5, who is being screened, can force O5 down or use a reverse pivot technique, avoid the contact, and beat O5 to the opposite block.

Forcing down is good because the defender maintains contact with his opponent, although he must do it without fouling. Warning: Watch for lobs. The reverse step-through means that the defender disengages and loses momentary contact with his opponent and then relocates across the free-throw lane in a three-quarter or front position. Practice both of these methods and use the one that fits your personnel.

SHELL DRILL VERSUS CROSS SCREENS

FOCUS

Communicating, getting ball side, and trailing on cross screens.

PROCEDURE

Players begin in a half-court shell set. Follow these steps:

1. The shell drill begins with a diagonal or around-the-horn passing drill.

2. When O1, a perimeter player, receives the pass, O5 relocates to the weak-side low block.

3. O4 moves to the strong-side free-throw line extended and receives a pass from O1, who then makes a basket cut in preparation for setting a cross screen for O5.

4. The goal for the cross screen is to establish a good low-post position for the inside big player.

5. X1 jumps to the ball, eliminating the ball-side cut by O1.

6. As O1 crosses for the screen on O5, X1 prepares to bump (that is, get in front of) O5 to disrupt the timing on the play.

7. X5 anticipates the screen by positioning himself a step off O5, preparing to force O5 baseline.

8. When O1 sets the screen on X5, X5 uses a step-back, step-through move, pivoting on the left foot, and then slides across the lane, seeing the passer and beating O5 to the spot. This technique permits X5 to front O5.

9. X4 must apply pressure on O4 and obstruct the passing angle.

10. As this action takes place, X1 continues to trail O1, looking for a pin-down screen.

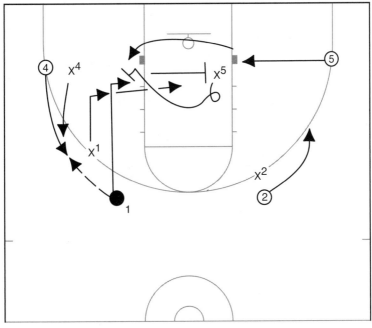

Shell drill versus cross screens.

Play 3: Defending the Up Screen

Many offensive sets, including the Hawk cut, UCLA action, and the 1-3-1 offense, use the up screen. During the late 1960s and early '70s when UCLA dominated college basketball under Coach John Wooden, the up screen became popular. The screen usually takes place at the elbow or a little higher, where the screener, an inside big, establishes stationary position. The perimeter player, trying to get his head and shoulders in front of the defender, cuts off the post, trying to rub the defender off the screen. He's looking for a direct pass and a layup. This initial cut can be deceptive, often catching the defender off guard. For that reason, the cutter's defender and the defender on the screener must communicate.

SHELL DRILL VERSUS UP SCREEN

FOCUS

Posting defense against the up screen.

PROCEDURE

Players begin in a half-court shell set. Follow these steps:

1. The shell drill begins with a diagonal or around-the-horn passing drill.
2. As O1 receives the ball and dribbles to the sideline at the free-throw line extended, O5 relocates to the strong-side elbow.
3. O2 positions himself in a direct line with O5, the defender, and the basket.

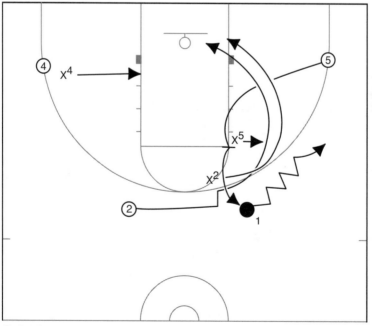

Shell drill versus up screen.

4. From here, O2 makes a hard cut to the basket, looking for a pass from O1.

5. X5, the key defender in this scenario, must communicate to X2 that a screen is coming. X2 must get through the screen and back to O2. X4 is the weak-side help position.

6. X5 must protect the basket first in case O2 gets open.

7. X5 looks to bump, or divert O2's direct path, to give X2 an opportunity to catch up with O2.

8. If O5 steps out and receives the pass, X5 must close out under control.

Play 3: Defending the Down Screen

A down screen is an effective way to free a shooter for an open catch-and-shoot. Dell Curry and Glen Rice, two great NBA shooters, illustrate different techniques in using down screens and getting shots off. Curry had an incredibly quick release. He worked hard at squaring up before receiving the pass so that he could quickly get off both the medium-range and long-range jumper. Rice would catch the ball, measure the distance, and then shoot, using his 6-8 height to shoot over the defender. Defenders will find it helpful to know the shooter's tendencies. Defenders must work to disrupt the shooter's rhythm by anticipating the down screen. The object is to get on the outside hip of the offensive player. This drill teaches defenders to trail hard.

SHELL DRILL VERSUS DOWN SCREEN

FOCUS

Executing on defense and influencing the opponent one way.

PROCEDURE

From a half-court shell set that begins with a diagonal or around-the-horn passing drill, players move into the following steps:

1. As O1 receives the last pass, O5 and O4 move opposite each other at the elbows and O2 relocates on the block (either side). O1 centers the ball and looks for O2 to pop out off the down screen.

2. As O5 starts to set the screen for O2, X5 should disrupt his movement by getting in front and slowing down the screen.

3. X2 influences O2 by directing him one way and then gets to O2's outside hip, trailing in anticipation of the screen by O5.

4. X2 must clear the screen, close out, and contest the shot.

5. X5 sees when O2 clears the screen, so he must get to the high side of O5, show hard to discourage the drive, and be ready to switch if X2 is caught up in the screen.

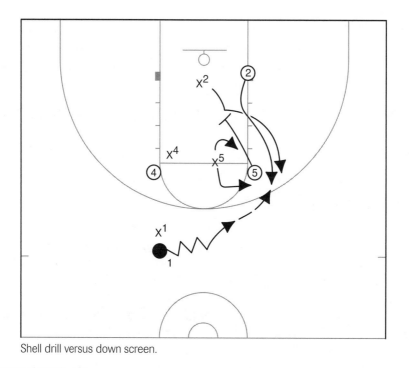

Shell drill versus down screen.

Play 3: Defending the Diagonal Screen

The diagonal screen, from the block to the opposite elbow, is set by a guard on O4 or O5 to help the big man relocate to post-up position. The Utah Jazz has used this screen effectively for years, and many NBA and college teams have copied them. The sequence begins with the guard making a UCLA or Hawk cut, setting up on the low-post block, and then crossing diagonally to set a screen on the opposite post man at the elbow.

The defense can defend this screen in two very different ways. In the first, X4 forces O4 high and to the middle; this action creates congestion and can become a physical play. In the second, X4 pushes O4 down toward the basket, where he gets a bump from O1. The bump gives X4 a chance to catch up to O4 and contest him for the low block. Both techniques are demanding and require good physical strength. This drill shows X4 pushing O4 over the top.

SHELL DRILL VERSUS DIAGONAL SCREEN

FOCUS

Preparing and setting a physical screen.

PROCEDURE

From a half-court shell set that begins with a diagonal or around-the-horn passing drill, players move into the following steps:

1. As O1 receives the pass, O2 goes to the deep block while O4 and O5 relocate at the elbows, opposite each other.

2. O1 dribbles to the free-throw line extended as O2 moves across the lane and sets a screen on X4.

3. X2 calls out the screen as O2 moves toward X4. X4 gets to the ball side and braces himself for the contact from O2.

4. X4 steps out and bumps O4 on contact, pushing him off the free-throw lane. X4's goal is to force O4 out on the floor and eliminate the low-post position. This is otherwise known as "riding him out."

5. X2 protects the basket. Should O4 go baseline, X2's job is to bump O4 and help X4 get back to his man.

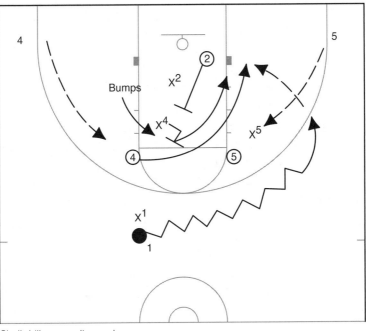

Shell drill versus diagonal screen.

Play 4: Defending the Post-Up on a Direct Pass

Teams with a good half-court offense are often winning teams, so your team must be properly prepared to defend multiple post-up situations. An offense can enter the ball to the low post in two basic ways—with either a direct or an indirect pass. A direct pass (one pass) occurs when the ball handler, typically in a half-court setting, dribbles to an area and then passes the ball directly to the low post. NBA teams that gear their offense to a great post-up player such as Shaquille O'Neal of the Lakers often use this approach. Direct passes are also used in secondary break or early offense situations when the guard or small forward dribbles to the free-throw line extended and passes to the first big to occupy the low block.

The secondary break is difficult to defend because organizing the defense is hard when all 10 players are in transition. For the purpose of teaching low-post defense, the direct and indirect passes will be illustrated. An indirect pass involves two or more passes on the half court before the ball goes to the post man.

Teams can defend the low post by playing behind the offensive player, by playing a three-quarter position, or by fronting him. Fronting, which works to keep the ball out of the middle, is the most difficult method. College and high school coaches should choose a way to defend the low post only after they judge the talents of their players. They should begin by teaching the fronting position.

SHELL DRILL VERSUS DIRECT POST-UP

FOCUS

Execution and technique versus direct pass to the post-up.

PROCEDURE

Players begin in a half-court shell set. Follow these steps:

1. The shell drill begins with a diagonal or around-the-horn passing drill.

2. As O1 receives the last pass and begins moving to the free-throw line extended, O5 moves to the strong-side low block. To get more movement, the big men can cross or the post man can establish low-post position to make the defender work to get in front. O5 moves to the low block from the corner.

3. X5 moves with O5 to the low post. As soon as O5 begins to post up, X5 steps in front

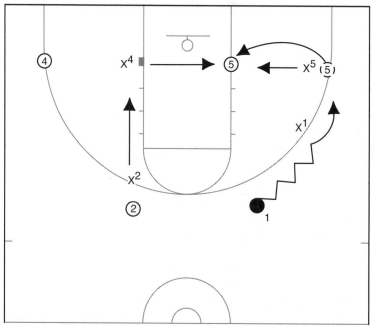

Shell drill versus direct post-up.

with his knees bent, butt in contact with O5, and arms extended up to discourage, deflect, or intercept a pass.

4. X1 applies hard pressure on O1.

5. X4 provides weak-side help, and X2 is ready to sink and fill.

6. X1 covers the first pass out if the ball goes to the post. If O1 cannot pass to O5, O1 rotates the ball to O2 weak side, O4 goes to the low post, and the offense attacks X4.

Play 4: Defending the Post-Up on an Indirect Pass

Indirect passes present an entirely different challenge because it's much harder to anticipate a pass to the post if the ball handler has several passing options. The following offensive sets involve indirect passes: baseline screens with weak-side pin-downs; pick-and-rolls in which the post man rolls to the basket or establishes weak-side low-post position; double high posts in which one big posts and the other pops out; cross screens, zipper action, turns and turnouts, motion, Hawk cuts, rip screens, UCLA action, and the triangle offense with post options. Most indirect post passes involve the passer to the post using a speed cut to the opposite corner and perimeter shooters spotting up to counter double teams and traps. The turnout illustrates the defensive demands imposed by indirect passes.

SHELL DRILL VERSUS INDIRECT PASS TO THE POST-UP

FOCUS

Reading and executing defense on post-up plays.

PROCEDURE

From a half-court shell set that begins with a diagonal or around-the-horn passing drill, players move into the following steps:

1. As O1 receives the pass, the other three offensive players relocate. O2 goes to the basket in line with the net, O5 moves to the strong-side low block, and O4 goes to the free-throw line extended on the same side. This is a post-up isolation for O5.

2. In the turnout, O2 works off O5 and receives the ball from O1 just beyond the three-point line. O2, a scoring threat, squares up to the basket and passes to O5.

3. O2 makes a diagonal speed cut to the far corner. O1 slides away and spots up. O4 can either go to the weak-side block or stay wide to crash the boards on the shot.

4. X2 trails O2 off O5's screen.

5. When O2 passes to O5 and speed cuts to the opposite corner, X2 makes sure that there is no ball-side cut and then goes through with O2 until they get to the basket.

6. X2 also has the responsibility to double back and trap O5 with X5 (not shown in the diagram). Important point: You must determine whether the guard goes high or low in the trap so that X5 knows which way to influence O5.

7. X4 drops to protect the basket, preventing O2 from sneaking in for a layup.

8. X1, at the free-throw line, sinks and fills and looks to block out O4. X1 is ready for long rebounds and has first-pass-out responsibilities in case O5 passes out of the double team.

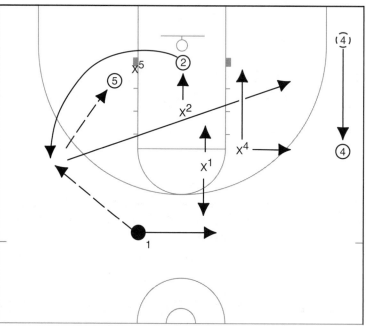

Shell drill versus indirect pass to the post-up.

Play 5: Defending Isolations on the Wing and at the Top of the Key

Isolations occur when a team clears a specific section of the floor, such as the side or the top of the key, to give a player space and opportunity to go one-on-one. Isolations occur more frequently in the NBA than in college ball because the prevalence of zone defenses in college nullifies their advantage. Although the NBA adopted the modified zone in 2001, it has not had the effect that many thought it would. NBA coaches are simply not comfortable using zones. Teams usually execute isolations from three key areas—the low post, the free-throw line extended wing area, and the top of the key. We will discuss defending the wing area and the top of the key.

SHELL DRILL VERSUS ISOLATION

FOCUS

Technique versus isolation at the free-throw line extended wing area.

PROCEDURE

Players begin in a half-court shell set. Follow these steps:

1. The shell drill begins with a diagonal or around-the-horn passing drill.
2. As O1 receives the last pass, O4 moves to the strong-side wing position at the free-throw line extended.
3. O1 passes to O4 and slides to the weak side.
4. O2 slides away toward the wing position.
5. O5 stays wide and crashes the boards when O4 begins his dribble drive.
6. O1 and O2 spot up, looking for a kick-out pass from O4.
7. In this drill, we implement the key principle of keeping the ball out of the middle and forcing the wing player baseline.
8. X4 has the responsibility of keeping the ball on the side and influencing his man to drive baseline.
9. Anticipating the drive on the weak side, X5 drops to the low box position and rotates across the lane, looking to draw the charge, block a shot, or trap O4. Ideally, X4's right leg and X5's left leg come together, preventing O4 from splitting the trap.
10. X2 rotates to the weak-side low block, looking to box out O5. X1 splits the difference between O1 and O2 and is responsible for the first pass out.

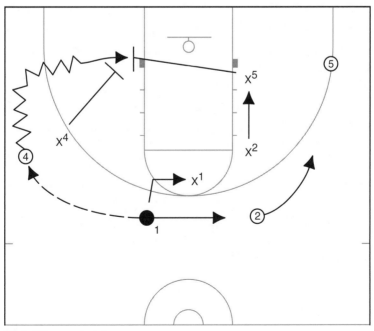

Shell drill versus isolation.

Play 5: Defending Top of the Key Isolations

Covering the ball handler one-on-one when he is at the top of the key is difficult because he is unrestricted and can dribble in either direction, which is why you want to keep the ball out of the middle of the floor. Allen Iverson of the Philadelphia 76ers, one of the NBA's leading scorers, illustrates the point. Early in his NBA career, the 76ers would run an offensive move for Iverson known as "the loop," in which he would run off two screens and receive the ball for wing isolation. Iverson soon realized that he would be more effective at the top of the key, so he began to deviate from his route, sprinting up the middle off a zipper or baseline cut. From the middle of the floor, he could let his quickness dictate his direction and rhythm. Great one-on-one offensive players will get a shot off this set. Let's look at the coverage options.

SHELL DRILL VERSUS TOP OF THE KEY ISOLATION

FOCUS

Technique versus isolation at the top of the key.

PROCEDURE

From a half-court shell set that begins with a diagonal or around-the-horn passing drill, players move into the following steps:

1. As O1 receives the last pass and dribbles to the wing at the free-throw line extended, O2 relocates on the strong-side low block.

2. O5 relocates to the strong-side elbow and sets a down screen for O2, who moves to the top of the key.

3. O5 relocates to the strong-side corner.

4. O4 stays in the weak-side corner, looking for a draw-and-kick pass from O2 on the dribble drive.

5. This offensive set is designed for O2 to either shoot, drive, or pass.

6. The best defensive option is to keep the ball on the side and not let it get back to the middle of the court. Accomplishing that is not always possible, so let's begin when O2 receives the ball at the top of the key. X2 could guard O2 one-on-one, but other options are better:

    a. X1 follows the pass and double-teams O2, staying with him in the double team until he passes the ball.

    b. The team could immediately realign into a 1-3-1, half-court zone and double-team the ball handler on dribble penetration. The key is to attack and be aggressive. Make someone besides O2 beat you.

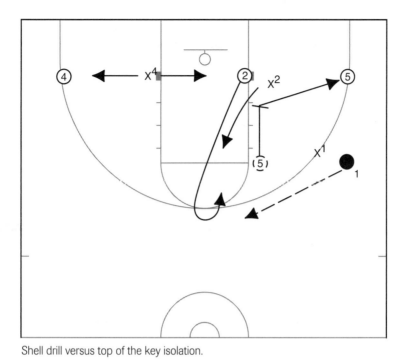

Shell drill versus top of the key isolation.

Play 6: Defending Motion Set

The motion offense is a great set for teaching defensive players how to adjust to both ball and player movement. In this drill, the coach instructs the offensive player with the ball either to pass and cut to the basket or to pass and screen away. The players without the ball can cross screen, use a screen and replace the screener, back screen a wing player, or use a down screen to free up a teammate. The idea is to keep the offense simple and create a lot of player movement.

The motion offense places a lot of pressure on the defense to react, and it reveals players' knowledge and understanding of team defensive principles. The defense must focus on keeping the ball on the side of the court, out of the middle, and out of the low post. Defenders must be ever alert for isolations, dribble drives, and defensive rebounding while communicating on all screens—cross, down, and up. Weak defensive players stick out like poor free-throw shooters.

SHELL DRILL VERSUS MOTION SET

FOCUS

Executing and communicating versus motion offense.

PROCEDURE

From a half-court shell set that begins with the diagonal or around-the-horn passing drill, players move into the following steps:

1. As O1 receives the last pass and sets the offense, O4 relocates to a wing and O2 slides to the opposite wing. O5 moves to either low-post position.
2. O1 passes to either wing player and screens away.
3. O5 sets up on the weak-side low block. O5 has the option of going to the strong-side block for a direct post-up. If O5 crosses to O4's side and O1 passes to O2, O1 screens O4, and O5 can set a back screen on X1. The play then becomes a sideline pick-the-picker.
4. X4 forces O4 baseline while X5 protects the basket.
5. If O1 screens for O2, X1 must open up and help X2 get through and back to O2. If O5 up screens X1, X5 must loosen up, protect the basket, and help X1 get through and back to O5.
6. If O5 relocates to the strong-side low post, X5 pushes O5 high and realigns in either a three-quarter or front position on the strong side.
7. This drill generates a lot of enthusiasm. Play through the possession until the defense captures the ball.

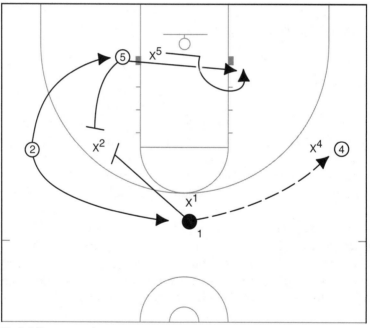

Shell drill versus motion set.

Transition Defense: Full-Court, Three-on-Two Catch-Up Drill

Good teams get about half of their points in transition. But as the season goes on and the team advances in postseason play, fewer fast break opportunities occur. Still, you must be prepared for a full-court offense. Teams like to fast-break off made and missed field goals, made and missed free throws, steals, jump-ball situations, against backcourt-out-of-bounds pressure with screens and long passes, or simply whenever they have an opportunity to push the ball. Here are six key points to emphasize when teaching transition defense:

1. Begin by properly aligning to slow down the outlet pass. The closest man to the outlet passer has the responsibility of getting his arms and hands up to deflect the outlet pass, a technique called "jamming the rebound."

2. The defense must contain the receiver of the outlet pass by staying in front of him and not getting beat off the dribble. The idea is to "retreat but don't get beat."

3. When caught behind the ball as it advances up the court, everyone is responsible for sprinting level to the ball, giving support to stop dribble penetration, and then finding their assigned man.

Holding the hands up to receive the pass.

Catching and shooting the jump shot.

4. A common defensive mistake is failure to see where the ball is. Players often have their heads down. Constant reinforcement is necessary to get players to see the ball and position their bodies with the correct posture for support and help. Alert players always see the ball.

5. In transition defense, the big man has the responsibility of sprinting to the paint, looking to help when opponents attempt dribble penetration. Just by getting to the paint and showing—that is, stepping toward the dribbler as if to double-team—helps seal off the middle drive.

6. Always assign one player the specific responsibility of protecting the basket. Eliminate any doubt about who that player is. Don't cloud the issue by saying it's either this player or that player who must rotate back. Be specific from the get-go: Name the player. If the point guard attacks the basket, the two guard is back. If both guards are involved in a fast break and end up under the basket, the small forward is back. If the point, two guard, and small forward are involved in attacking the basket, the power forward is back.

The better your opponent, the fewer people you can send to the offensive boards. At times you may have to keep two or three people back to stop the fast break. Here's an all-purpose transition drill that teaches floor balance, proper coverage, and basket protection. After you understand the drill, you can add the fourth and fifth players to each side.

TRANSITION DEFENSE VERSUS FULL-COURT ATTACK

FOCUS
Movement communication technique during transition.

PROCEDURE
Players begin on the full court. Follow these steps:

1. Six players, three offensive and three defensive, participate in this drill, without regard to position.

2. The three offensive players line up across the free-throw line, O1 on the free-throw line and O2 and O3 at the free-throw line extended at the wing position.

3. Two of the defender's, X2 and X3, match up with the wing players, and X1 lines up under the basket.

4. The coach with the ball also lines up on the end line. The coach passes to O1, who attacks the defenders in a three-on-two transition break.

5. As O1 catches the ball, X1 sprints to catch up. O2 and O3 stay wide, with O1 in the middle in a three-on-two alignment.

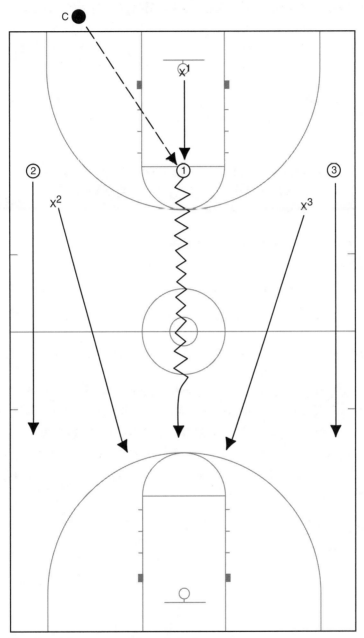

Transition defense versus full-court attack.

Play 7: Transition Defense Versus Offense Advantage

The previous diagram shows the beginning of the drill, and the following diagram shows its completion. The end of the drill develops into a basic three-on-two ball-handling and shooting drill. This drill is excellent for teaching player reactions, evaluating the ability of players to make good decisions on the run, and teaching techniques for players caught behind the ball. Certainly, other defensive transition drills are available, but none is better for teaching transition principles.

TRANSITION DEFENSE VERSUS NUMBERS DISADVANTAGE

FOCUS

Defending three-on-two full court and catching up.

PROCEDURE

Players begin on the full court. Follow these steps:

1. When O1 catches and attacks, X2 and X3 sprint back to the basket, setting up in tandem.

2. The first player back, X3, takes the low position at the bottom of the free-throw lane circle.

3. The second player, X2, stops between the top of the key and the free-throw line.

4. As O1 attacks, X2 has the responsibility of stopping O1's dribble penetration. X2 then drops toward the basket, looking for a pass to the opposite wing man.

5. X3, closest to the basket, fires out and takes O1's first pass to O2 or O3.

6. As all this unfolds, X1 sprints back to get to the level of the ball, looking to match up with either O1 or O3, whoever is open.

This situation basketball drill is one of the best methods for teaching players how and when to react in game situations.

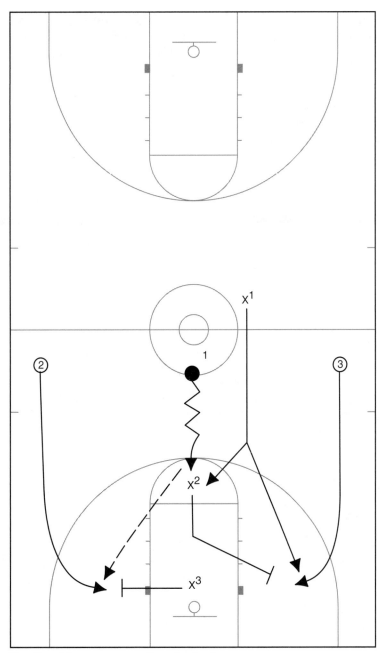

Transition defense versus numbers disadvantage.

In summary, defense is the one constant in the game of basketball. On those nights when your shooters can't make shots, good defense can keep you in the game and give you a chance to win. In addition, great defensive teams do well on the road, where effective defense can negate the home-court advantage by taking the crowd out of the game. My attitude about defense is grounded in more than four decades of working with teams that were usually short on offense but long on hustle and desire. Manufacturing points is the hardest thing to do in coaching, but by having a strong philosophical commitment to defense and an understanding of the right defensive principles, you can realize success.

CHAPTER 9

Situational Tactics

Failure to prepare is preparing to fail. A cliche, but it's true. A coach owes it to his players to have them ready for any tactical maneuver the opposition might employ. He should cover all realistic strategic options with the team in practices leading up to the game. The more fully prepared players are before competition, the more confident they'll be in executing both planned and spontaneous efforts to thwart the opponents' attack. Conversely, unprepared squads are susceptible to confusion, panic, and ultimately, defeat.

Pregame Analysis

One of the major differences between high school basketball, college basketball, and the NBA is game preparation. High school and college teams usually play 2 games per week, whereas NBA teams have stretches during the season when they may play 4 games in 5 nights or 8 games in 12 nights. High schools play approximately 25 games per season, colleges play 30, and the pros play around 100, counting preseason games and the playoffs. Many times NBA teams lose a day of practice because they play so many games back to back. Although the volume of games varies, the pregame preparation routine with films, scouting reports, personnel tendencies, and walk-throughs is much the same.

Let's look at a specific play and point out the differences in preparation. To prepare for a pick-and-roll set, high school and college teams can practice against it for two days to perfect their technique. Seldom would they have to modify their strategy from practice to game. An NBA team, however, may face four different pick-and-roll attacks in a week, executed by a variety of talented players. By following an NBA squad through a four-game road trip, you can see how difficult it is to prepare.

Practice and preparation time for NBA teams diminishes as the season progresses. When playing four games in five nights, game preparation for the first game is the best. Preparation will involve practicing against the opponent's offense, a game-day morning walk-through showing an edited video of the opponent's play sets, a review of the opposing team's individual personnel, and defensive matchups against the opposition's play sets with specific player assignments. Just before the game, there is a scouting review and videotape session.

Following the game, the NBA team boards a charter flight to the next city, arriving at their hotel sometime between 1 and 3 A.M. Players meet the next morning for an 11 A.M. breakfast and watch the previous night's game film or a film on the opponent for that night. Players then rest until it's time to go to the arena. The early bus with rookies and seldom used players leaves at 5:30 P.M. so that they can get in extra work. The veterans leave the hotel around 6 P.M. Following pregame shooting, a coach will go over the scouting report and show an edited video highlight film. After the game, the team repeats the travel procedure of the night before. Practice the next day is generally light because the men who play major minutes need to let their bodies recuperate.

On the day of game 3, the players repeat the breakfast, film, rest, bus ride, pregame shooting, and locker room procedures. After the game, they bus to the airport and travel to the next city. The fourth game on a road trip like this is difficult because fatigue, lack of adrenaline, and diminishing concentration begin to take their toll on the players; preparation is mostly scouting reports and videos. Quality of play suffers, and some teams are blown out when they are on the road for an extended time.

One of the crucial aspects of game preparation involves objective analysis of the two teams' comparative speed and quickness. The faster team should look to exploit that quickness advantage, both as a unit and in individual matchups.

The slower team must try to control the pace of the game and emphasize fundamentals, ball fakes, and positioning. If the opponent has quicker guards, the coach should identify a player at another position who is capable of handling the ball in the backcourt.

The NBA Hornets did that by using power forward Anthony Mason to help bring the ball up. When I coached at UNC Charlotte, we did it by having center Cedric Maxwell use his quickness advantage over virtually every center he played against to dribble the ball across the time line. Both of those big men had the skill and confidence to dribble the ball under pressure and initiate the offense. The daily full-court dribble drill is thus an important source of information for the coach and his team. UNC Charlotte upset number-one Michigan in the NCAA Mideast Regional to go the 1977 Final Four, even though Michigan's guards were too quick for the 49ers' guards. Similarly, poor-shooting teams have to find other ways to score. Defense is often a great equalizer in such circumstances. Presses, traps, and a variety of zones—such as the box-and-one, matchups, and run-and-jump traps—can confuse opponents and make them tentative. Changing defenses can also create turnovers that result in run-out baskets. Those easy shots created by the defense certainly improve a team's field-goal percentage. Poor-shooting teams also have to hit the boards, both on the offensive end to convert missed shots into put-backs and on the defensive end to prevent second-shot scoring opportunities for the opponent.

This chapter highlights six key tactical situations that require significant pregame preparation:

1. Attacking full-court pressure defense
2. Scoring plays from the backcourt
3. Backcourt inbounds plays against pressure, side out-of-bounds
4. Short-clock plays from the frontcourt, side out-of-bounds
5. Scoring plays from the frontcourt, baseline out-of-bounds
6. Executing against disruptive zones

Allow sufficient practice time to cover each situation thoroughly, especially those in which quickness and pressure have significant effect. These six situations represent four major areas of the game in which an offensive team lacking speed and quickness can be helpless if the coach has not adequately prepared his team. Three of those plays involve getting the ball inbounds against hard pressure in the backcourt; one play entails scoring from the frontcourt, side out-of-bounds with a short clock; one play includes scoring from the front court against pressure from baseline out-of-bounds plays; and the last one requires that the coach be prepared for irregular zone defenses. When the opponent is quicker or a team has to face a box-and-one, triangle-and-two, or diamond-and-one, the coach must be prepared to execute the offensive strategy with the correct play calls. All these situations are special because the defense forces the action with pressure and disruptive configurations. The offense must respond with an effective attack of its own.

Attacking Full-Court Pressure Defense

The coach must consider four major areas when designing a full-court offensive attack versus man-to-man and zone pressure. Teams must carry out four specific steps to complete the possession and establish a defensive position. First, a team has 5 seconds to get the ball inbounds. Second, after the ball is touched inbounds, high school and college teams have 10 seconds, and pro teams have 8 seconds, to get the ball across midcourt. Third, after the ball is in the frontcourt, the coach must decide whether to attack immediately or to set the offense and run a play. Fourth, after the attacking team scores or loses possession of the ball, it must get into a specific defensive alignment. Each step requires individual strategies dictated by the skills of the players

The Special Situation Game Chart is a quick study of offensive plays that a coach can use when confronting pressure and disruptive defenses. This chart is shown in table 9.1. Teams must practice these tactical options with the player alignment that produces the best results. Coaches should be prepared to run more than one option to counter different looks and matchups.

Table 9.1 Special Situations Game Chart

Defensive attack	Offensive counter
Pressure full court (man or zone)	• Alignment 1-4 Option 1 guard pass Option 2 big-man pass
Pressure full court (man)	• Scoring plays from backcourt The bomb The line Fake-and-go
Pressure sideline backcourt *(SOB)	• Backcourt – sideline inbounds The line
Pressure frontcourt (man) vs inbounding the ball vs 2-point shot vs 3-point shot	• Frontcourt (SOB) scoring plays X-out alignment X-out into pick and roll X-out into a 3-point shot
Pressure baseline frontcourt **(BOB)	• Frontcourt (BOB) scoring plays Pick-the-picker Box – cross 2 The line
Disruptive zones on the half court vs 1-3-1 vs box-and-one vs triangle-and-two vs triangle-and-two	• Attacking disruptive defenses LA offense Triangle overload attack Guards to block alignment 3-man overload shot spots

*SOB = Sideline out-of-bounds
**BOB = Baseline out-of-bounds

1-4 SET VERSUS FULL-COURT DEFENSE

FOCUS

Proper alignment when pressured full court.

PROCEDURE

Play begins in the backcourt. Follow these steps:

1. The team lines up in a 1-4 alignment with the two ball handlers lining up at the wing positions and the big men lining up on opposite elbows.

2. For identification purposes, 1, 2, and 3 will be the ball handlers, and 4 and 5 will be the big men.

3. The coach must put each team member in his strongest position on the court, the place where he can be most effective.

4. Basic inbounding rules apply. Following scores, the player has five seconds to inbound the ball, and he can run the baseline. The player should never throw in from under the basket. He should use a two-handed pass and be aware that he cannot bounce the ball on the end line.

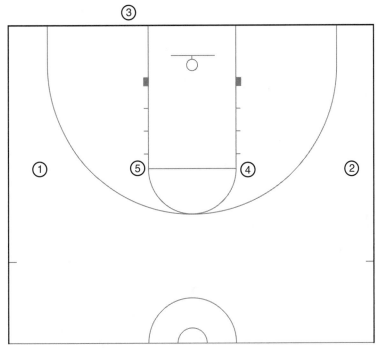

1-4 set versus full-court defense.

GUARD PASS: OPTION 1

FOCUS

Forward O3's first pass versus full-court pressure.

PROCEDURE

Players begin in a 1-4 alignment in the backcourt. The wide lanes, designated right and left, are described from the perspective of the offensive attack.

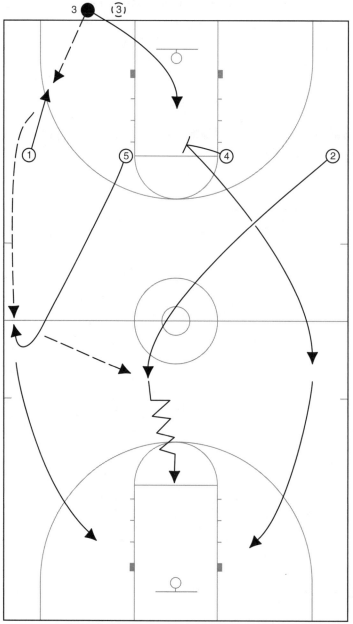

Guard pass: option 1.

Follow these steps:

1. The 1-4 alignment depends on all five offensive players to get the ball inbounds. This position is an effective attack against both man-to-man and zone pressure.

2. In this scenario, O3 is a good passer, so O1 and O2 line up at the wing positions and become ball handlers. No matter which way O3 goes, to O1 or O2, the play is the same.

3. The diagram has O3 throwing the ball in on the right-hand side, but teams must also practice going left.

4. O3 passes to O1 and relocates to the middle of the free-throw lane.

5. O5 cuts diagonally across the midcourt line and looks for a pass.

6. O1 catches, pivots, and faces the defender before dribbling. He passes to O5 if O5 is open.

7. On O1's pass to O5, O2 sprints across midcourt and looks for a pass from O5. O4 releases and goes opposite O5, filling the outside left lane.

8. O5 passes to O2 and fills the right lane.

9. From here, O2, O4, and O5 attack the defense, looking to score.

GUARD READS AND REACTS

FOCUS

Execution, passing, and reading versus full-court pressure.

PROCEDURE

Play begins in the backcourt with an inbounds pass. Follow these steps:

1. Continuing option 1, if O1 is unable to pass to O5, his next look is to O4 or O3. Dribbling in the backcourt is the last option.

2. As O5 vacates, O4 cuts to the ball, making himself visible to O1.

3. If O4 receives the pass, he turns and looks for O2. If O2 is covered, O4 passes to O3.

4. When O3 receives the ball from O1 or O4, he looks to rotate the ball to O2; O3 may need one dribble to establish a passing angle.

5. After the ball gets to O2, he looks to pass to O1, cutting into the middle. O2 then fills the left lane.

6. O5 fills the right lane.

7. When O1 gets the ball, he attacks the basket, with O2 and O5 filling the lanes. O1 looks to pass, drive, or shoot the ball.

8. After the ball enters the frontcourt, the offense aggressively attacks the basket. Aligning the attack with balance and spacing is crucial to good execution.

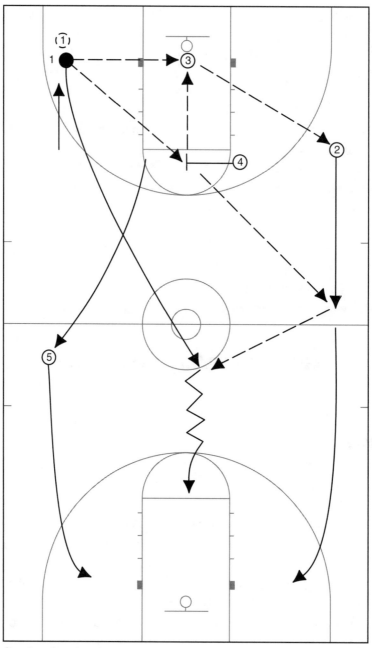

Guard reads and reacts.

FIND THE BIG MAN: OPTION 2

FOCUS

Forward O3's second pass to O4 or O5 versus full-court pressure.

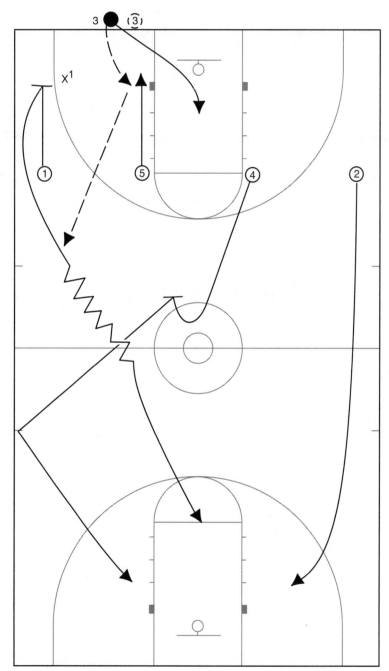

Find the big man: option 2.

PROCEDURE

Play begins in the backcourt with an inbounds pass. Follow these steps.

1. The first inbounds option is always O1, but if a hard denial prevents O1 from receiving the ball, O1 still breaks to the corner looking for a pass.

2. O3's second option is the big man on the strong side, who should come straight down the lane. Seldom do big men, especially 5s, defend deep in the backcourt, so O5's defender is usually smaller than he is.

3. The pass to O5 is a high pass over a smaller defender's head, especially when a defender is on the ball. As O5 gathers the pass, his first look is for O1, who takes his man to the baseline, plants his right foot, uses a quick reverse pivot, and sprints ahead of his man looking for O5's pass.

4. On the weak side, O4 sees O5 break for the ball, so he sprints to midcourt, finds the open space, and button hooks, looking for a pass from O5.

5. Now that O4 has the play in front of him, if he sees O5 pass to O1, he continues diagonally to the hash mark on the strong side and fills the right lane.

6. On the weak side, O2 sees the play develop and fills the left lane.

7. O1, O4, and O2 attack the basket.

MAKE THE SURE PASS

FOCUS

Full-court pressure attack with pass to O5 or O4.

PROCEDURE

Play begins in the backcourt with an inbounds pass. Follow these steps:

1. The second passing option for O5 presents itself when O1 is unable to get open on the sideline cut. O5 has three options—O4 in the middle of the floor, O3 stepping inbounds, and O2 on the far sideline.

2. If the pass goes to O4, he has two options—O1 and O2. If the pass goes to O2, he has O4 in the middle and O1 cutting diagonally across the middle.

3. O5's easiest pass is to O3, who is stepping inbounds. Should the pass go to O3, his action is to move the ball to O2 and stay behind the ball in the middle of the floor as an outlet against pressure.

4. O2's action is to push the ball with a couple of dribbles, pass to O1, and then run the left lane.

5. When O4 realizes that he will not be involved in the backcourt, he clears diagonally to the frontcourt hash line and runs the right lane, with O1 in the middle and O2 on the left lane.

6. As they attack, O1 decides whether to drive, shoot, or pass.

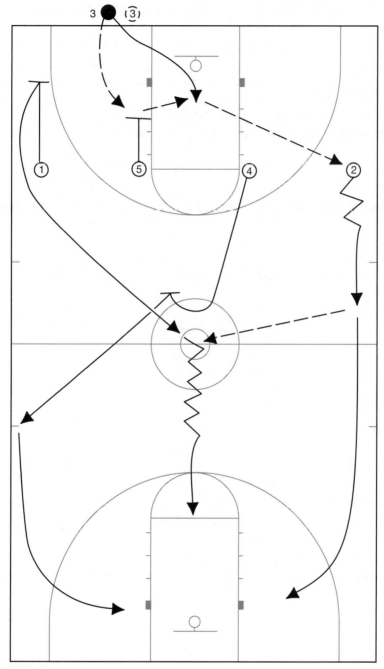

Make the sure pass.

Scoring Plays From Backcourt

The step-out bomb play can be run only following a score when a team is permitted to run the baseline. Teams use the bomb play when the defensive team is desperate and gambling all out to get the ball. This play is effective only when all five defenders are in a full-court man-to-man press. This timing play takes practice and a touch of deception to be effective. Only through practicing the play can the coach assign positions. The player who shoots the ball should have good speed, and the passer must be skilled at throwing the long baseball pass. To illustrate in the following diagram, the players will be numbered, but when running this play in a game situation, specific skills determine player positions. The play is specifically designed to score against a denial defense. O2 handles the ball out of bounds. O1 lines up at the strong-side elbow with O4 on the same side at the wing position, free-throw line extended. O5 lines up on the low block on the weak side, with O3 at the elbow. O3 can also line up in the weak-side deep corner and just step out of bounds if his lack of speed is a factor.

THE BOMB

FOCUS

Scoring from the backcourt when the defense overplays.

PROCEDURE

Play begins on the end line in the backcourt after a score. Follow these steps:

1. The play begins just before the official hands the ball to O2. O5 fakes a screen for O3, but O3 ignores the screen and sprints out of bounds on the baseline, where he receives a pass from O2.

2. During this action, O1 fakes a screen for O4 and screens O2's man on the baseline. O2 passes to O3 and immediately sprints off O1's screen, running down the sideline looking for the long pass from O3.

3. For inbounds options, O1 looks for the ball in the middle. O5 sets up at the top of the key and lets O4 run off him toward the sideline. O2 is the primary option.

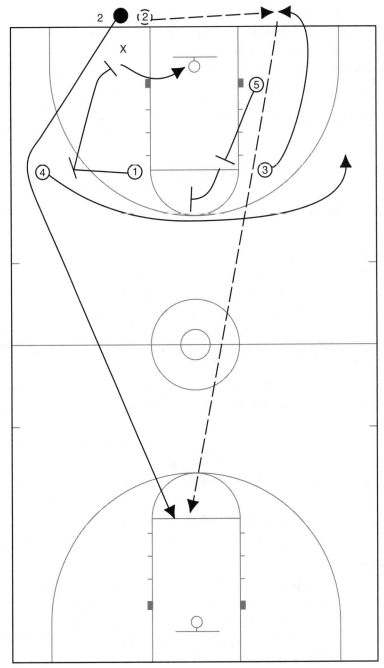

The bomb.

The Line

When no big men are available and the 1-4 formation is not an option, the line is a great alternative against man-to-man pressure. Proper execution of this play depends on correct alignment of the players. The line can be run from both the spot, meaning that the inbounding player can't move the pivot foot on the throw-in, and when the inbounder can run the baseline following a score. For the offense to score on this play, all five defenders must be guarding a man in backcourt.

THE LINE

FOCUS

Backcourt scoring play with inbounds options.

PROCEDURE

Play begins on the end line in the backcourt. Follow these steps:

1. Player O3 has four passing options. All four players line up facing O3, approximately 12 to 18 inches apart. The players' routes are not scripted; instead, each reacts to the player in front of him and goes to an open area. When O4, the first player in line, runs out, O5's defender must guard against the bomb, which allows O5 to get open going to the ball.

2. When the official hands the ball to O3, O4 goes away from defensive pressure and sprints to midcourt, looking for the bomb. O4 has the option to go either right or left.

3. O2 breaks in the opposite direction of O4, and O1, the third player, cuts opposite O2. O5 breaks toward O3, with both hands high, looking for the ball.

4. The line is an effective way either to score or to get the ball inbounds.

5. Once the ball is inbounded, the offensive players space themselves out and work the ball up the court. O3 is the safety.

Fake-and-Go

This play can be run effectively 10 to 15 times a season. Use the play at the end of the half or at the end of the game when little time remains on the clock and you are 94 feet from the basket. Designing a set play with multiple options is better than just having someone go long and heaving the ball toward the basket. The fake-and-go is a good one in this situation.

FAKE-AND-GO

FOCUS

Backcourt scoring against pressure with a short clock.

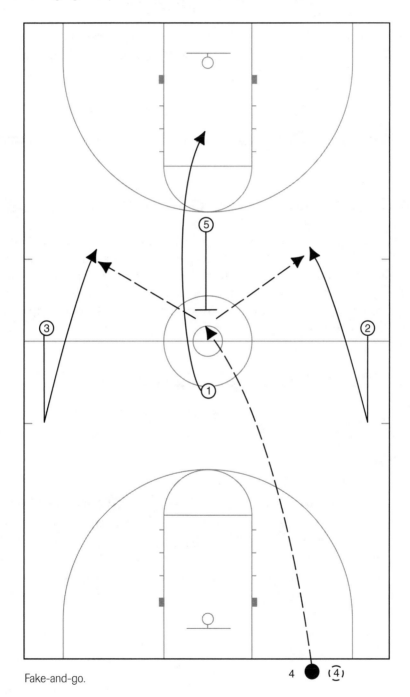

Fake-and-go.

PROCEDURE

Play begins on the end line in the backcourt. Follow these steps:

1. This skill-specific play requires a player, O4, who can throw the long pass, two good shooters, O2 and O3, on the wings, and a big man, O5, who sets a screen for a small man, O1, at midcourt.

2. When the referee hands the ball to O4, O5 moves to the midcourt area and sets a screen for O1, who sprints to the basket. The strategy is to get O5 open for a baseball pass from O4.

3. As O1 makes his move, O2 and O3 sprint into the backcourt, where O4 fakes passing to them. O2 and O3 sprint to the hash line as though they are going to receive a pass. They then reverse pivot as O4 passes to O5.

4. O5 uses a touch pass to either O2 or O3 for the shot.

Attack Versus Backcourt Pressure, Side Court

One reason that the line is such a good play is that it can be used effectively for all three inbounding areas—the backcourt baseline, the side court, and the frontcourt baseline. The play is not complicated, and with just a few modifications, it is adaptable and effective in most situations. On the side court, when the defense applies tight pressure, the players line up directly in front of O3, approximately 12 to 18 inches apart.

BURN THE DEFENSE: RUN THE LINE

FOCUS

Backcourt scoring play against defensive pressure, side out-of-bounds.

PROCEDURE

Play begins in the backcourt, side out-of-bounds. Follow these steps:

1. O4 lines up 10 feet off the sideline with O2, O1, and O5 behind him in that order.

2. On O3's command of, "Hike," or, "Go," O4 peels off, circles the line, and sprints toward the basket. O2 breaks opposite O4. O1 breaks opposite O2, and O5 steps into the open area toward O3.

3. All four players are options. O3 must choose the right one and get the ball inbounds.

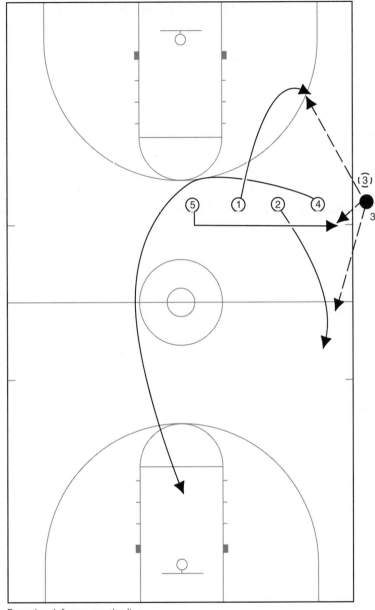

Burn the defense: run the line.

Frontcourt, Side Out-of-Bounds

The amount of defensive pressure dictates whether the goal of the play is to get the ball inbounds and initiate a play, or to attempt to score off the initial pass. This play, called "the box double," is run from the free-throw line extended to midcourt and is designed to produce a score off the initial pass.

BOX DOUBLE

FOCUS

Looking to score from the frontcourt, side out-of-bounds.

PROCEDURE

Play begins from the frontcourt, side out-of-bounds. Follow these steps:

1. Players line up in a box set. O5 and O2 are on the low blocks, and O4 and O1 are at the elbows. The player in the O4 position must be a good jumper because this play is a lob for him.

2. O4 sets a cross screen for O1. O1 fakes a screen on O2 and comes off O4.

3. O2 sets a back screen for O4 and continues to the sideline off O5's screen.

4. O5 steps up to the free-throw lane, sets a screen for O2, and opens to the ball.

5. O3 has four possible receivers—O4 on the lob; O1, who is coming to him; O2 in the left corner; or O5, who is stepping to the ball after O2 clears the screen.

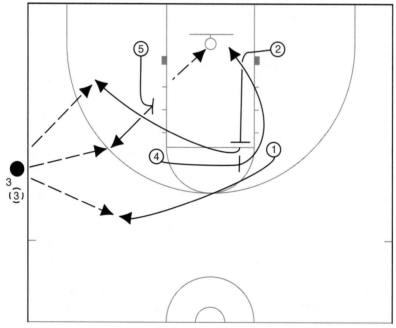

Box double.

Scoring Plays in Short-Clock Situations in Frontcourt, Side Out-of-Bounds

In a last possession situation when a team is behind by three or fewer points and has a time-out, specific issues arise. The biggest concern is getting the ball to the player who has the best chance of making the play. Coaches must keep in mind that whatever play the team runs must work against all types of defense. Therefore, if the defense denies the player designated to receive the pass, the other players must be alert and available for the inbounds pass. If the game clock shows four seconds or fewer, the player receiving the inbounds pass must make the play. His teammates should flatten out in the corners and not obstruct him. The player who receives the pass has plenty of time to catch, face up, and dribble a couple of times before shooting. The ball handler does not have time to run a play or gamble on a pass that may be deflected, bobbled, or mishandled. If the clock has between 5 and 10 seconds remaining, the player receiving the inbounds pass has time to run a pick-and-roll, looking to penetrate or draw and kick. The X-out play can be used in both situations, assuming that the player can create and get his own shot. The following drills cover X-out alignment and first cuts.

X-OUT ALIGNMENT

FOCUS
Execution and proper alignment, down two points, side out-of-bounds.

PROCEDURE
Play begin in the frontcourt, side out-of-bounds. Follow these steps:
1. O1 lines up under the net and uses O5's screen to get open at the top of the key.
2. O2 and O3 line up at the free-throw lane extended, just above the three-point line. O3 cuts first and goes to the left-hand corner. O2 cuts off O3's back and goes to the right-hand corner.
3. After O2 and O3 make their cuts, O5 turns and sets a down screen for O1, whose job is to get open by going either way off O5.
4. O4 inbounds the ball and dives to the same-side block to rebound. The alignment is now set to run a specific play.

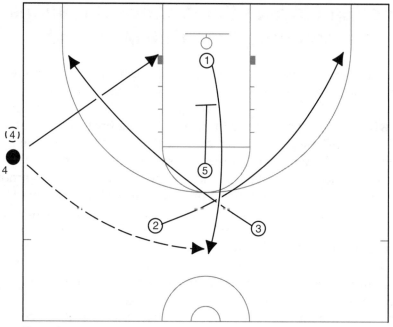

X-out alignment.

X-OUT INTO PICK-AND-ROLL

FOCUS

Execution and proper alignment, down two points, side out-of-bounds.

PROCEDURE

Play begins in the frontcourt, side out-of-bounds, X-out. Follow these steps:

1. In most situations, the inbounds pass will go to the point guard because he is generally the team's best ball handler and can penetrate.

2. The following diagram illustrates the X-out with seven seconds on the clock and the offensive team down two points. The team aligns to run a middle pick-and-roll.

3. When O1 clears O5 and O4 inbounds the ball, O5 relocates at the top of the key and sets a screen for O1. O5 then pops for a spot-up.

4. The team's best shooter spots up in the corner on the side to which O1 drives. The offensive team is down two points, so O1 looks to turn the corner and attack the basket.

5. O1 has three viable options—his drive, a pass to O5, or a pass to O2.

This play is designed to get the best shooters in the corners, with the point guard penetrating to the basket for the layup or a draw and kick. If O2 is a good ball handler as well as the best shooter, it may be wise to have O1 and O2 switch positions. When diagramming these plays during time-outs, the coach should put his players in positions where they are comfortable. Coaches should know their players' strengths, such as which side of the floor they like to shoot from or whether they prefer to go right or left on drives. Practicing special situations, a crucial aspect of game management, allows coaches to gain this knowledge. The X-out play provides excellent opportunities for scoring by several players in a variety of ways.

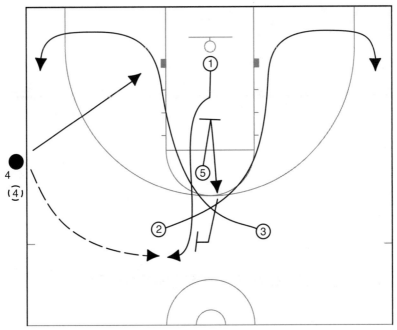

X-out into a pick-and-roll.

THREE-POINT X-OUT

FOCUS

Execution and proper alignment, down three, side out-of-bounds.

PROCEDURE

Play begins in the frontcourt, side out-of-bounds. Follow these steps:

1. This side inbounds play (SOB) is designed to get a three-point attempt.
2. The play begins with the X-out formation, which properly aligns the players.
3. Instead of going wide to the corner on their cuts, O2 and O3 dive to the low blocks and then flare to the corners.
4. After O1 clears O5's screen, O5 steps out of the three-second lane and prepares to set the last screen in the pick-the-picker set for O3.

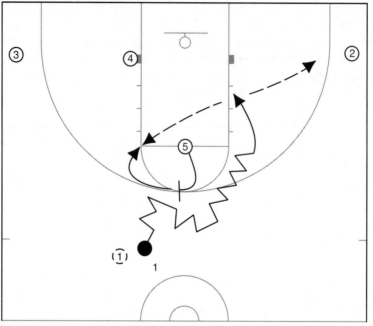

Three-point X-out.

X-OUT INTO SINGLE-DOUBLE

FOCUS

Execution and proper alignment, down three points, side out-of-bounds, baseline set.

PROCEDURE

Players begin in the X-out formation. O1 has the ball at the free-throw line extended, beyond the three-point line. Follow these steps:

1. O1 begins the play by dribbling to the wing position, free-throw line extended.

2. O3 sets up about 12 inches higher than O2 and steps into the free-throw lane for a cross screen for O2. O2 uses a jab step to the middle and goes off a staggered double screen, with O4 being the second screen.

3. After O2 clears O3, O3 uses O5's screen and cuts to the top of the key.

4. O1 passes to O3, who has the option of shooting or rotating the ball to O2 for a three-point shot.

5. The three best perimeter shooters occupy the O1, O2, and O3 positions.

Frontcourt, Baseline, Out-of-Bounds Plays

There are two theories about baseline out-of-bounds plays. One promotes getting the ball inbounds and running a play, and the other advances the goal of scoring off the inbounds pass. The coach must take into consideration the normal variables of score, time of game, shot clock, floor position, and players in the game. This play, inside pick-the-picker, is designed to produce a score off the initial pass. The play works best when O2, or whoever is designated to run O2's route, is a great shooter. During the Michael Jordan era with the Chicago Bulls, this play was good for at least one basket a game, with Jordan being the shooter. The basic play is normally run for O2, the shooter, to come off a double stagger set by O5 and O4 for a catch-and-shoot jump shot from the corner.

INSIDE PICK-THE-PICKER

FOCUS
Setting good screens with ball fakes and good passes.

PROCEDURE
Play begins in the frontcourt, baseline. Follow these steps:

1. After running the basic set a couple times, the play call changes and O2 becomes a decoy. Instead of going to O2, the play goes to O5 or whoever sets the first screen.

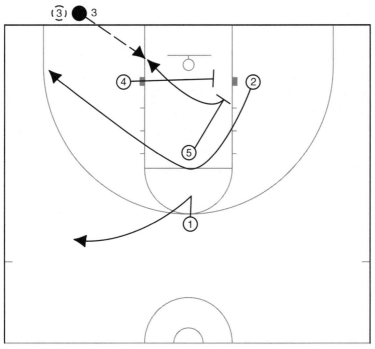

Inside pick-the-picker.

2. Usually O5 turns and lets O2 work off him, but when the play is run for O5, O2 holds a little longer and O5 goes and screens for him.

3. This puts O5 at the low block opposite the player inbounding the ball. O4 then back screens the defender guarding O5, and O5 cuts to the vacated open space for a layup.

Box: Cross 2

Sometimes the simplest plays are the most effective ones. The box set can be highly successful and easily disguised. Players need to learn three calls—cross, diagonal, and up. Each call indicates a screening angle. The players can then line up at any of the four spots and execute the play. For instance, in the cross action, the hot spot, or the shooting spot, is the elbow opposite the player inbounding the ball. The call "Cross 2" means that the play is designated for O2 coming off a cross screen. "Cross 3" indicates that O3 is on the hot spot and so on. If the call is "Diagonal 4," O4 lines up diagonally to the player inbounding and the player who lines up in front of the player passing the ball inbounds sets the screen. The offensive team should pick on a weak defender and get a layup or a foul by attacking the basket.

BOX: CROSS 2

FOCUS

Alignment, screens, cutting angles, and passes.

PROCEDURE

Play begins in the frontcourt, baseline. Players are in a box set. Follow these steps:

1. O1 takes the ball out-of-bounds and calls, "Cross 2." O5 fakes inside as if he's going to get the pass and moves to the corner, pretending to be the primary target.

2. O3 calls out, "Back screen" and moves toward the defender guarding O2. O2 jab steps to the sideline, setting up a cross screen by O4, who sets a cross screen on O2's man.

3. O2 uses the screen and cuts down the middle, looking for a lob or layup. O4 holds the screen on X2, opens to the ball, and goes to the basket as the second option. O1 fakes to O5 and looks for the O2 and O4 options. O3 relocates high as the safety.

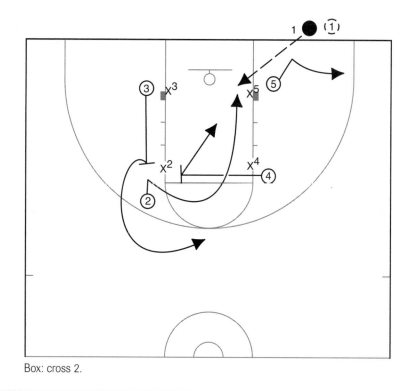

Box: cross 2.

The Line

The line inbounds play is one of the most effective alignments. The line play can be used underneath the basket to score or to inbound and get the ball in play. The play permits the coach to assemble the line to his best advantage, changing the player alignment to inbound to a passer, a ball handler, or a shooter.

THE LINE

FOCUS

Inbounding the ball versus hard defensive pressure.

PROCEDURE

Play begins in the frontcourt, baseline. Follow these steps:

1. Players line up approximately 12 inches apart. O2 is in the front of the line, and he lines up on the low block on the ball side.
2. O1, O4, and O5 line up behind O2. O3 takes the ball out of bounds.
3. O1 cuts toward the baseline, goes around O2, and sprints up the middle, veering to the sideline and looking for the inbounds pass. As O1 makes his move, O5 jab steps to the middle and goes to the corner, looking for the inbounds pass.

4. O4 steps inside the free-throw lane and screens down on O2's man. O2 comes up the lane, veers to the elbow, and moves to the sideline, looking for the inbounds pass.

5. Following his down screen, O4 steps to the ball as a possible receiver. O3 looks over the options and decides where to throw the ball. Regardless of who receives the inbounds pass, O1 seeks the ball to set the offense.

If a coach could choose only one out-of-bounds alignment, the line would be it. This play works against pressure, and with proper spacing, it is the most adaptable. When the defense applies hard pressure on the baseline, the line provides several effective options. The objective is to get the ball inbounds and into the hands of the point guard quickly. All four players in the line are possible options and must get open to receive a pass. The offensive players must be aware that defenders will try to hold them, so a determined mind-set to get open is required.

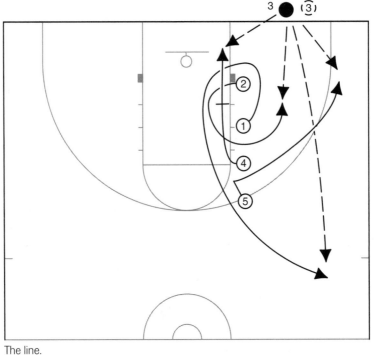

The line.

Attacking Disruptive Defenses

The traditional theory for attacking a zone with a one-man front is to align the offense in a two-man front. And if the zone is a two-man front, the offense aligns in a one-man front. After the offense aligns itself properly, the players try to create a triangle, or an overload, pitting three offensive players against two defenders. The team's best shooters occupy at least two of the spots. This offensive strategy is sound until the defense throws up a box-and-one, triangle-and-two, or 1-3-1 half-court trap. Why? Because these defenses are designed to disrupt the normal zone attack. The offensive team must be prepared, and preparation comes from practice. Zone defenses, especially those designed to disrupt, require special attention. Most coaches cover the basic 2-3 and 3-2 zones within their normal offensive sets, but defenses that disrupt the offense with traps, denial of the ball to the best player, and gimmicks demand special preparation. Coaches need a well-designed plan of attack to make sure that the right players are in the right spots to get their shots.

Let's look at three disruptive half-court defenses—the 1-3-1, the box-and-one, and the triangle-and-two. In all cases, the offense needs to be patient, align in an overload, maintain proper floor balance and spacing, and use player and ball movement to attack the offensive boards for rebounds. A 1-3-1 defense is designed to keep the offense on the perimeter and eliminate layups. The LA guard-to-forward set (see chapter 6) is an excellent 1-3-1 example because it puts shooters in open areas and gives an opportunity to lob to a big man. In this misdirection play, the ball starts on one side and reverses to the other side for the attack. The first drill covers the alignment and first cuts, and the second drill continues the play and shows where the shots come from.

ALIGNMENT VERSUS 1-3-1 ZONE ON THE HALF COURT

FOCUS

Alignment and execution versus disruptive defenses.

PROCEDURE

Players begin on the half court. Follow these steps:

1. O2 starts the play with a pass to O4 and then cuts through to the opposite corner.
2. O5 screens away for O3 and relocates to the low block and out of the low defender's vision.
3. O3 cuts from the wing to the ball-side elbow, looking for a pass and a shot. O1 uses a V-cut to get open at the top of the key.

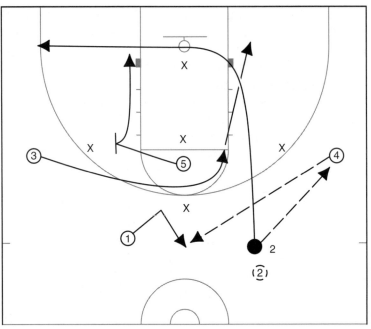

Alignment versus 1-3-1 zone on the half court.

MOVEMENT WHEN ATTACKING THE 1-3-1 ZONE

FOCUS

Attacking disruptive defenses with movement and shots.

PROCEDURE

Players begin on the half court and continue the play. Follow these steps:

1. As the offense begins to move and players realign, O4 looks at O3 coming in behind the middle man on defense. If O3 does not get the pass, he continues to the baseline on the ball side.

2. O4 passes to O1, who looks to lob to O5 as he steps into the lane behind the defense. If that is not available, O1 passes to O2, who may have a shot or a pass inside to O5.

3. Following his pass to O1, O4 relocates to the elbow and forms a triangle with O2 and O5. This set offers many opportunities for good shots, and someone is always on the boards.

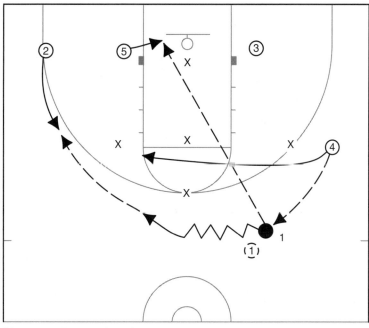

Movement when attacking the 1-3-1 zone.

Box-and-One

The box-and-one is designed to guard one player man-to-man and to zone the rest of the team. The intent is to shut down a high scorer or at least limit his good view of the basket and reduce his points. Sometimes coaches assign the one man (in the box-and-one) to the opposing team's best ball handler, hoping to disrupt their playmaker. With some modification, the LA set (see chapter 6) accommodates our needs on offense.

ALIGNMENT VERSUS BOX-AND-ONE

FOCUS

Proper alignment and execution versus box-and-one.

PROCEDURE

Players begin on the half court in the LA offense. Follow these steps:

1. X2 is assigned to O2. The offense begins by attacking the box. O1 initiates by passing to O3 and getting a return pass. O1 passes to O2, who passes to O4. O2 dives to the strong-side block and screens X4.

2. O3 uses the screen on X4 and clears to the strong-side corner.

3. O4 passes to O3 and clears to the weak-side block. O1 replaces O4 on the wing, and O5 remains at the high post in the middle and opens to the ball.

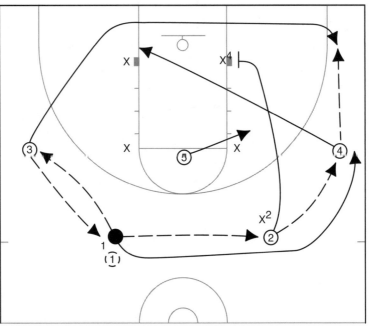

Alignment versus box-and-one.

SHOT SPOTS VERSUS BOX-AND-ONE

FOCUS

Alignment and shooting areas versus disruptive box-and-one.

PROCEDURE

Players begin on the half court and continue the box-and-one attack with these steps:

1. The realignment places O1 with the ball at the wing position, O3 in the ball-side corner, O5 at the high-post elbow ball side, O4 on the weak-side block, and O2 on the ball-side block, setting a screen on X4 and attempting to occupy two defenders.

2. O1, O3, and O5 establish a passing triangle, with each looking for an open shot. The objective of the offense is to find the open holes in the defense and get the best shooters to those spots.

3. If the point guard decides to reverse the ball on the dribble, O2 uses O4's screen for a turnout. In this scenario, O5 stays at the high post and crosses the free-throw lane to form a triangle with O4 on the block and O2 on the wing.

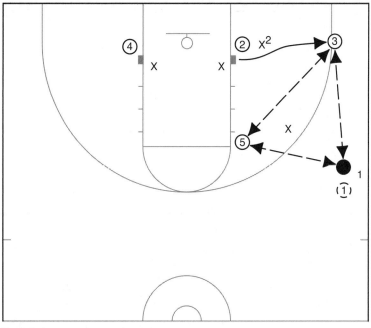

Spot shots versus box-and-one.

Triangle-and-Two Disruptive Defense

The intent of the triangle-and-two defense is to place enormous pressure on players who are not good perimeter shooters. These players may be effective close to the basket but are not skilled at face-up jump shots. The triangle-and-two is a mind game, inviting nonshooters to do things outside their comfort zone while applying constant pressure on the good shooters. But with patience and disciple, the offense will get good shots.

The triangle-and-two defense can be extremely effective. Auburn did a great job with it in playing eventual champion Syracuse to a one-point loss in the 2003 NCAA tournament. The Auburn defense slowed the normally potent Syracuse offense by disrupting the tempo and flow of the game. When key players, scorers, and playmakers passed the ball, Auburn made it difficult for those players to get the ball back. Other Syracuse players then had to make big plays, such as getting rebounds, making assists, and scoring baskets, and they did. Syracuse won, but not before being tested by what many described as a junk defense. The defense that Auburn used is designed to keep constant pressure on two players, even denying them the ball when possible, while zoning the middle in a triangle set. Teams with big men who are poor shooters and faulty ball handlers have a difficult time scoring when defenses man-up on the guards and invite the inside players to shoot on the perimeter.

ALIGNMENT VERSUS TRIANGLE-AND-TWO

FOCUS

Proper alignment versus triangle-and-two.

PROCEDURE

Players begin on the half court. Follow these steps:

1. Defenders X4 and X5 work in tandem to cover the baseline. When one slides out to cover a baseline jump shooter, the other slides across and covers the low block. X3 covers the middle and the top.

2. The defense is man-to-man on the guards, inviting shots from O3, O4, and O5. The defense gambles that by constantly applying pressure to O1 and O2, they can eliminate guard play, control the boards, and keep the offense off balance.

3. The offense will get open shots because the defense is designed to give nonshooters semicontested shots.

4. One way to attack this defense is to relocate the two players with man-to-man coverage to the low blocks, occupying two defenders.

5. O1 passes to O5. O1 and O2 dive to their same-side low-block positions. O1 and O2 create congestion. They can screen the baseline defenders or cross screen to get open. Discipline is the key.

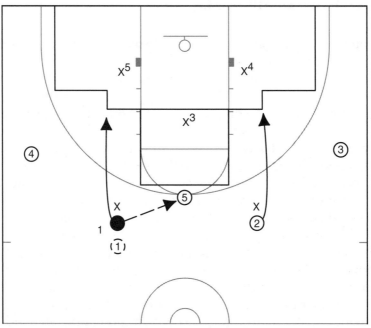

Alignment versus triangle-and-two.

FINDING SPOTS VERSUS TRIANGLE-AND-TWO

FOCUS

Triangle overload for shooters and rebounders versus triangle-and-two.

PROCEDURE

Players begin on the half court. Follow these steps:

1. If the triangle-and-two is going to take a team out of its offense, this diagram illustrates where the team can expect to get open shots.

2. The important issue is to get the right players in the right spots and aggressively attack the offensive boards. The blocked-off space indicates the open areas that the three undefended players can occupy.

3. The baseline corners, wings, and top of the key are the shooting areas.

4. For identification purposes, O3 has the ball, O4 is at the top, and O5 is in the corner. When working the right side of the court, O3, with the ball, creates a two-on-one situation with either the corner, O5, and the baseline defender, X4, or with the top, O4, and the defender, X3. The left side is the same except that its baseline defender is X5.

5. Ball movement with good passes between O3, O4, and O5, and taking up slack toward the basket will establish shooting range with open shots. Make sure that the shooter is the right player and that rebounders attack the glass.

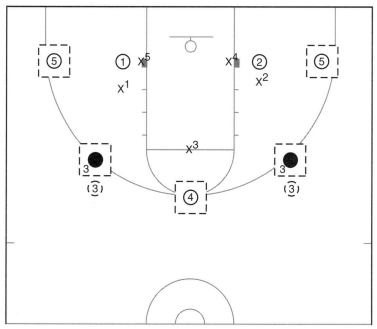

Finding spots versus triangle-and-two.

Disruptive defenses can cause problems for most teams. Going into a season-ending tournament, coaches must address the possibility that their opponent might try one of these unorthodox defenses. Teams that have nothing to lose will sometimes rally around a defensive gimmick such as the box-and-one, triangle-and-two, diamond-and-one, or 1-3-1 half-court trap to pull an upset, as Auburn almost did. Successful coaches prepare for full-court presses, inbounding the ball against pressure, and disruptive defenses rather than wait until game time to make adjustments.

INDEX

Note: The italicized *f* and *t* following page numbers refer to figures and tables, respectively. The italicized *ff* and *tt* following page numbers refer to multiple figures and tables, respectively.

ABOUT THE AUTHOR

Lee Rose began his coaching career as a teacher-coach at Versailles (Kentucky) High School in 1958, and he's been involved in the game ever since. He joined the collegiate coaching ranks in 1959 at Transylvania College and held subsequent positions at the University of Cincinnati, University of North Carolina at Charlotte, Purdue University, and the University of South Florida. He joined the NBA ranks in 1986 as an assistant coach with the San Antonio Spurs and remained in the NBA for the rest of his career.

Rose's passion and intelligence for the game are well documented throughout his 45-year career. As a college head coach, Rose finished with a .705 winning percentage (388-162), including a 72-18 (.800) record in three seasons at UNC Charlotte. He was named the *Sporting News* National Coach of the Year in 1977 after leading UNC Charlotte to the NIT Finals in 1976 and the NCAA Final Four in 1977. Rose went on to lead Purdue to the NIT Finals in 1979 and the Final Four a year later. Rose has been named Coach of the Year in every conference he has coached in: Kentucky Intercollegiate Athletic Conference (KIAC), Sun Belt, and Big Ten. He was inducted into the Kentucky Athletic Hall of Fame in 2001.

As an NBA consultant for National Basketball Developmental League coaches, Rose continues to benefit the sport with his superior teaching and talent-assessment skills. Lee and his wife, Eleanor, live in Charlotte, North Carolina.